THE DICKENS
THEATRE

THE DICKENS THEATRE

A REASSESSMENT OF THE NOVELS

BY

ROBERT GARIS

OXFORD
AT THE CLARENDON PRESS
1965

Oxford University Press, Amen House, London E.C.4

GLASGOW   NEW YORK   TORONTO   MELBOURNE   WELLINGTON
BOMBAY   CALCUTTA   MADRAS   KARACHI   LAHORE   DACCA
CAPE TOWN   SALISBURY   NAIROBI   IBADAN   ACCRA
KUALA LUMPUR   HONG KONG

PRINTED IN GREAT BRITAIN

FOREWORD

It is a pleasure to acknowledge the advice, aid, and encouragement of teachers, colleagues, and friends: Reuben Brower, Douglas Bush, Ruth Michael, Anne and David Ferry, Martha Craig, Constance and Richard Harrier, Ruth Vande Kieft, Mary Ann and William Youngren, Martin Green, Joan Hartman, Thomas Wilcox, and Richard Poirier. I dedicate this book to them and also to B. H. Haggin, whose music criticism first showed me that critical judgement of the arts can express moral passion and intellectual integrity.

I am grateful also to the English Department, the President and the Trustees of Wellesley College for awarding me the leave of absence during which I wrote the major portion of this book. And I thank Elizabeth Ames and the Corporation of Yaddo for providing a particularly helpful environment for writing.

R. G.

CONTENTS

PART I

THE DICKENS PROBLEM

1

STYLE AS THEATRE

THERE is a fundamental oddity about Dickens's art which makes his novels hard to judge by ordinary standards: there is 'a Dickens problem'. But you could hunt for ever through criticisms of Dickens without finding much straightforward treatment of it. Dickens's contemporaries were largely unaware of it, just because they were his contemporaries and in an immediately intimate relationship with him and his work. But as the novels of the beloved family entertainer, the 'Inimitable Boz', entered the body of past literature and began to be discussed in terms ordinarily used about classics in the novel form, the problem began to make trouble, though its existence was registered only indirectly, by the confusions, the uncertainties, the bluster, and defensiveness of so much Dickens criticism. The problem has in fact led to actual and grave distortion only recently, in the widespread view, endorsed by some high authorities, that the most interesting and significant part of Dickens's work is that which can be regarded as seriously symbolic and prophetic. It is because this exciting but seriously misleading view may already have hardened into the new orthodoxy about this great and strange writer, that I propose, in the following pages, to set forth as straightforwardly as possible the 'Dickens problem', together with some suggestions about solving it.

Dickens is a great genius, a great artist—everybody recognizes this—and his works can hardly be called anything but novels. His name, then, is inevitably associated with certain other names: Fielding, Tolstoy, Henry James, Flaubert, Joyce. All these writers (many others might of course be added to the list) were highly gifted in the basic skills of fiction, and Dickens was too—perhaps as highly gifted as any. But the other names are on the list for another reason. *The Portrait of a Lady* is a great novel because James's remarkable

verbal skill—a human faculty in itself pleasurable to exercise and to observe in action—was directed to making a large,
complex, and coherent image, which maintains a consistent
'illusion of reality', and an organic interrelationship between
its parts, which makes the whole structure seem alive. And
it is exactly its coherence and organic complexity that make
The Portrait of a Lady a 'vision' of human nature and human
conditions worth the serious attention of people with serious
interests. The old view of Dickens was a confused one because
it tacitly accepted this standard, yet denied it in practice.
Dickens was admittedly weak in coherence and organic complexity of structure, yet separate elements were brilliant and
the whole work was informed with some quality—energy,
passion, humour, gusto, heart—which made it great. Hence
the eager welcoming of the new view, which maintains that
Dickens's darker novels do in fact turn out to be coherent
complex organisms when they are properly identified as
symbolic in method. Earlier critics who failed to make this
identification must, it appears, have been enslaved by un-
questioned realistic criteria—look at Bradley on Shakespeare,
Tolstoy on *King Lear*. Today, after G. Wilson Knight, T. S.
Eliot, and Kafka, we are simply luckier by virtue of the
generally developed skill in apprehending poetic and symbolic
structures. Dickens is discovered to have been ahead of his
time, not only in prophetic message, but in literary method
as well.

The honourable motive in the recent apologetics has been
an eagerly misdirected piety. Dickens is a great writer and the
new interpretation has defined his work in an appealing way,
with the result that sophisticated people have been sent back
to reading him: this is the optimistic way of understanding and
forgiving the distortions of Edmund Wilson, Lionel Trilling,
J. Hillis Miller, and others. But these well-intentioned distortions are bound in the long run to produce uneasiness, blurring
of standards, mute questionings, which will, in the longer run,
work against Dickens's reputation rather than for it. Intelligent
and sophisticated readers will not in fact find what they have
been sent back to Dickens to find and, looking for what is not
there, they will miss what is there. A more serious danger is
that they will find something disarmingly close to what they

expected to find, for the new Dickens criticism argues not only
with eloquence but with an apparently conscientious analysis
of detail. Readers excited by its promises will indeed find
symbols and patterns in Dickens, but they will find the actual
working of the symbolic instruments very different from what
they expected—much less powerful, much less valuable. And
this is the very worst effect that criticism can have, for it
suggests all too clearly what is all too often true: that criticism
is a mode of finding plausible ways of defending vested
interests. The pitiful irony in this instance is that it should be
the greatest popular writer in the English language who seems
to be the vested interest that needs defending. It is in order to
restore something like the popular understanding of Dickens
that I should like to set forth what seems to me the true facts
of the Dickens problem.

These facts are, in brief: that the 'great novelists' were
deeply schooled in certain disciplines, which came to be their
habits, which were their necessary and appropriate procedures
in shaping their literary structures and expressing their moral
vision, and which were utterly unfamiliar to Dickens and
utterly antithetical to his essential nature and genius. For
Dickens characteristically worked in a literary and moral
mode that ordinarily is taken by readers seriously interested
in art to be incapable of producing 'high art'. Dickens's extraordinary gifts produced, in this mode, literary objects that are
permanently beautiful and valuable but which did not, through
their beauty and value, accomplish the impossible transmu-
tation of this mode into a vehicle for what we ordinarily understand as high art.

The salient characteristics of this special mode in which
Dickens composed all his novels are visible everywhere in his
work, in its smallest as well as its largest elements. For my
purpose the most convenient as well as the most legitimate
place to look for them is at the very beginning of one of his
novels. I quote the opening description of Marseilles in *Little
Dorrit*:

Thirty years ago, Marseilles lay burning in the sun, one day.
A blazing sun upon a fierce August day was no greater rarity
in southern France then, than at any other time, before or since.
Everything in Marseilles, and about Marseilles, had stared at the

fervid sky, and been stared at in return, until a staring habit had
become universal there. Strangers were stared out of countenance
by staring white houses, staring white walls, staring white streets,
staring tracts of arid road, staring hills from which verdure was
burnt away. The only things to be seen not fixedly staring and
glaring were the vines drooping under their load of grapes. These
did occasionally wink a little, as the hot air barely moved their
faint leaves.

There was no wind to make a ripple on the foul water within
the harbour, or on the beautiful sea without. The line of demarca-
tion between the two colours, black and blue, showed the point
which the pure sea would not pass; but it lay as quiet as the
abominable pool, with which it never mixed. Boats without awnings
were too hot to touch; ships blistered at their moorings; the stones
of the quays had not cooled, night or day, for months. Hindoos,
Russians, Chinese, Spaniards, Portuguese, Englishmen, French-
men, Genoese, Neapolitans, Venetians, Greeks, Turks, descendants
from all the builders of Babel, come to trade at Marseilles, sought
the shade alike—taking refuge in any hiding-place from a sea too
intensely blue to be looked at, and a sky of purple, set with one
great flaming jewel of fire.

The universal stare made the eyes ache. Towards the distant line
of Italian coast, indeed, it was a little relieved by light clouds of
mist, slowly rising from the evaporation of the sea, but it softened
nowhere else. Far away the staring roads, deep in dust, stared from
the hill-side, stared from the hollow, stared from the interminable
plain. Far away the dusty vines overhanging wayside cottages,
and the monotonous wayside avenues of parched trees without
shade, drooped beneath the stare of earth and sky. So did the
horses with drowsy bells, in long files of carts, creeping slowly
towards the interior; so did their recumbent drivers, when they
were awake, which rarely happened; so did the exhausted labourers
in the fields. Everything that lived or grew, was oppressed by the
glare; except the lizard, passing swiftly over rough stone walls, and
the cicala, chirping his dry hot chirp, like a rattle. The very dust
was scorched brown, and something quivered in the atmosphere as
if the air itself were panting.

Blinds, shutters, curtains, awnings, were all closed and drawn
to keep out the stare. Grant it but a chink or keyhole, and it shot
in like a white-hot arrow. The churches were the freest from it. To
come out of the twilight of pillars and arches—dreamily dotted
with winking lamps, dreamily peopled with ugly old shadows
piously dozing, spitting, and begging—was to plunge into a fiery

river, and swim for life to the nearest strip of shade. So, with people lounging and lying wherever shade was, with but little hum of tongues or barking of dogs, with occasional jangling of discordant church bells, and rattling of vicious drums, Marseilles, a fact to be strongly smelt and tasted, lay broiling in the sun one day. (I. i) (pp. 1–2)[1]

We can legitimately examine the style of this passage in and for itself and legitimately take what we discover as representative of Dickens's general methods, because the first pages of a novel actually offer themselves as representative. At any rate, they are taken by even the most casual reader as representative, which is to say that they are read with a kind of close and alert inspection not unlike the close analysis of literary study. They introduce us, if not necessarily to the leading characters and their situations, then at least, and always, to the characteristic interests and methods of the novelist. Highly self-conscious writers will introduce themselves with considerable finesse, economy, and power, but the least self-conscious writer will be, in his less knowing way, equally anxious to get on the best terms with his reader as soon as possible. The writer is beginning his work of creating an illusion—a mode of being that is not that of actual existence —and the reader is beginning his work of co-operating with that illusion, his work—in Dr. Johnson's word—of 'crediting' the illusion. The question is not one of the willingness of belief, for that can be taken for granted, but of the mode of belief. The first question the reader asks, then, consciously or unconsciously, is, 'How am I to believe, and in what?' And it is in this respect that Dickens's prose immediately presents a problem.

For our first impression of this prose is that it is immensely contrived; to a degree, in fact, that automatically blocks ordinary modes of belief. The machinery, the 'works', that produces the expressive effects is puzzlingly, almost embarrassingly visible. The prose is thick with verbal artifice, which actually forces itself into our consciousness. Nor is there the slightest suggestion of an attempt to hide the presence of the

[1] All quotations from Dickens's novels are followed by two kinds of reference: in the first parenthesis, to the chapter number; in the second parenthesis, to the page number in the *New Oxford Illustrated Dickens*.

artificer: our sense of his presence does not gradually disappear as we become aware of the objects his language is embodying, the feelings it is evoking, though those objects and feelings are unquestionably embodied and evoked. There in front of us, gradually taking shape as a 'fact to be strongly smelt and tasted', is the city of Marseilles on a hot day. But, as we credit this illusion we also continually notice, and credit, the agency by which this illusion has been produced, the verbal contrivances and, behind them, the verbal contriver. And if we continue reading with pleasure it is partly because we enjoy watching the contriver at his work.

More specifically there is the remarkably full-blown and explicit pattern of repetition of the words 'stare' and 'glare' about which the whole description is organized. There is the final clause, which we encounter with no subtle or vague sense that rounded completeness has been achieved but with distinct recognition that this clause is an intensified recapitulation of the first sentence of the description. We know this because the prose points it out to us. When we recognize that 'broiling' in the last sentence is an intensification of 'burning' in the first we are not 'analysing the way the effects are achieved' but grasping with confidence and pleasure what has been directly proffered with confidence and pride. Likewise, the opening sentence announces itself, by its shape and tone, to be a statement of the theme of the whole description.

One might say that this prose is characterized by a profusion of verbal figurations, or, to use the word from Renaissance rhetorical analysis, 'schemes'. But would-be-technical definition is misleading. By the time the novel came to the fore as an important literary form the seventeenth-century revolution in prose style had been fully effected; the kind of prose style that might seem to concentrate on words rather than on things had been discredited, and the plain style had come to be accepted not only as the norm but as, generally speaking, the only permissible prose style. And thus, by the time Dickens began to write, a style that displayed a high incidence of verbal schemes was no longer one of the many styles from which a writer could choose freely, nor is it so for us today. Only in public oratory is such a style admissible, and the example of Winston Churchill shows that even in oratory such a style has an archaic flavour—which is perhaps only to say that oratory itself is an anachronism in the modern world. With Churchill it was only the urgency, the sheer practicality of his attempt to recall England to a national ideal of heroic courage and persistence, that saved him from the imputation of being only and merely a stylist; and as we read those speeches today it takes a considerable effort of the historical imagination to find them perfectly sincere.

But since we cannot think of Dickens's prose as oratory (though I shall show later that it is something like oratory), we must find some other way of accounting for his explicit artifice and for our acceptance and enjoyment of it as we read. Were this prose less professionally secure and confident, we might condescend to its high-flown floridity as to something countrified and ill-educated. But the assured brilliance of the manner, the richness and power of the verbal resources—not to speak of the supreme success with which it achieves its purpose of registration and evocation—these make condescension impossible. There is nothing clumsy or inadvertent about it. This is a successfully functioning artistic enterprise, and we are left with the necessity of defining and accepting its conditions. These conditions amount to the fact that there are two 'presences', two illusions being created in this description: the illusion of Marseilles, a 'fact to be strongly smelt and tasted', and also the illusion of 'seeing' the skill of the describer itself, almost palpably present to us as he goes about his professional work of evoking the illusion of Marseilles.

This describer, this artist, is present before us not as a personality, with particular personal feelings, attitudes, and habits, but as a performer, as a maker and doer. We do not attend to his personality or his personal feelings (as, in the famous instance, we are invited occasionally to attend to the personality and personal feelings of Shelley). Our response to Dickens's presence in his prose takes the form of an impulse to applaud. The performer is 'there' in the sense that he is displaying his skill, and we respond to him appropriately by applauding his skill, just as the illusion of Marseilles is 'there', and we respond to it by crediting it and entering it. But of course the crediting is of a different order from that to which we are accustomed, because the impulse to applaud does not ordinarily come upon us when we are reading other great novelists. When it does, something has gone wrong. In the work of Conrad, for instance, whenever we sense the presence of conscious brilliance of expression we resent the intrusion of the artist calling for our applause: we think of such an occurrence as a vice of style, and so it is, because it interrupts the kind of illusion the prose is creating. Not so with Dickens, which is to say that Dickens's art thrives on a state of affairs that would be a vice in other novels. But this is also to say that Dickens's art creates a different kind of illusion from that of Conrad.

The licensed presence of the performer in this description accounts for and makes acceptable another oddity that faces us when we inquire into the function of the description in the novel as a whole. The description is not subject to the standards of relevance ideally governing the procedure of other novelists, yet again this oddity does not impress us as a defect.

Consider the standards of relevance that govern this description from *Middlemarch*:

Mr. and Mrs. Casaubon, returning from their wedding journey, arrived at Lowick Manor in the middle of January. A light snow was falling as they descended at the door, and in the morning, when Dorothea passed from her dressing-room into the blue-green boudoir that we know of, she saw the long avenue of limes lifting their trunks from a white earth, and spreading white branches against the dun and motionless sky. The distant flat shrank in uniform whiteness and low-hanging uniformity of cloud. The very furniture in the room seemed to have shrunk since she saw it before: the stag in the tapestry looked more like a ghost in his ghostly blue-green world; the volumes of polite literature in the bookcase looked more like immovable imitations of books. The bright fire of dry oak-boughs burning on the dogs seemed an incongruous renewal of life and glow—like the figure of Dorothea herself as she entered carrying the red-leather cases containing the cameos for Celia. (XXVIII)

In this description, to spell it all out slowly, we are not presumed to be interested in a description of a cold day in the English provinces for its own sake, nor to be interested in an account of how people in general might respond to such a day. We are interested only in the cold day in relation to the experience of a created character in whose experiences we have become engaged. A concrete scene is evoked, as in Dickens's description, but every detail in it is relevant to Dorothea Casaubon. The language of the second, third, fourth, and the first half of the fifth sentences is not a realistic imitation of Dorothea's feelings or of the words she would use about the scene to herself, but our perspective on the scene is hers and the feelings evoked by the scene are those evoked in her. And in the last sentence it is by a nice accordance with Dorothea's own habits of ironic self-scrutiny (but recently developed in her, to be sure) that we rise to a larger and more ironic view of the scene, of which Dorothea herself has become a part.

When a novelist describes a city or a countryside, then, he will normally be describing the environment, permanent or temporary, of a character with whose career we have become engaged. And if he begins his novel with such a description he will have a special reason for wanting us to understand the environment before he has introduced us to the character. In *The Portrait of a Lady* one of James's themes is the relationship of the spirit to the material things that surround it, and he opens his novel by describing the rich and fine texture of the civilization at Gardencourt because his heroine's first great choice in the novel will be to reject this kind of 'thing'. In the first pages of *Nostromo* we seem to be on a ship entering the harbour of Sulaco accompanied by a guide who instructs us in the economic geography of what we are looking at: we enter the Golfo Placido as students of international politics. And Conrad continues to interest himself throughout the novel in the relationship between individual human lives and large economic and political movements. George Eliot begins *The Mill on the Floss* with a description of the river and the country surrounding it, not only because the river is to play an important 'role' in the climax of the novel, but also because the heroine is dominated throughout the novel by a quasi-Wordsworthian piety towards the family and the landscape with which she grew up. And the description is couched in an appropriately personal tone of voice:

Just by the red-roofed town the tributary Ripple flows with a lively current into the Floss. How lovely the little river is, with its dark changing wavelets! It seems to me like a loving companion while I wander along the bank and listen to its low placid voice, as to the voice of one who is deaf and loving. I remember those large dipping willows. I remember the stone bridge.

This is a particularly instructive example. The unabashed presence of the narrator here, and the presence of the narrator's personal feelings, actually further the illusion rather than interrupt it; for those feelings strike (and, in the word 'deaf', with what marvellous concreteness!) the first note of familial piety towards nature, which will be echoed and confirmed by the feelings of the heroine. Conversely, the narrator's personal feelings validate the heroine's feelings. This example shows precisely that when a novel begins with a description it is ordinarily saying, 'This is what you need to know in order to understand what follows.'

But Dickens's opening description in *Little Dorrit* says nothing of the kind and will puzzle, if not irritate, readers who expect it to. Dickens's Marseilles is not an environment and his description of it does not promote our understanding of the characters in the first chapter. They are minor characters, as a matter of fact, but this is less significant than the fact that they are astonishingly unrelated to the Marseilles Dickens has been describing. The characters in this first chapter, Monsieur Rigaud and John Baptist, turn out to be in a foul prison where the glaring and staring sun cannot enter, a prison that is 'like a well, like a vault, like a tomb', damp and dark. And this new place is embodied in some new verbal contrivances only slightly less full-blown than the description of Marseilles itself.

The prison is, to be sure, connected with the preceding description by being called 'so repulsive a place that even the obtrusive stare blinked at it, and left it to such refuse of reflected light as it could find by itself'. It is an interesting and ingenious transition. Dickens's large theme in *Little Dorrit*, as Lionel Trilling and others have demonstrated, has to do with many kinds of imprisonment and with their effect on the human spirit, and one might be tempted to say that the effect of this transition is to show that even the overpowering glare and stare of a hot day in Marseilles are unable to penetrate the atmosphere of prison, which is always a self-contained and isolated world of its own. And in this reading we may discover a fine irony: if the real world is hostile, it is at least real, whereas one of the horrors of imprisonment is that prisoners in Marseilles wish they were in the sunlight when the sun is, in fact, staring and glaring. This reading is already pretty elaborate, but one might go further and read the irony backwards, to see that the people suffering under the stare and glare of Marseilles are in truth just as effectively imprisoned as if they were in the 'villainous' dark and damp place officially designated as a prison. One might indeed go further, go anywhere, because the fact is that in all these 'readings' we are on our own, making up our own novel, the kind we may like to read but not the kind Dickens wrote. Modern Dickens criticism has spawned many such 'free' readings, for the discovery that he is a symbolic novelist has apparently exempted his critics from even the most elementary standards of relevance.

Judged by such standards, however, there is no organic relationship between the description of Marseilles and the description of the prison, and the interesting ironic meanings suggested above can properly grow only out of such a relationship. Dickens's transitional sentence makes a little bridge to new material: it is ingenious and (such is the nature of the art we are dealing with) highly successful, but its ingenuity does not produce a meaningful organic relationship. Rather it clears the stage for a new performance, and when, in the prison, Monsieur Rigaud growls, 'To the Devil with this Brigand of a Sun that never shines in here!' we are dealing, simply, with a different sun. It might be argued that sensations so strenuously, so insistently evoked as the stare and glare of the opening paragraphs are not to be so lightly laid aside. But of course exactly the opposite is true. The insistence of Dickens's expressive devices has set the whole literary enterprise going at a certain pitch, which it will have to maintain thereafter: the stare and glare have been evoked by the strong force of the rhetoric in the performer's voice, and when that force, that presence, is withdrawn, the evocation collapses immediately, nor will the stare and glare return until they have been reactivated by similarly insistent and strenuous verbal artifice. And when we enter the prison the narrator's art is devoted to the new task of evoking the dampness and darkness of this new scene, and the sound of his voice at this new task fills our ears.

The loudness of Dickens's voice and of its expressive devices is virtually a physical, even an acoustic, phenomenon: it produces a condition in which the explicit intention of the insistent voice all but totally fills our consciousness, and it follows from this that we have little occasion to think of other intentions it might be pursuing, and which in another kind of prose it ought to be pursuing. In the second chapter of *Little Dorrit* Dickens introduces some of his main characters to us and he is almost totally occupied with the procedures necessary for doing so. We find these characters conversing without discomfort in the shade of a parapet, while their conversation pays no attention whatever to the stare and glare of their environment. The narrator alone remains conscious of the weather and offers occasional reminders to the reader: 'what cool refreshment of sea-breeze there was, at seven in the morning', 'they made little account of stare and glare, in the new pleasure of recovering their freedom'. But the characters themselves are unaffected by these reminders, and when they have finished their encounters it is again the narrator alone who is conscious of the effects of that opening description:

The day passed on; and again the wide stare stared itself out; and the hot night was on Marseilles; and through it the caravan of the morning, all dispersed, went their appointed ways. And thus ever, by day and night, under the sun and under the stars, climbing the dusty hills and toiling along the weary plains, journeying by land and journeying by sea, coming and going so strangely, to meet and to act and react on one another, move all we restless travellers through the pilgrimage of life. (I. ii) (p. 27)

Marseilles, then, is not an environment for Dickens's characters, but a setting for them: when the characters are on stage, so to speak, we are aware only of them and they happen not to be aware of the glare and stare; but when they make their exit we are left again with the stage-setting, and the chapter is rounded off with a little moralization of the setting itself, which has no specific relevance to the particular travellers we have seen.

If Dickens's description of Marseilles is not governed by the standards of relevance to which we are accustomed from other novels, this fact merely demonstrates that Dickens is writing in a totally different mode, for we do not consider these opening chapters of *Little Dorrit* unsuccessful. Dickens's descriptions are perfectly relevant—not to the characters but to another 'presence', that of the artificer, the performer, and to his intentions, which are always clear enough. In those first paragraphs the artist presents himself to us as a master of descriptive prose who has assigned himself a certain subject, and he has fulfilled the assignment with considerable power and intensity. We need nothing else; the occasion is complete; and he proceeds to his next assignment. All of which is to say that the centre of our attention in this prose is the artificer himself, his skills, and his purposes, and every event in the prose is related primarily to this centre.

Gissing noticed this fact—only once, apparently—and objected to it. He was discussing the opening of *Bleak House*:

London. Michaelmas term lately over, and the Lord Chancellor sitting in Lincoln's Inn Hall. Implacable November weather. As much mud in the streets, as if the waters had but newly retired from the face of the earth, and it would not be wonderful to meet a Megalosaurus, forty feet long or so, waddling like an elephantine lizard up Holborn Hill. Smoke lowering down from chimney-pots, making a soft black drizzle, with flakes of soot in it as big as full-grown snow-flakes—gone into mourning, one might imagine, for the death of the sun. Dogs, undistinguishable in mire. Horses, scarcely better; splashed to their very blinkers. Foot passengers, jostling one another's umbrellas, in a general infection of ill-temper, and losing their foothold at street-corners, where tens of thousands of other foot passengers have been slipping and sliding since the day broke (if this day ever broke), adding new deposits to the crust upon crust of mud, sticking at those points tenaciously to the pavement, and accumulating at compound interest. (1) (p. 1)

This wonderful writing is distinctly superior to the description of Marseilles: more agile and flexible in rhythm, bolder and more adventurous in the play of its imagination and wit. The whole is charged with resilient, spirited energy. But it is exactly to this that Gissing objected:

This darkness visible makes one rather cheerful than otherwise, for we are spectators in the company of a man who allows nothing to balk his enjoyment of life.[1]

Gissing is right, of course, that we sense throughout this passage a delighted observer and that it is from his point of view, with his attitude, that we see the London streets, not from that of the observed people who are supposedly having a bad time of it. And this passage *is* perhaps exceptional, but only because Dickens, in his joyful delight in making the scene effective and alive, has momentarily forgotten perhaps to make it perfectly clear that the people in the scene are not enjoying themselves. Except for this inadvertence, the passage is thoroughly representative. Whenever Dickens is at his best this odd thing happens: all the landscapes, all the dramatic scenes come to us in a voice in which we hear an infectious delight in what it, itself, is doing—infectious because the pleasure often spills over on to the material itself. And so I would amplify Gissing's remark to say that the source of Dickens's enjoyment here is not only the scene before him but his own skill in rendering that scene, and that he consciously and proudly offers us that skill for our enjoyment and our applause.

The first impression, and a continuing one, in Dickens's prose is of a voice manipulating language with pleasure and pride in its own skill. In the first paragraph of *Bleak House* it is the staccato rhythms, the vocal force in the epithet 'implacable', that command our attention first, before there are any objects to observe. And it is not without significance that the first object is in a double sense an imaginary object—that Megalosaurus 'forty feet long or so, waddling like an elephantine lizard up Holborn Hill'. That imaginary dinosaur, so vividly registered, so charmingly waddling, is a concrete embodiment in language of the self-delighting fancy of our performer's skilful voice—he has 'made it up' before our very eyes. It is not something we seem to experience from within the scene. No one has ever come within miles of even imaginary discomfort in looking at it—the insouciance of the language ('forty feet long or so'), the comic diminution ('waddling'), these easy devices keep us from inwardly imagining it.

[1] *Charles Dickens* (New York, 1924), p. 228.

Similarly the flakes of soot—snow-flakes 'gone into mourning, one might imagine, for the death of the sun'—register vividly enough, with a lively inventive point made about them, but this is a free-wheeling, self-delighting wit and inventiveness, and the inhabitants of the scene are no more touched by these flakes of soot than the visitors in Marseilles were by the glare and stare. The dogs exist just because we hunt for them in the mire and can't see them, the horses because of their minutely observed blinkers, the foot passengers because of their umbrellas.

But, it will be argued, the scene is concrete, the objects are realized in language and are really *there*. Yes, but in an odd way. Let me exaggerate by saying that these objects are there in the way the magician's rabbit is there. We give that rabbit its due as kicking flesh and blood, but we are more interested in giving the magician his due, for the rabbit seems to us mainly a concrete embodiment of his skill. You might say that although the rabbit exists, lives, and moves in its own flesh and blood, it has its 'reality' in the magician's skill that produced it out of the hat. Nor is this a distinction too subtle for something as crude as the performance of a magician: we know our way around among such distinctions very well indeed, when it comes to practice, and we signal our recognition of the kind of existence enjoyed by this rabbit by our response to the 'act', the response of applauding the magician. We make something of the same response to those horses, 'splashed to their very blinkers', which have been produced by the verbal skill of Dickens, the artificer, of whose presence we are never unaware.

There is another word for a magician—'illusionist', or 'illusion-artist'. Being a good audience for an illusionist requires not willing suspension of disbelief but almost the opposite. To get the point and pleasure we must almost encourage ourselves to disbelieve, because only by 'knowing' that the rabbit is not in the hat can we feel the impact of its *surprising* appearance when we see the magician pulling it out. It is this shock, the shock of belief in what we seem to know can't be 'really there' but do in fact see, that impels our applause. Dickens, it is true, does not actively encourage our disbelief in quite this way, but his art does not ask for, or get, willing suspension of disbelief as we commonly understand the phrase. He is an illusionist in the sense that the creation of an illusion is something he does only at certain moments, and with spectacular effect; he is not producing a *continuous* illusion of reality. It is a puzzling mode of art, and I can perhaps dramatize the nature and the difficulty of the Dickens problem by suggesting that his art is something that Partridge in *Tom Jones* would have appreciated. Tom and Mrs. Miller have taken Partridge to see Garrick's *Hamlet*:

> Little more worth remembering occurred during the play, at the end of which Jones asked him, 'Which of the players he had liked best?' To this he answered, with some appearance of indignation at the question, 'The king, without doubt.'—'Indeed, Mr. Partridge,' says Mrs. Miller. 'You are not of the same opinion with the town; for they are all agreed that Hamlet is acted by the best player who ever was on the stage.'—'He the best player!' cries Partridge, with a contemptuous sneer; 'why, I could act as well as he myself. I am sure, if I had seen a ghost, I should have looked in the very same manner, and done just as he did. And then, to be sure, in that scene, as you called it, between him and his mother, where you told me he acted so fine, why, Lord help me, any man, that is, any good man, that had such a mother, would have done exactly the same. I know you are only joking with me; but indeed, madam, though I was never at a play in London, yet I have seen acting before in the country: and the king for my money; he speaks all his words distinctly, half as loud again as the other.—Anybody may see he is an actor.' (Bk. xvi, ch. v)

Likewise, we may say, 'Anybody may see that Dickens is a writer', for the art of the actor who played the king has much in common with the prose we have been discussing.

When Partridge says 'Anybody may see he is an actor' he is both sneering at Tom's dullness and defining the actor's purpose as he understands it, which is to be loudly obvious about doing a spectacular thing called acting, but not in the least to create a continuous illusion. 'Acting' is very close to oratory, and requires a highly artificial speaking style, the essential virtue of which is to be 'loud and distinct'. When Garrick convincingly expresses fear, Partridge takes it for granted that this is not acting but Garrick's own emotion, and just because it convinces him he does not admire it. Indeed, he barely notices it except when he is arguing against Mrs.

Miller or defending himself against the charge of cowardice:
'Nay, you may call me coward if you will; but if that little
man there upon the stage is not frightened, I never saw any
man frightened in my life.' He is deeply moved by the closet-
scene, and therefore puzzled to hear it called a scene and
especially puzzled to hear Garrick's 'acting' in this scene
praised: 'Why, Lord help me, any man, that is, any good man,
that had such a mother, would have done exactly the same.'
'Good acting' in the closet-scene would be some extraordinary, artificial, peculiar way of 'behaving': it is because Garrick
behaves ('acts') so well that Partridge sees nothing to admire
in his *acting*. For 'acting' has really nothing to do with the
creation of an illusion as we ordinarily understand it, and in
fact has very little to do with expressivity either. During the
play within a play, Partridge asked her, 'If she did not imagine
the king looked as if he was touched; though he is,' said he, 'a
good actor, and doth all he can to hide it'—here Partridge gets
everything upside down because he hardly conceives that it
is the purpose of acting to express emotion at all. Convincing
expression of emotion and a convincing illusion of reality are
really wasted on him, just because he is so susceptible to being
convinced by them.

It is clear enough that Partridge would be a good audience
for Dickens's art, not of course in the sense that he would be
experienced enough to appreciate the rich mastery of Dickens's
style, but in the sense that the overtness of that mastery
would create no problems for him. He would also be an ideal
audience for the performance of a magician, since he would
believe so very firmly that the hat was empty that his surprise
and admiration when the rabbit appeared would be enormous;
and one can imagine him making this response again and again.
If he were to learn to appreciate Dickens's much more sophisticated version of pulling rabbits out of hats, his admiration
would be equally great. All this is clear enough, but it is also
clear that Partridge will not seem a very dignified model for
imitation, and that an art that appeals to him will not seem
a very dignified art; for Fielding is certainly making fun of
Partridge's provincial gullibility, and we are meant to realize
that the actor who played the king was a vulgar roarer. Yet
the issues raised by Fielding's ironies are fairly complex. The

implication throughout is that Partridge is experiencing a kind
of art which is new to him, and in fact Garrick seemed to
far more cultivated people than Partridge to be a new kind
of actor. Fielding, indeed, reports that Garrick apparently
wasn't able to find enough actors of his own kind to fill out the
whole cast, since a very important role had to go to an actor
of Partridge's kind. What then is Garrick's kind? The fact
that his acting 'fooled' Partridge is surely some kind of compliment to Garrick, and this means not that Garrick aimed
at fooling people like an illusionist but that his art worked
somehow in that direction. Yet Mrs. Miller and Tom have also
come to the theatre to see 'acting', to see a 'performance' by
'the best player who ever was on the stage', and they are able
to admire his performance instead of taking it for a real happening. What is at issue here is the permanent difficulty of
the word 'illusion'. One of the most famous attempts to deal
with it was made by Garrick's tutor, Dr. Johnson:

The truth is, that the spectators are always in their senses, and
know, from the first act to the last, that the stage is only a stage,
and that the players are only players. They came to hear a certain
number of lines recited with just gesture and elegant modulation. . . . It will be asked, how the drama moves, if it is not credited.
It is credited with all the credit due to a drama. It is credited,
whenever it moves, as a just picture of a real original; as representing to the auditor what he would himself feel, if he were to do
or suffer what is there feigned to be suffered or to be done.[1]

Johnson's powerful argument creates a forum of sophisticated
rational common sense in which the puzzles connected with
the word 'illusion' vanish as smoothly as Berkeley's nonsense
vanished under the rhetoric of the famous kick. The value of a
dramatic illusion vanishes too. Johnson's rhetoric invites us
to join the society of urban, civilized, and rational men who
go to the theatre not to lose their senses in an illusion but to
become expert judges, judging the degree of 'justness' in the
gesture and 'elegance' in the modulation achieved by those
who are 'reciting' the lines. Tom and Mrs. Miller are members
of this society, always in their senses; Partridge would be
excluded because he finds it so hard to remain in his senses.

[1] Walter Ralegh, *Johnson on Shakespeare* (London, 1925), pp. 27–28.

He is in fact merely uneducated. What he responded to in Garrick's performance was exactly its 'justice' and 'elegance', but he is below the level of being interested in or even aware of these civilized achievements. He can therefore offer no significant testimony about what happens at the theatre beyond that of inadvertently emphasizing, by contrast, the rational civilization achieved by the Augustan temperament.

Dr. Johnson's argument makes no significant distinction between an art which maintains a continuous illusion, like Garrick's, and an art which creates an illusion only intermittently, like that of the actor who played the king and that of Dickens. But if we move out of the range of Johnson's seductive rhetoric of common sense we again become aware of other possible alternatives. We remember that there are states of mind more complex than either 'being in one's senses' or 'not being in one's senses', and we return then to our interest in and our problems about the word 'illusion'. Here is another attempt to deal with the word 'illusion', from a far more subtle and professionally expert thinker about theatrical matters than Johnson, Bernard Shaw:

But Duse has been helped to her supremacy by the fortunate sternness of Nature in giving her nothing but her genius. Miss Ellen Terry is a woman of quite peculiar and irresistible personal charm. Miss Achurch has been kept in constant danger of missing the highest distinction in her art by having, as an extra and cheaper string to her bow, an endowment of conventional good looks, and a large share of that power of expressing all the common emotions with extraordinary intensity which makes the vulgar great actress of the Bernhardt school. . . . But in Duse you necessarily get the great school in its perfect integrity, because Duse without her genius would be a plain little woman of no use to any manager. . . . Duse, *with* her genius, is so fascinating that it is positively difficult to attend to the play instead of attending wholly to her. The extraordinary richness of her art can only be understood by those who have studied the process by which an actress is built up. You offer a part to a young lady who is an enthusiastic beginner. She reads it devoutly, and forms, say, half a dozen great ideas as to points which she will make. The difficulty then is to induce her to do nothing between these points; so that the play may be allowed at such moments to play itself. Probably when it comes to the point, these intervals will prove the only effective periods during her performance, the points being ill chosen or awkwardly executed. The majority of actresses never get beyond learning not to invent new points for themselves, but rather to pick out in their parts the passages which admit of certain well worn and tried old points being reapplied. When they have learnt to make these points smoothly and to keep quiet between whiles with a graceful air of having good reasons for doing nothing, they are finished actresses. The great actress has a harder struggle. She goes on inventing her points and her business determinedly, constantly increasing the original half-dozen, and constantly executing them with greater force and smoothness. A time comes when she is always making points, and making them well; and this is the finishing point with some actresses. But with the greatest artists there soon commences an integration of the points into a continuous whole, at which stage the actress appears to make no points at all, and to proceed in the most unstudied and 'natural' way. This rare consummation Duse has reached. An attentive study of her Marguerite Gauthier, for instance, by a highly trained observer of such things, will bring to light how its apparently simple strokes are combinations of a whole series of strokes, separately conceived originally, and added one by one to the part, until finally, after many years of evolution, they have integrated into one single highly complex stroke. Take, as a very simple illustration, the business of Camille's tying up the flowers in the third act. It seems the most natural thing in the world; but it is really the final development of a highly evolved dance with the arms—even, when you watch it consciously, a rather prolonged and elaborate one. The strokes of character have grown up in just the same way. And this is the secret of the extraordinary interest of such acting. There are years of work, bodily and mental, behind every instant of it—work, mind, not mere practice and habit, which is quite a different thing. It is the rarity of the gigantic energy needed to sustain this work which makes Duse so exceptional; for the work is in her case highly intellectual work, and so requires energy of a quality altogether superior to the mere head of steam needed to produce Bernhardtian explosions with the requisite regularity.[1]

Shaw's distinctions yield a much sharper focus than Johnson's on the performance of *Hamlet* in *Tom Jones,* and for our purposes on Dickens. Inspecting Shaw's four kinds of actress, we see that Partridge would have liked and understood Bernhardt, whereas Tom Jones and Mrs. Miller would have found

[1] *Our Theatres in the Nineties,* 3 vols. (London , 1932), i. 146–8.

Duse more to their taste. In his next review, Shaw described Bernhardt's method more fully:

Her lips are like a newly painted pillar box; her cheeks, right up to the languid lashes, have the bloom and surface of a peach; she is beautiful with the beauty of her school, and entirely inhuman and incredible. But the incredibility is pardonable, because, though it is all the greatest nonsense, nobody believing in it, the actress herself least of all, it is so artful, so clever, so well recognized a part of the business, and carried off with such a genial air, that it is impossible not to accept it with good-humour. One feels, when the heroine bursts on the scene, a dazzling vision of beauty, that instead of imposing on you, she adds to her own piquancy by looking you straight in the face, and saying, in effect: 'Now who would ever suppose that I am a grandmother?' That, of course, is irresistible; and one is not sorry to have been coaxed to relax one's notions of the dignity of art when she gets to serious business and shews how ably she does her work. The coaxing suits well with the childishly egotistical character of her acting, which is not the art of making you think more highly or feel more deeply, but the art of making you admire her, pity her, champion her, weep with her, laugh at her jokes, follow her fortunes breathlessly, and applaud her wildly when the curtain falls. It is the art of finding out all your weaknesses and practising on them—cajoling you, harrowing you, exciting you—on the whole, fooling you. And it is always Sarah Bernhardt in her own capacity who does this to you. The dress, the title of the play, the order of the words may vary; but the woman is always the same. She does not enter into the leading character: she substitutes herself for it.[1]

Partridge would respond to this—'Anybody may see she is an actress.' More importantly one sees that, despite the force of Shaw's witty and impudent abuse, he too responds to Bernhardt's art and recognizes her as having achieved consummate perfection in a certain style of acting. The fact that he actually resents her power over him emphasizes its intensity, and the problem it causes. The problem arises because when he is in the presence of Bernhardt, Shaw is caught in the dilemma of deciding which of two equally valid 'truths' to emphasize: the truth that Bernhardt's kind of acting is inferior to Duse's in dignity, and the truth that it is very different in kind, since it

[1] i. 149–50.

does not create a continuous illusion, and that she is superbly good at it. He is in no doubt as to which of these kinds he thinks is the greater, yet Bernhardt's kind obviously appeals to certain of his interests, and these interests, when she is performing, become final and absolute: they cannot be resisted by remembering that he prefers to attend to other more dignified interests. Bernhardt brought to perfection the art of the actor who played the king. It is very different from the art of Garrick, and if the king had been a better performer in it there would have arisen a problem of conflicting interests for the audience. The art of Dickens is also different in kind from what we expect to find in the novel, and because he is a consummate performer there is a Dickens problem.

The kind of art Dickens practises I propose to call 'theatrical art'. This is clearly appropriate for the kind of art practised by Bernhardt, and there is an obvious similarity between the characteristics of a Bernhardt performance as Shaw describes them and the characteristics of the opening chapters of *Little Dorrit* and *Bleak House*. There is the constant and overt intention to dazzle us with verbal devices, leading us through our impulse to applaud to a continual awareness of the artificer responsible, a self-exhibiting master of language. There is the fact that the presence of this artificer does not interfere with the workings of the language in the medium of prose fiction, since the objects and feelings created by Dickens's devices do indeed come into existence, though not in the mode of illusion to which we are accustomed (just as Shaw reports that Bernhardt did her 'work' ably when she got down to 'serious business', the work consisting of making the audience 'follow her fortunes breathlessly' and indeed of 'fooling' the audience). Finally, there is the fact that the several effects or 'points' made by the artist are not 'integrated' into a 'continuity' as we ordinarily understand the word, and do not need to be, since each one is sponsored directly by the artist to achieve his obvious moment by moment plans and purposes, one of which is self-display. Above all, by the word 'theatrical' and by the comparison of Dickens and Bernhardt, I am pointing to the fact that these qualities in their performances, which may seem to us so much less dignified than those of most of the art we take seriously, are 'irresistible' when we are in contact with a consummate performer in the medium of which they are the leading characteristics.

I had better use Shaw's distinctions also to make a cautionary statement of what I do not intend by 'theatrical'. I do not mean, for instance, that Dickens's art is merely a non-realistic art. Garrick's art, were we to see it today, might perhaps seem 'realistic', and Duse, of course, acted mainly in plays of the nineteenth-century realist school. But it is not to her realistic style that Shaw is drawing attention. He is stressing the *form*, the structure, of her performance, not at all the fact that she used, as the separate 'strokes' of this performance, representations of the actual surface and texture of everyday life; nor is Shaw primarily making the opposite point about Bernhardt, though he is surely referring to it in his description of her stylized physical beauty. The illusion which Duse created, and which derived from the 'integrated continuity' of her acting, was not so much an illusion of reality as an illusion of naturalness—she 'appears to make no points at all, and to proceed in the most unstudied and "natural" way'. Shaw claims, it is true, that Duse gives the audience 'the charm, in short, belonging to the character she impersonates', whereas he says of Bernhardt that 'she does not enter into the leading character: she substitutes herself for it'. But Duse's art is not that of realistic impersonation, as Shaw's description of her 'highly evolved dance with the arms' shows. On this point we have the curiously corroborative testimony of a much more superficial observer than Shaw who is all the more trustworthy for just that reason. Max Beerbohm almost hated Duse, he thought her arrogant and egotistical, because she never deigned to use the elementary instruments of illusion that are furnished by make-up or the more obvious mimicry of impersonation.[1] She was not, to use Beerbohm's habitual and significant word, a good 'mime', or even a 'mime' at all. Now, on the question of Duse's greatness one simply takes Shaw's testimony as more trustworthy than Beerbohm's, but one can accept Beerbohm's factual report too, for it does not essentially contradict Shaw's or cast any doubt on his judgement. Beerbohm's key word is 'mime', Shaw's is 'natural'. And the word 'natural' happens to be a word we use to praise the most excellent performances

[1] *Around Theatres* (New York, 1954), pp. 81–82.

in highly stylized, distinctly non-realistic arts. We use it, for instance, in speaking of ballet, and we use it with particular force to praise the dancing of certain dancers in abstract ballets, in those of Balanchine, for example. When such a dancer, in such a ballet, looks 'natural' and makes one 'believe' in his or her identity as a 'person' while making highly stylized non-representational movements, this illusion is created, as Shaw says, because these separate movements have been integrated into a continuous flow. Why an integrated continuity should seem natural is another matter, to which I must give some attention later; at the moment I wish only to emphasize that it does, and to suggest that the kind of illusion we expect to find in serious art is less misleadingly described as the illusion of naturalness than as the illusion of reality. If Dickens's art is theatrical then, it is not because it is non-realistic.

Another possible implication of the word 'theatrical' that I want to avoid is one that may have arisen through the words 'loud' and 'distinct', or through Shaw's reference to Bernhardt's 'explosions': the implication that the difference between theatrical art and the other kind lies in the restraint, the quietness, the good taste of the latter, and the loud brilliance of the former. The 'points' of theatrical art may indeed *seem* more brilliant than those of Duse, since they are not integrated into a continuity but sponsored directly by the artist. But Shaw's praise makes it clear that Duse's was a very strongly inflected art, as does Beerbohm's hostility. It is even likely that Beerbohm's hostility was occasioned partly by the very power of Duse's expressivity: his mild and humorous refusal to 'rave' about her may have been his way of saying 'Not English'. There is evidence elsewhere in the dramatic criticism that Beerbohm suffered under a profound misunderstanding about taste in the arts, a misunderstanding which makes the deepest experience of art inaccessible to many cultivated people. These are people who have learned that Bernhardt's explosions are not in good taste, but they have learned it only negatively, not positively—as Shaw did—by learning what an integrated continuity in the arts looks like and how intensely interesting and beautiful it is. Out of this negative taste a conception of the arts can be developed in which, though explosions are known to be in bad taste, it is discovered that bad taste can be 'fun'—and one gets the cult of 'good theatre'. The devotees of this cult have often claimed Dickens for their own, and I am anxious to save him from this kind of enthusiasm. For the 'good theatre' cult, serious art is likely to be identified as the mere opposite of vulgar brilliance: quiet restraint, modesty, conventional and respectable good manners, and regularity. Consider, for instance, those music-lovers who have learned to despise—or, in the next convolu-tion, to find amusing—the brilliant explosions of the star performers, but have learned to respect and admire instead only the pallid and correct regularity which some musicians, equally deceived, produce by fearfully avoiding brilliance and power of inflection. An art so produced by a gifted artist may indeed be very beautiful, but an exclusive preference for it— and especially for its superficial earmarks—is an unfortunate and even a vicious taste. Responsiveness to musical correct-ness may in fact be a lack of responsiveness to musical life, and one knows cultivated people who are not only unresponsive but actually hostile to the powerfully inflected continuity of impulse in the very greatest musical performances—those of Toscanini, Schnabel, Casals, Glenn Gould. Consider also the current problem of the dancer Nureyev. His dancing seems to most people incontestably powerful and expressive, but the applause he gets is equally powerful; and his lack of conven-tional modesty and Royal Ballet 'good form' has blinded many judges of correctness to the powerful continuity of his dancing and the very powerful illusion which that continuity creates. Indeed, what is condemned as bad taste may, ironically, be the fact that Nureyev creates a powerful illusion of which he is inevitably the centre. And D. H. Lawrence's offences against good taste and good form will never cease to infuriate those who cannot hear his genius and follow the continuity of his original structures.

It may well be that Beerbohm was unable to banish such a negative standard of refined and restrained good taste from his mind when he came to the obviously 'serious' art of Duse, which is to say that he created his own Duse problem. But with the superb fooling of Bernhardt the elegant Max had no problem whatsoever. Shaw, in arguing that Bernhardt could

not be taken seriously, actually took her very seriously indeed,
since he described her method from the inside, he knew the
mode she was working in by experiencing it. To Beerbohm,
Bernhardt was *connue*, a known and laughable quantity, and
her Hamlet provided (understandably enough) the occasion
for one of his own performances: 'Yes! the only compliment
one can conscientiously pay her is that her Hamlet was, from
first to last, *très grande dame*.'[1] Such amused affection for the
'theatre' of Dickens is far from what I am attempting to
convey. Bernhardt at her worst must have been very silly, and
even at her best her art may always have been faintly meretricious. Dickens's art is famous for the remarkable innocence
of its spirit, and on the question of his skill and power there
need be no interrogation of witnesses—it is still there, extraordinarily alive, on almost every page. But although Dickens's
innocence and his genius make his theatrical art far too large
and important a matter to be handed over to the good-theatre
cult, these qualities only augment the Dickens problem; for
that problem exists only for those who know what Shaw meant
by an integrated continuity and who share his intense admiration for it.

In one respect, my term 'theatrical' will occasion no
surprise, and need no defence, inasmuch as it has been very
frequently used to describe Dickens's art in the past. But it
has been a pejorative use, and I want to avoid the implication
that it is the bad, the melodramatic, the trashy Dickens who
is a theatrical artist. Let me point instead to a well-known
fact about Dickens to confirm my contention that the word
'theatrical' is appropriate to almost all of Dickens's art, good
and bad alike. Not only did he spend much of his energy in
amateur theatricals, but he also virtually acted out the
theatrical nature of his art in the public readings which
eventually exhausted even that immense energy. His desire,
his need, to enact his special kind of art on an actual stage and
in the living physical presence of his audience amounted to an
obsession, to which he was driven against the advice of his
physicians and his friends and against his own reason. But no
one has ever seen anything in the least puzzling about his
public readings of the death of Paul Dombey and the murder

---

[1] *Around Theatres* (New York, 1954), p. 37.

of Nancy. Everyone understands why he did it, just as everyone understands why George Eliot did not give public readings
of the death of Maggie Tulliver, and why Tolstoy's need for a
closer relationship with the people did not take the form of
public readings of the death of Prince André.

The recent view of Dickens as a serious symbolic and prophetic artist is supposed to have put an end once and for all
to the old superficial view of his work as merely 'entertainment', and my word 'theatrical' will perhaps seem merely to
be ignoring what the new Dickens criticism has demonstrated.
But there is in Dickens's kind of symbolism nothing antithetical to the theatrical mode of all his work. The basic
argument of the recent criticism claims that readers in the past
were not aware of the symbolic structure of his novels, which
they regarded as journalistic improvisations for the serial-
novel audience. Accordingly, external and internal evidence
has been offered to prove that Dickens planned his novels
with complete consciousness of his own symbolic proclivities
and intentions. And we have heard much about the fog and
Chancery in *Bleak House*, prisons in *Little Dorrit*, the river
and the dust-heap in *Our Mutual Friend*. Edmund Wilson's
words can stand as the rationale of all this recent work:

The people who talk about the symbols of Kafka and Mann and
Joyce have been discouraged from looking for anything of the kind
in Dickens, and usually have not read him, at least with mature
minds. But even when we think we do know Dickens, we may be
surprised to return to him and find in him a symbolism of a more
complicated reference and deeper implication than these metaphors
that hang as emblems over the door. The Russians themselves, in
this respect, appear to have learned from Dickens.[1]

On this basis a large body of symbolic interpretation of
Dickens's work has been built up, much of it just and illuminating. The fallacy lies in the claim that those readers who
did not name Dickens's structures 'symbolic' were unaware of
them. For the truth of the matter we can return to Partridge:
'Anybody may see that Dickens's novels are structures of
symbols.' Dickens's novels are all of a piece, and the large
symbolic patterns of *Little Dorrit* are offered to us as insistently
as the verbal schemes in the opening description of Marseilles.

[1] *The Wound and the Bow* (Cambridge, Mass., 1941), pp. 37–38.

A theatrical artist displays in front of us his skills and the special illusions he creates by means of those skills, but he may also, by means of the same methods and under the same circumstances, perform before us a large structure of these illusions, which, by virtue of their planned interconnexions, will amount to a statement about the world and about human nature. If such is his aim he will, in accordance with his theatrical instincts, make it perfectly clear in theatrical terms. I simply do not believe in the existence—now or in the middle of the nineteenth century— of the unknowing readers against whose insensitivity to Dickens's symbols so much of the current criticism is triumphantly directed. Who are these deaf entertainment-lovers who can encounter the following passage from the first chapter of *Bleak House* and remain unaware that the London fog and mud are 'symbolic of' the tendency of institutions to stifle human interests? 'Never can there come fog too thick, never can there come mud and mire too deep, to assort with the groping and floundering condition which this High Court of Chancery, most pestilent of hoary sinners, holds, this day, in the sight of heaven and earth.' (i) (p. 2) What reader will fail to see that in the second chapter Dickens wants to introduce him to another instance of the same thing? 'It is but a glimpse of the world of fashion that we want on this same miry afternoon. It is not so unlike the Court of Chancery, but that we may pass from the one scene to the other, as the crow flies.' (ii) (p. 8) And with each new instance, and with each recurrence of each instance, these loud and distinct connexions are made for us by the theatrical artist. Often he makes them explicitly, and even when he does not he always sees that we are conscious of his plans, his meanings, his structures.

If there are readers who are aware of these meanings, as they cannot help being, and who nevertheless do not connect this kind of writing with Kafka's, they are responding to an important difference between two different kinds of art. And if they have reserved the work 'symbolic' for Kafka's kind and left themselves with no appropriate word for Dickens's kind, they are again responding accurately to what I have called 'the Dickens problem'.

2

THE MORAL BASIS OF NON-THEATRICAL ART

THERE is a Dickens problem because we ordinarily do not regard the theatrical mode as capable of 'serious' artistic effects and meanings. There is then another mode which does seem capable of these high matters, a mode for which we have no name because it is the only mode which we take 'seriously', to use the dangerous word again. In Shaw's terms, this is Duse's mode, and its essential characteristic and method is to integrate separate 'points' into a continuity which creates the illusion of 'naturalness'. I propose now to raise the question why this mode seems the best and how it comes to be the only generally recognized vehicle for serious effects and serious meanings in art.

It is not only for ironic effect that I go to Edmund Wilson, one of the critics against whose view of Dickens this study is directed, for another definition of the 'serious' mode of artistic creation: Edmund Wilson's common sense is so dependable that his definitions will not easily be suspected of special pleading or fancy professionalism. My text is taken from his 1944 review of Katherine Anne Porter's *The Leaning Tower*: 'She is absolutely a first-rate artist, and what she wants other people to know she imparts to them by creating an object, the self-developing organism of a work of prose.'[1]

This definition is a distinction rather than a description: you have to know what Mr. Wilson means by the 'self-developing organism of a work of prose' before you can understand his sentence. The question he is answering, in fact, is not 'What is art'? but 'Which, of the various elements in a work of art, is the distinguishing one, without which art cannot be said to be first-rate'? Mr. Wilson is specifically praising the fact that Katherine Anne Porter does not 'tell' us her 'general opinions' about life. But his words have the larger implication that, in

---

[1] Reprinted in *Classics and Commercials* (New York, 1950), p. 222.

the work of a first-rate artist, we tend not to be *in any respect* conscious of the artist but only of the work of art in itself, and the work of art in itself does not *tell* us anything but instead *develops*, in accordance with its own internal, 'organic' life. What Mr. Wilson is describing and praising seems, at first glance, a mysterious and even a paradoxical state of affairs. The work of art is a construct made by the artist, yet it turns out to be a self-developing organism. Nevertheless, most readers will accept this account of the distinctive quality of the highest art; most of us use it as a standard of judgement.

Everybody agrees, for instance, that when Faulkner's work is at its best, his special vocabulary (of which 'indomitable' will be a sufficient example) seems to be actually generated by the people and situations about which he is using it, and thus disappears from our consciousness as a special vocabulary. But in his worst work it does not disappear, but rather seems to have been imposed upon the characters and their situations, and thus shows itself to be exactly a special vocabulary which someone, some voice, which we may legitimately call Faulkner's, enjoys using because of the thrilling sensations it affords. Demonstrating which passages are of the one kind and which of the other is a subtle business and one would expect to find different critics in disagreement with each other about particular works. But these disagreeing critics would agree that the difference between the two kinds of writing is both crucial and recognizable, and that the first kind is good and amounts to what Mr. Wilson describes as a self-developing organism in prose, and that the second kind is bad because it is not self-developing nor an organism, but a construct validated only by the voice, and behind the voice by the *will*, of the writer.

Faulkner's work is a useful example because the intensity of his special vocabulary leads to effects which are equally intense and therefore easy to see and analyse. When 'indomitable' is joined to the words surrounding it by the nerves of a living organism, the power generated is very strong indeed. But when this does not happen, the 'effect' is actively irritating and repellent. We feel that the elements of the fiction have been deliberately contrived and manipulated as pretexts for the use of these exciting words and that the motive is to thrill the writer and to exploit the feelings of the reader. We find ourselves in a repellently direct contact with the author's will, which seems to be interested in dominating the real world instead of understanding and revealing it. And this means that we are asking Faulkner not for a miracle of creation but for something much closer to our everyday concerns and our everyday practices; we are asking him for a certain moral attitude towards what his artistic talents have called into being. If, when his work is not at its best, we are repelled by the presence of his will, then it follows that we are asking him to discipline that will, to get beyond it and its interest in dominating the world, and that in his best work he succeeds in doing this. And there is a positive way of describing how he does it.

Henry James speaks with unusual authority on this question. Through the systematization of his views by Percy Lubbock and others, his name has come to represent only a specialized technical interest in the modes of achieving a dramatic illusion in the novel. But Henry James was by no means a mere technician; he was constantly alert to the moral implications of his technical concerns:

'Balzac aime sa Valerie', says Taine, in his great essay—so much the finest thing ever written on our author—speaking of the way in which the awful little Madame Marneffe of *Les Parents Pauvres* is drawn, and of the long rope, for her acting herself out, that her creator's participation in her reality assures her. He has been contrasting her, as it happens, with Thackeray's Becky Sharp or rather with Thackeray's attitude toward Becky, and the marked jealousy of her freedom that Thackeray exhibits from the first.[1]

James is describing a 'self-developing organism' which in this instance is not the whole work of fiction but one of its elements, the fictional representation of a human being. Madame Marneffe derives her freedom from her creator's 'participation in her reality', and, conversely, he can participate in her reality only because he lets her be free to act herself out, because he does not force his own will on her. Taine and James bring the great word to bear on their subject without senti-mentality: 'It was by loving them—as the terms of his subject

---

[1] *The Question of our Speech, The Lesson of Balzac* (Boston, 1905), pp. 96–97.

and the nuggets of his mine—that he knew them; it was not by knowing them that he loved.' James's language moves easily and expertly through the paradoxes: it is the artist's subject but the terms of it exist for themselves, in themselves, in a realm of being which he can only know by loving; it is his mine, but the nuggets in it are *there*, to be found and owned only in loving knowledge. Here, too. there is a viable bridge between moral and technical concerns. Thackeray's jealousy of Becky Sharp is not only an ugly moral spectacle in itself, but also simply a practical disadvantage for the artist, because it cuts him off from 'knowledge' of the terms of his own subject.

For an amplification of what James means by 'her creator's participation in her reality', we may go to another of James's teachers, George Eliot:

We are all of us born in moral stupidity, taking the world as an udder to feed our supreme selves: Dorothea had early begun to emerge from that stupidity, but yet it had been easier to her to imagine how she would devote herself to Mr. Casaubon, and become wise and strong in his strength and wisdom, than to conceive with that distinctness which is no longer reflection but feeling—an idea wrought back to the directness of sense, like the solidity of objects —that he had an equivalent centre of self, whence the lights and shadows must always fall with a certain difference.[1]

Here the moral question and the technical question merge completely. George Eliot is distinguishing between two kinds of love. There is a love which imposes an identity on the loved one and is therefore wilful and egotistic, however honourable the identity imposed and however total the lover's devotion to that identity. And there is another kind of love, more disinterested, less egotistic, more imaginative, by means of which alone Dorothea can penetrate to the inner 'centre of self' of Mr. Casaubon, participate in his reality, and truly know him. More important, George Eliot is here pointing to the essence of her own artistic mode and its appropriate procedures, procedures of which she is clumsy enough to let us see the machinery from time to time. In the opening of Chapter XXIX, for instance, she writes: 'One morning, some weeks after her arrival at Lowick, Dorothea—but why always Dorothea? Was her point of view the only possible one with regard to this

[1] *Middlemarch*, XXI.

marriage ?' However clumsily explicit the voice of the narrator is here, there is no important interruption of the action or the illusion, for the significant action in *Middlemarch* is the artist's attempt to conceive the centre of self of her characters, and that attempt is surely, though too explicitly, continuing in these sentences. There are, elsewhere in the treatment of Dorothea, failures of objectivity which Dr. Leavis has pointed out with his usual accuracy, failures which testify to the fact that imaginative disinterestedness, the highest kind of creative gift, was not always easy even for this large mind and imagination. But *Middlemarch* is concerned throughout with the centre of self of its various characters, and it is in fact George Eliot's amplitude and patience of analysis that allows her to achieve that participation in the character's reality of which James speaks. Most of the characters in *Middlemarch* are given an unusally long rope for acting themselves out.

I have gone far away from Edmund Wilson's words and it may seem that I have even gone counter to them. For Mr. Wilson's point is that Katherine Anne Porter does not tell us her general opinions about life, and George Eliot is famous for doing exactly that. But 'the George Eliot problem' seems to me to derive from critical dogma and not from her novels. The general understanding that a great work of art is a self-developing organism has narrowed and hardened in the practice of some critics into a mechanical rule of thumb which automatically interprets any explicit authorial commentary, analysis, or generalization as a sure signal that the work of art has failed. But the life of a work of art is not commensurate with such mechanical rules. The created life in *Middlemarch* is not threatened or even interrupted by George Eliot's moral generalizations; on the contrary it actually lies in the explicit 'analysis'. On the other hand, modern literature is full of completely dramatized works of art which claim to be self-developing organisms and are actually sterile contrivances of the will. A completely dramatized work of art may be the highest kind, and yet an exclusive taste for this kind of art may be a vicious taste. James's preoccupation with 'total dramatization' has the grandeur of a fatal obsession, and it drove even his immense talent and intelligence into inadvertent, unnecessary, and even self-destructive ambiguities.

Lesser talents will often produce total dramatizations which
are closer to the efficiency of a gadget than to the miracle of
creation. Discovering whether a work of art is in fact a self-
developing organism is a function of the whole sensibility, and
it is, if the word be granted a wide and flexible enough definition, an essentially *moral* function. Our response to Faulkner's
failures in this respect is a kind of distaste which has moral
implications; likewise, our deep admiration of his successes
is a matter of moral judgement too, a matter of recognizing
and honouring the *best* kind of relationship between the human
being and his materials and his world.

To those who may object to George Eliot's explicitly moral
language, let me point out a striking connexion between her
words and those of a writer who will at least not be accused of
sharing her moral tone. 'To conceive with that distinctness
which is no longer reflection but feeling—an idea wrought back
to the directness of sense, like the solidity of objects'—these
words bring to mind T. S. Eliot's description of the ideal poetic
sensibility which feels its thought 'as immediately as the odour
of a rose'. To me, George Eliot's discursive language seems
subtler and more exact in reference than T. S. Eliot's rather
banal simile; but both Eliots are trying to describe the same
high achievement. T. S. Eliot's account of what happened in
Donne's mind is a device for describing what happens in the
poetry as we experience it, and his word 'immediately' leads
us on to his related dictum about the 'objective correlative'—
that the feeling must 'arise' out of the literary objects presented.
And in the word 'arise' there is again the implication of im-
mediacy: the poet does not wilfully mediate between us and
his objects, but lets the objects speak for themselves. One is
reminded, too, of T. S. Eliot's continual concern for the im-
personality of the artist.

Edmund Wilson, Henry James, George Eliot, and T. S.
Eliot are each in their own way describing the same quality
and honouring it as the best. T. S. Eliot emphasizes discipline,
tradition, and authority. His terms will satisfy those to whom
the warmer and more explicitly moral vocabulary of James
and George Eliot is displeasing. But what they are all pointing
to—the self-developing organism—is in fact generally accepted
as the desideratum in art, and it seems to me that the moral

language of James and George Eliot is the only language which can account for the immense prestige this kind of art enjoys. When from this sense of what is highest in art we derive criteria for judging particular works, we do so with assurance and passionate intensity only because we are, perhaps unconsciously (and perhaps for that reason the more boldly and sincerely), expressing a preference for the most honoured moral ideals in our culture: for disinterestedness, for a love which is morally intelligent, for the sympathetic imagination.

These are the ideals of that other mode of art against which I have set Dickens's 'theatrical mode'. That they seem impossibly high ideals for a merely human art is logical, even tautological in view of the fact that our culture has conceived its art 'seriously', as an endeavour worthy of its highest faculties. These impossible ideals turn out, moreover, to be eminently and happily practical; they have kept our art fresh and self-renewing. Even the studied triviality of a Firbank is 'serious' when it is properly identified as a move, however weirdly indirect, toward these ideals. Only in this light can we see the real dignity in what might otherwise seem the disheartening flux of fashion in literary taste. The reputation of George Eliot is up again, T. S. Eliot's idealization of the impersonal artist has come to seem suspect to many besides Dr. Leavis—and so it goes. But these fluctuations, which have already been the occasion for many a chic analysis of the literary stock-market, are serious and necessary events in the dialectic of the literary conscience when they are viewed and experienced properly, from the inside of the experience of art and with respect to the ideals by which they are motivated. If an external view promotes dilettantish relativism, that is merely another argument against a foolish and inhumane perspective.

Likewise, the intensity of literary warfare will seem preposterous and ludicrous only to those who do not take literature seriously. The battle between Joyce and Lawrence, for instance: on the one side we can envision Lawrence denouncing Joyce for 'doing dirt on life'; on the other side, Joyce identifying Lawrence as an almost unbelievably perfect instance of that inferior art which is both pornographic and didactic. Here is a fine Hegelian drama, yet the dialectical struggle is both

serious and fruitful. Nothing is clearer than that both writers
share the same goal and are indeed quite explicitly dedicated
to the discovery of a morally intelligent love of life. Out of such
a dialectic as this, literary history takes its form and direction.

The greatest works of art lead us to these high questions
naturally, and modern literature tends to do so quite consciously. Although the same questions are at stake in all
serious art, the terms in which I have described them are
perhaps too extreme to seem relevant to many valuable works
of art which nevertheless belong to the non-theatrical mode.
For, just as the supreme moral ideal of a disinterested
imaginative love has in our everyday life descended to bodies
in the not contemptible form of good manners, good breeding,
and good form, so the achievement of this ideal in works of art
has often been a matter of conventional forms of decorum. In
science there are the imaginative leaps of the great minds, but
there is also the accurate reporting of lesser minds which is
nevertheless honourably selfless and disinterested. In literature
there are the supreme moments of imaginative sympathy, in
Homer, Dante, Shakespeare, Tolstoy; but there are also the
lesser works which, by their accurate reporting, their tact and
taste, their disciplined craftsmanship, their decorum, convince
us that they stand in a morally intelligent relationship to their
subjects. There are, too, the works against which we use the
words 'good form' as a contemptuous dismissal, and it is again
only a subtle action of the whole sensibility that can judge
between the wheat and the chaff in this respect. But below
the level of the supreme imaginative artists, there is an art
governed by what might be called a code of literary good manners, morally intelligent without being sterile and merely well
bred, and capable of producing its own kind of imaginative insight.

It is against this code of literary manners that Dickens
offends most obviously. The first 'rule' our civilization teaches
any writer is not to 'show off his style', not to show that he is
trying to delight us with verbal tricks and dazzle us with his
virtuosity. This is the area of simple *good taste* and *good
manners*: the tasteful artist will never seem to be seeking our
applause. It is moreover only *good sense* that the novelist
should not work hard to make us believe in his illusion and

then let us catch a glimpse of him behind the scenes, manipulating the whole business. Everybody scolds poor Thackeray, and with the greatest confidence, for calling his characters puppets (for this reveals his radical uncertainty about his whole career and his whole moral perspective). We feel pretty complacent about these rules of good taste and good form. 'Our hero' and 'our heroine' appear only as parody now. And, on another level of taste altogether, I am sure that other readers have shared my affectionate pleasure at seeing the strict Jane Austen forget herself in those curious sentences towards the end of *Mansfield Park*:

Let other pens dwell on guilt and misery. I quit such odious subjects as soon as I can, impatient to restore every body, not greatly in fault themselves, to tolerable comfort, and to have done with all the rest.

My Fanny indeed at this very time, I have the satisfaction of knowing, must have been happy in spite of every thing. (III. xvii) (XLVIII) (p. 461)[1]

Jane Austen breaks the rules here, and everybody must be aware of it momentarily, though no important interruption of the illusion has taken place. Dickens, however, breaks these rules from start to finish in all his books: he is always the self-conscious virtuoso and we never lose sight of him for a moment.

Consider the reception the opening of *Little Dorrit* would get, today or in Dickens's time, if it were submitted as a piece of student writing to a teacher of English prose composition. Perhaps genius would be recognized, making vain all thought of discipline. But judged by conventional standards of 'stylistic purity', decorum, or educated good form, this description of Marseilles is almost beneath criticism. The writer seems never to have heard of the rules. As it happens, the description is just laboured enough to arouse the shadow of such standards in our minds as we read, though we see easily enough that they are really irrelevant to what we are experiencing. The sound of genius in the opening pages of

[1] All quotations from Jane Austen are followed by three kinds of reference: in the first parenthesis to the chapter number in editions which divide the novels into volumes; in the second parenthesis to the chapter number in editions which do not; in the third parenthesis to the page number in the *Oxford Illustrated Jane Austen*, third edition.

Bleak House, one hopes, would silence the sternest discip-
linarian. 'Anyone may see' that the writer is 'writing for
effect', but the impulse to scold is immediately dissolved by
the impulse to applaud—after which the rules never cross
our minds again. Yet this fact has very rarely been straightforwardly put down on paper.

The explanation for this conspiracy of silence is of course a
simple one. Even the darkest symbol-reader takes Dickens for
granted as a humorist, and humorists are licensed exceptions
to the rules of writing. They can not only 'try to be funny'
without annoying us, but they are expected to try. They annoy
us only if they don't succeed.

Anyone who opens one of Dickens's novels, then, is prepared
to enter a 'theatre' and to co-operate with the 'theatrical mode'
because he knows that he is going to find 'humorous' writing
soon and he knows, without consciously defining it as such,
that humorous writing is theatrical in nature. Humorous
writing is expected to reveal itself openly as 'trying to be
funny', and the reader will not be at all surprised to find the
humorous writer openly trying for whatever other kinds of
effect he might be interested in. We know our way around in
the Dickens theatre.

It is my contention, of course, that the recent Dickens
criticism has totally lost sight of this theatre, else I could
hardly ask my reader to be very excited to discover that
Dickens was a humorist. I do indeed believe that Dickens
was essentially and radically a humorist, certainly that he
was *first* a humorist. I believe, also, that he became what
must be called, for lack of a better word, 'serious'. The fact
that he was from the beginning, and remained, committed to
the theatrical style means not only that he expressed his serious
concerns in a unique mode but that he felt and saw them from
the first in a strange way. Nor should we be surprised to find
that this amazing theatrical performer, who is largely exempt
from the ordinary rules of literary procedure, is also largely
exempt from, and ignorant of, and indeed hostile to the moral,
intellectual, and emotional disciplines and habits which we
accept as normal to serious concerns. From which it follows
that Dickens's way of 'loving' his characters and his world is
not the way we are accustomed to find in high art.

3

DICKENS AND THE INNER LIFE

THE methods of a work of fiction amount to its mode of 'seeing' its subject, and the subject of fiction is human beings and their relationships. It is precisely Dickens's method of characterization which has from the beginning seemed the one obvious critical problem about his work.

The problem itself has been most fluently by-passed by the recent view of Dickens as a symbolic artist. Dickens criticism today proceeds by means of critical terminology and critical strategy in comparison with which the word 'characterization' itself may seem almost provincial. But an even more outlandish kind of critical language has been used about Dickens: it often used to be said that his characters are not 'real'. Sophisticated people shoot this one on sight now, to ward off sentimental nonsense about the girlhood of Shakespeare's heroines. But we can take it for granted that characters are not people and that Hamlet is an illusion made up entirely of words, and yet at the same time hope that so valuable a word as 'real', a word so centrally useful to all our thinking about ourselves and everything around us, may remain available in literary discussions. Marianne Moore has made a famous request for 'real toads' in the 'imaginary gardens'[1] of poetry. What does she mean by 'real', and is it the same thing that people used to mean when they said that Dickens's characters were not real?

Miss Moore's 'garden' is the conventional ideal garden of poetry and by accepting this she accepts the fact that the world of art is of a different order of being from that of actual existence. Beyond this, she implies that she doesn't want entry to this world of art limited by a narrow and precious standard of what is attractive or agreeable; there should be toads as well as flowers. But she wants 'real toads', and this artful

---

[1] 'Poetry', *Collected Poems* (New York, 1951), p. 41.

(perhaps arch) verbal trick needs some exigesis. Since Miss
Moore wants everything in the imaginary garden to be 'real',
it is by her choice of the word 'toad' that she shows us how
reality can be achieved. The trick here, I think, is that Miss
Moore's plain words and syntax, which apparently merely
state her prescription, actually enact an experience, the experience of seeing a little patch of undifferentiated earth in
a garden suddenly come alive in the form of a hopping toad.
Toads are nearly invisible in an actual garden; and when we
survey a garden, we normally use a kind of idealizing, conven-
tionalizing 'eye' for the whole effect, which is destroyed by
our catching a glimpse of (or perhaps by touching) a toad, an
experience which unexpectedly activates powerful sensuous
and kinesthetic responses. Then our view of the garden
changes from conventional idealization to an immediate sense
of the concrete particularity and individuality of its separate
objects. Miss Moore's 'real' suggests the shock of concreteness. And she is asking for a kind of art which can, without
interrupting the illusion of the imaginary garden, transform
sterile aesthetic contemplation into a concrete experience of
living reality.

Miss Moore's prescription—asking as it does for an almost
shocked awareness of this 'reality'—has only a limited relevance to the general procedures of art, but that is no important
criticism of it, as long as the limitations are recognized. The
real toad is an apt analogy for the aliveness of space in Van
Gogh's *The Artist's Bedroom*, for instance, but it seems too
excited and tricky to have much to do with the aliveness of
space in Cézanne's *Mont Sainte Victoire* in the Metropolitan
Museum, with its quietly grand harmony that is nevertheless
completely alive. Yet 'real toads in imaginary gardens' seems
at first glance distinctly relevant to the kind of aliveness and
concreteness that is virtually the Dickens trademark.

Consider the lizard and the panting air in the description
of Marseilles, or the Megalosaurus, the dogs and horses in the
description of London from the opening of *Bleak House*—these
dogs and horses seem to share with Miss Moore's toad exactly
the quality of near-invisibility and therefore the same shocking
actuality. Consider, too, Mrs. Pardiggle in *Bleak House*:

She was a formidable style of lady, with spectacles, a prominent nose, and a loud voice, who had the effect of wanting a great deal of room. And she really did, for she knocked down little chairs with her skirts that were quite a great way off. As only Ada and I were at home, we received her timidly; for she seemed to come in like cold weather, and to make the little Pardiggles blue as they followed. (VIII) (pp. 100–1)

Or Mr. Vholes, who 'takes off his close black gloves as if he were skinning his hands'. (XXXIX) (p. 549) Or the windows in Mr. Vholes's office, which 'have but one piece of character in them, which is a determination to be always dirty, and always shut, unless coerced. This accounts for the phenomenon of the weaker of the two usually having a bundle of firewood thrust between its jaws in hot weather'. (XXXIX) (p. 547)

These brilliant, thoroughly representative passages only superficially fulfil Miss Moore's requirements for 'reality'. Again it is a question of the self-developing organism, the continual illusion. Those windows, with their 'determination' and their 'jaws', derive their animation from the felt and known presence of the theatrical performer too obviously to be really very much like Miss Moore's toads, which—and this is the main point about them, I think—seem to move *by themselves*. It is hard to find accurate words to describe the sense in which Dickens's windows are alive and concrete and real. The whole theatrical enterprise is so wonderfully alive that one wants to avoid language implying that the windows are a contraption worked by the theatrical artist, that Mrs. Pardiggle 'knocking down little chairs' is a puppet manipulated by the puppeteer. Nevertheless, the *intention* to animate those windows, and the *agency* by which this is achieved, are thoroughly obvious to us at all times, and this does make a difference.

When Miss Moore asks for real toads in imaginary gardens she is taking for granted, I believe, what you cannot take for granted in Dickens, the self-developing coherence of the 'garden' of the basic illusion. She is describing the way this garden comes to life and becomes significant to human beings and their interests. This happens when we make contact with the inner life of the garden, the suddenly discovered 'real toad'. But she never for a moment doubts that the garden itself should seem to be a self-sponsoring, self-developing coherent illusion. Readers who call Dickens's characters unreal

are taking this for granted too. The charge that Mrs. Pardiggle
is not real, that she does not 'come alive', is a perfectly literate
way of saying that Dickens has not created an imaginary
garden as we ordinarily understand it. Mrs. Pardiggle does
move, she 'knocks over little tables', but that movement does
not seem to come from inside her and she does not seem to come
from inside the garden either. She does not seem to be alive in
and for herself; she does things because the author makes her
do them.

To point out something like this in the work of serious
novelists is, of course, to make an important charge against
them. But in reading Dickens such a charge becomes impossible if only because one has to make it all the time. In
Dickens's theatrical art the will of the artist is always a felt
presence, and Mrs. Pardiggle seems no more and no less real
than the fog, the horses, the dogs in the opening description.
Nothing moves by itself, everything is sponsored directly by
the theatrical artist's voice. Everything is the brilliant achievement of an 'illusionist', and nothing is real.

But when people say that Dickens's characters are not real,
they may also mean that they are not 'believable', not true
to life. Here we enter a more complex question. It is precisely
the vivid concrete particularity of Dickens's characters that
seems to inhibit some people's belief in them. What Mrs. Gamp
looks like, what she does, what she says, is too brilliant, too
sharp, too 'loud and distinct' to be believed in. Yet much
recent Dickens criticism has made a point of demonstrating,
and it has been a fairly easy demonstration, that people really
do look like that, people really do say things like that, again
and again. Clearly we are dealing with a question of attitude,
not of fact. There is something about Dickens's way of looking
at people which is unacceptable by the ordinary standards of
serious fiction.

For an analysis of this matter, we may turn again to George
Eliot. Before Celia Brooke, in *Middlemarch*, learns that Casaubon has been a successful suitor for her sister's hand, she
expresses a hope that he will not be the only guest at dinner:

'I hope there is some one else. Then I shall not hear him eat his
soup so.'

'What is there remarkable about his soup-eating?'

'Really, Dodo, can't you hear how he scrapes his spoon? And he always blinks before he speaks. I don't know whether Locke blinked, but I'm sure I am sorry for those who sat opposite to him, if he did.'

'Celia,' said Dorothea, with emphatic gravity, 'pray don't make any more observations of that kind.'

'Why not? They are quite true,' returned Celia, who had her reasons for persevering, though she was beginning to be a little afraid.

'Many things are true which only the commonest minds observe.'

'Then I think the commonest minds must be rather useful.' (v)

George Eliot, in the best pages of *Middlemarch*, maintains an ironic balance between Dorothea's way of seeing human beings and Celia's. In the passage quoted, Dorothea seems to be rejecting physical appearances as an accurate witness to spiritual identity: there are things about human beings which uncommon minds simply do not observe, their attention being fixed on spiritual essences. But Celia uses the same word that Marianne Moore uses:

> Hands that can grasp, eyes
> that can dilate, hair that can rise
>   if it must, these things are important not because a
> high-sounding interpretation can be put upon them but
>   because they are
> useful.

Sensuous response to concrete particularity is 'useful'—and it is interesting that the sensuous responses Miss Moore lists are those of fear. Celia trusts her response to Casaubon, the repulsion and the disgust, because it seems useful. For Dorothea such a response is common. But she has herself her own standards for reading the indices of spiritual nature in the face. 'He is one of the most distinguished-looking men I ever saw. He is remarkably like the portrait of Locke. He has the same deep eye-sockets.' When Celia complains that Mr. Casaubon is sallow, Dorothea expresses scorn for a man like Sir James Chettan, 'with the complexion of a *cochon de lait*'. And there are other views represented—Sir James, for instance, says, 'Look at his legs!' George Eliot fixes all these responses in terms of the habits, the expectations, the personal standards of each of the characters. Her mastery lies in affirming all these readings of Mr. Casaubon's spiritual nature, whilst in her own practice transcending them by an appeal to the sympathetic imagination capable of achieving another kind of vision which sees human beings with another kind of concreteness. Let me quote the great passage again:

We are all of us born in moral stupidity, taking the world as an udder to feed our supreme selves: Dorothea had early begun to emerge from that stupidity, but yet it had been easier to her to imagine how she would devote herself to Mr. Casaubon, and become wise and strong in his strength and wisdom, than to conceive with that distinctness which is no longer reflection but feeling—an idea wrought back to the directness of sense, like the solidity of objects —that he had an equivalent centre of self, whence the lights and shadows must always fall with a certain difference.[1]

With this goal in mind, George Eliot looks at the loud and distinct visible manifestations of that inner life, and tries to see them as accurately as possible, the moles along with the deep eye-sockets; she listens to Casaubon scraping his spoon and also to his thoughtful and deliberate speech. But she is eager (too eager, some would say) to pass beyond these external manifestations: not to deny them nor merely to 'analyze' the motives that produced them, but to make imaginative contact with, to 'conceive' with 'distinctness', the inner life that makes the gestures and feels the motives. Observe that the crucial word is 'conceive', not help or comfort or even love. When Dorothea goes to visit Rosamund, she wants to help her and does succeed in comforting her; and it is true, as Dr. Leavis has pointed out, that George Eliot is guilty here of a rapturous over-valuation of Dorothea's actions and motives. But George Eliot's theoretical statement of this ideal contact with the inner life of human beings is as disinterested as Joyce's image of the creative artist, her statement being an adequate description of what Joyce achieves in his characterization of Leopold Bloom. It is, in fact, an accurate description of what we expect to find at the heart of all significant dramatic literature—what people who cannot 'believe' in Dickens's characters are puzzled to find lacking at the heart of Dickens's work.

[1] *Middlemarch,* XXI.

Contact with the inner life of created characters is established by various means in serious literature, but it always takes the form of an 'action' because we ordinarily assume inner life to be an action. Two chief modes of contact may be distinguished: continuous registration and sudden revelation.

The most familiar example of the continuous registration of the inner life is the Shakespearian soliloquy. Through familiarity it has come to seem eminently natural and straightforward, but it is actually an accident in the history of language and therefore a very dangerous model to imitate. This frank and direct address to the audience produces, in the work of Shakespeare and some of his contemporaries, a remarkably convincing, continuous, and fully rendered registration of inner happenings; but it is of course the 'Shakespearian' condition of the language to which is due our sense of the participation in the reality of the inner life of Hamlet:

> This is most brave,
> That I, the son of a dear father murther'd,
> Prompted to my revenge by heaven and hell,
> Must (like a whore) unpack my heart with words
> And fall a-cursing like a very drab,
> A scullion! (II. ii. 610–15)

We know Hamlet's self-disgust by means of Shakespeare's language; through our own experiencing of the 'action' of the language, we participate in the action of his inner life, which can then be said to have been enacted for and by us. Otherwise Hamlet would seem merely to be telling us what and how he feels. The imitation of this dramatic device is remarkably successful in Ahab's soliloquies in *Moby Dick*, but notoriously unsuccessful in the lurid sensationalism of Shelley's *The Cenci*, and the luxurious upholstery of Tennyson's blank-verse tragedies.

Since Richardson the novel has had at its disposal an equally straightforward technical device for the continuous registration of inner happenings, one perhaps even more dangerous to use than the dramatic soliloquy. Yeats claimed that the modern realistic drama was incapable of poetry because it had to be true to the expressive habits of modern, educated people, who, when they are disturbed about anything, look moodily into the fire and remain silent. He added that the modern psycho-logical novel does not labour under this disadvantage, because the novelist can 'follow the thoughts of the man looking into the fire', and thus need not be at pains to develop conventions and devices for registering the inner life of his characters. The novelist can produce, that is, a *narrative* or analysis of inner happenings, and of course most modern novelists do this at great length as an important part of their method. The notorious problem is that this narrative or analysis can re-main only *statement*, lacking entirely that 'distinctness which is not reflection but feeling': it has become possible for us to know everything *about* a character without 'knowing' him in the special sense which art can achieve. Indeed, one of the received opinions of yesterday was that George Eliot's in-teresting and 'wise' moral and psychological essays about her characters were in just this sense deficient in drama and crea-tive imagination.

Everyone agrees that the modern novel has become a very complex medium of artistic expression: the question is whether one should substitute the less graceful word 'complicated' for the word 'complex'. To some tastes, which to me seem inhumanly pure, no literary form besides the short lyric is capable of the highest excellence. But even a much less rigorous taste might well find a structure like *Middlemarch* disturbingly unshapely, very far indeed from the pure spontaneous flame of passionate utterance—'simple, sensuous and passionate' are the last words one would apply to this 'study of provincial life'. But the critic's duty is to discover where the life in a work of art really lies, rather than to com-plain that it doesn't lie where he would like it to. Only a naïve anti-rationalism would claim that there is an *essential* antithesis between George Eliot's analytic methods and true creativity. And the complicatedness of the modern novel can be explained by the impossibility of clear action in the modern world, which makes it necessary for the novelist to bring us into so close a knowledge of such complicated *terms* of life in order to show us what action is exactly or what it can be in any modern person's life.

This is not the place to attempt the long and careful analy-sis that would be necessary to prove that *Middlemarch* is an 'imitation of an action' which does achieve that 'distinctness which is no longer reflection but feeling'. I am confident that such a demonstration is possible and that it could broaden considerably the general conception of the way the creative imagination works and perhaps must work today. I will say in passing, though, that the mode of action in *Middlemarch* is that of the narrator's and reader's search, beyond the surface of conventional social life, for the inner life of human beings in a provincial society, and that this search is not completely unlike the action in *Oedipus Rex*. Sophocles' question-and-answer technique creates for the audience a continuous registration of the action of the inner life of Oedipus, though of course this happens more indirectly than in the Shakespearian soliloquy. Yeats did not see that Ibsen made his own kind of poetry out of an adaptation of Sophocles' methods. In *Ghosts*, for example, the continuous mutual interrogation of the characters, carried on in colloquial language of the very flattest kind, deliberately inexpressive, nevertheless enacts Mrs. Alving's self-discovery in an action which we must call poetic. But Yeats could of course have pointed to the sterilities of the well-made play which imitate the same device. We must expect to find in serious literature plenty of failed attempts to register, in a continuous dramatic enactment, the inner life of human beings; and there will always be some argument whether anything but the full Shakespearian, or Jamesian, method is sufficiently dramatic. But we may assume that serious literature will always try to find a way to achieve this continuous vision of the inner life, for it will always need one in order to seem serious.

For an example of a sudden revelation of inner life, rather than continuous registration, we may go again to *Hamlet*.

Polonius: My honourable lord, I will most humbly take my leave of you.

Hamlet: You cannot, sir, take from me anything that I will more willingly part withal—except my life, except my life, except my life. (II. ii. 218–21)

Here, out of the brilliant contrast of the two social tones and the two syntactical structures, there is generated, with extraordinary vividness, an illusion of the inner life in Hamlet. With this speech, one can perhaps argue persuasively against those who are becalmed in their discovery that 'Hamlet' is made up of words and that all talk of his inner life is illegitimate and unsophisticated speculation. For it is out of the action of the *words* here, that is, out of the tension between the two tones of voice, that there is bred the illusion of a deeper life in which that tension is taking place as conflict. Just as we have throughout the play the illusion that 'Hamlet' is 'speaking', so we at this point have the illusion that the 'inner life', the centre of self, of Hamlet is finding its kind of utterance. Observe that we *hear* the language, but *envision*—conceive— the centre of self. 'Except my life, except my life, except my life', expresses an inner feeling which exists in tension with the contemptuous irony of the rest of the speech, which we can call Hamlet's 'behaviour'. We hear both the behaviour and the feeling. The feeling does not merely 'explain' the behaviour, as might happen in the work of a cruder artist. Although we are interested in understanding the motive for Hamlet's behaviour (particularly since Polonius himself voices such an interest in this scene), we do not rest in the solution we have found, as Polonius does. Our main concern is with vision, not with explanation, though explanation is a viable and legitimate pathway to vision, with Shakespeare as well as with George Eliot. Thus, when I say that this speech suddenly reveals Hamlet's inner life, I am not saying that it reveals the inner feeling which accounts for Hamlet's behaviour; but that out of the tension between the feeling and behaviour, that is, out of the verbal action, there is generated the illusion of Hamlet's self, which is the field for both his feeling and his behaviour.

This particular device is so prevalent in all drama and fiction that it is likely to seem not a device at all, but nature itself. Perhaps it is nature. Certainly the confusion of art and life is in this respect a daily occurrence for us all: we read the speech of our friends as if it were drama, often with surprising success. This is inevitable for the deeper reason that we expect serious drama and serious literature in general to enact an approach towards human beings which accords with the way we approach the people we know in real life, when we are taking them seriously.

We seldom speak of 'taking people seriously', but we speak often enough of 'not being able to take them seriously'. This piece of ordinary language is worth considering, for in using it we voice, casually and confidently, an entire moral system. When we say—of a fool, or a clown, or a mass-murderer—that we cannot take him seriously, we are voicing a moral condemnation of a human being who does not seem truly human because he does not seem to have a 'self'.

The existence of a self behind or beneath or beyond or above visible and audible behaviour is the creation of our own act of imagination and faith; we create the self of others. Yet this creation is, in ordinary experience, so automatic, so habitual as hardly to deserve the name. The question hardly interests us until the habit is frustrated, and only then do we learn that the kind of self we are trying to create and are in the habit of creating is not merely an inner life which can suffer feelings and breed motives, but an inner life which is the field for a moral activity. This moral activity tends towards self-awareness, self-criticism, but must at the very least involve a *sense* of the problematical relationship between two separate things—the self and what is not the self—and a sense of responsibility concerning that relationship. All this we presume, in an almost mechanical act of faith, to be taking place inside people we meet. When an Adolf Eichmann, for instance, interrupts the mechanism of our faith, we react by instituting a search for signs of that moral activity. We are not inquiring whether that activity has been carried on to good effect; we are already certain that it has not. We are inquiring whether that activity has taken place at all, whether, indeed, there actually is a field, a self, in which that activity could possibly take place.

If the reader can be said to encounter human beings (and not merely patterns of words) in the mode of illusion we call fiction or drama, then it seems to me that his normal, habitual, almost mechanical expectation is that he will encounter human beings whom he can take seriously, human beings with an inner life which is the field for this moral activity of self-awareness and self-criticism. The responsibility of the artist, in the face of this expectation, is that he will never frustrate it pointlessly. He will often frustrate it pointedly. The normal procedure in satirical comedy of manners, for instance, is to surround a hero or heroine whom we can take seriously with other characters whom we cannot take seriously; *The Way of the World* is a classic instance. At another level, Albany in *King Lear* shares and speaks the reader's discovery that Regan and Goneril cannot be taken seriously as human:

> Tigers, not daughters, what have you perform'd?
> A father, and a gracious aged man,
> Whose reverence even the head-lugg'd bear would lick,
> Most barbarous, most degenerate, have you madded.
> Could my good brother suffer you to do it?
> A man, a prince, by him so benefited!
> If that the heavens do not their visible spirits
> Send quickly down to tame these vile offences,
> It will come,
> Humanity must perforce prey on itself,
> Like monsters of the deep.   (IV. ii. 40–50)

It was George Eliot's habit (some would say her limitation) to take all her characters seriously; only at the end of her career, in the figure of Grandcourt in *Daniel Deronda*, did she turn her attention to a human being whom even her immense generosity could not quite take seriously as human.

The reader's expectation of encountering human beings whom he can take seriously may be frustrated for other purposes besides moral condemnation. In a successful farce, the audience learns very quickly to abandon the expectation, not only that the characters will have an inner moral life, but also that they will have inner feelings or even physical sensations. But many people dismiss farce as a barbarous form of art altogether. Even Shaw, so canny in theatrical matters, scolded Oscar Wilde for not touching his heart in *The Importance of Being Earnest*. But Shaw's best plays are heartless intellectual farces, and his attempts at more 'serious' forms, as in *Saint Joan*, only make us realize that we cannot take *him* seriously when he deserts his natural style.

Shakespeare's theatre, a remarkable (perhaps precarious) hybrid of realistic and conventional modes, enacts a wide variety of ways of taking human beings. It is generally accepted by now that Polonius's advice is spoken by a conventional role, 'the father giving advice', and not by the fool whom Hamlet cannot take seriously until he has killed him. The

Duke in *Measure for Measure* is not taken seriously for a different reason: as a manipulator, a deviser, the Duke of dark corners inhabits a level of illusion with which we are only now becoming familiar. Even Shakespeare himself may have been guilty of some uncertainties in the manipulation of his rich repertory of conventions; how to take Iago is a moot question still. When Coleridge spoke of Iago's 'motiveless malignity' he was taking him as Albany takes Goneril and Regan, as a monster within which there is no self. E. E. Stoll answered, much too crudely, that Iago was a role, a device, a 'villain'. Dr. Leavis suggests that the focus of the action is never really on Iago, but on the attitudes of Othello which made the success of Iago's schemes possible. Perhaps it is impossible for modern readers to be as sensitive and knowledgeable an audience for Iago as Shakespeare asks; but the possibility remains that Shakespeare himself miscalculated.

In the Shakespearian theatre it is the audience's responsibility to keep all these possibilities open and ready. Yet even here the normal attitude that the audience—at least the modern audience—takes towards the represented persons is the serious one, and any deviations from it must be recognized as deliberate and understandable exceptions to the norm. Certainly this is true of most of the fiction and drama after Shakespeare, when the realistic mode became dominant. And thus when people say that Dickens's characters are not 'real' or 'believable' or that they do not 'come alive', they are saying that they cannot take these characters seriously and yet at the same time do not understand why this should be so. The difficulty is not likely to be experienced by a reader co-operatively engaged in the theatrical situation in which Dickens always works, however. And to criticize certain elements of the performance after one has left the theatre and forgotten the special circumstances of the theatrical situation and its appropriate kind of art is simply to be irrelevant.

Theatrical art is not an appropriate mode for dealing with the inner life, nor is an artist who works in this mode likely to be interested in the inner life. The elements of serious dramatic art—the self-developing, continuous, and integrated illusion, the self-effacement of the artist, the disinterested, morally intelligent search for the centre of self of human beings—these elements are the harmonious manifestations of an attitude of mind and an attitude towards the world totally at variance with the procedures and attitudes of theatrical art. In theatrical art the primary object of our attention is the artist himself, on the stage of his own theatre, performing his brilliant routines. The characters he 'creates' on this stage will come to us, and be consistently known to us, as the embodiments of his brilliant gift for *mimicry*. And his art inevitably will represent an attitude towards human beings which is in harmony with this skill. A mimic will see what can be mimicked; he will see what can be seen.

Again we come back to one of the commonplaces of the old Dickens criticism, the fact that Dickens's characterization is rendered from an external perspective. George Eliot praised Dickens for his brilliant achievement in this mode, but expressed a faint—and quite unreasonable—hope that he would give some attention to the inner life:

> We have one great novelist who is gifted with the utmost power of rendering the external traits of our town population; and if he could give us their psychological character—their conceptions of life, and their emotions—with the same truth as their idiom and manners, his books would be the greatest contribution Art has ever made to the awakening of social sympathies. But . . . he scarcely ever passes from the humorous or external to the emotional and tragic, without becoming . . . transcendent in his unreality.[1]

To check George Eliot's judgement, let us examine what happens when Dickens does attempt to vary his normally external perspective with some attention to the inner life. Here is an external view of Lady Dedlock in *Bleak House* which is thoroughly representative of his normal methods:

> Both before and after saying it she remains absorbed, but at length moves, and turns, unshaken in her natural and acquired presence, towards the door. Mr. Tulkinghorn opens both the doors exactly as he would have done yesterday, or as he would have done ten years ago, and makes his old-fashioned bow as she passes out. It is not an ordinary look that he receives from the handsome face as it goes into the darkness, and it is not an ordinary movement, though a very slight one, that acknowledges his courtesy. But, as

---

[1] 'The Natural History of German Life', *Essays* (Edinburgh, 1884), pp. 236–7.

he reflects when he is left alone, the woman has been putting no common constraint upon herself.

He would know it all the better, if he saw the woman pacing her own rooms with her hair wildly thrown from her flung back face, her hands clasped behind her head, her figure twisted as if by pain. He would think so all the more, if he saw the woman thus hurrying up and down for hours, without fatigue, without intermission, followed by the faithful step upon the Ghost's Walk. (XLI) (p. 581)

The dramatic method in this scene is what any reader would call theatrical, in the ordinary sense of the word, and the word melodramatic is likely to come to mind too. The pregnant mute interchange at the door, the thrilling shift in Lady Dedlock's behaviour when she is alone—these are 'effective pieces of business', exciting theatrical 'points', beyond any question. And Lady Dedlock's gestures and postures when she is alone are Dickens's transcriptions of the methods of melodramatic and operatic heroines. We can easily think of all this as 'stagey' because this melodramatic mode of theatrical art is still with us, in parody or in the tissues of absurdity rescued from oblivion by Verdi's music. But it is my contention that Dickens's methods here are no different from his methods elsewhere.

Dickens is doing exactly what Shakespeare was doing in the scene between Hamlet and Polonius: he is setting up a tension between behaviour and inner feeling. Why then does he not, from this tension, create an illusion of the centre of self of Lady Dedlock? The answer does not involve a mere question of taste: it is not merely that Lady Dedlock's actions have become a crude theatrical cliché, whereas Hamlet's speech has retained its freshness. For we must ask why this difference exists.

When we take Lady Dedlock's actions as a 'theatrical effect', we do so because we are instructed to do so by Dickens himself, by the voice of the theatrical artist, and instructed by no subtle hints but by 'loud and distinct' contrivances: 'It is not an ordinary look . . . it is not an ordinary movement'—devices in which the master theatrical showman's hand and intention is clearly visible. 'Taken seriously', these devices could at best invite us to supply the missing concreteness out of our own repertory of 'extraordinary' theatrical movements and looks.

But we do not even go so far as this. We respond directly to what is in fact the primary object of our attention, the narrator's voice; and that voice is working us up into thrilled excitement at the brilliant spectacle he has mimicked for us. Dickens follows Lady Dedlock into her own rooms ('He would know it all the better, if he saw the woman pacing her own rooms') to excite us about what is going on there, which he mimics in turn. If we are obedient to Dickens's voice, we simply have no time or energy to make contact with the inner life of Lady Dedlock as we do with Hamlet's; nor is there any occasion to, since we are already making a satisfactory contact with Dickens. But if we are not obedient, and ponder privately on Lady Dedlock's inner life, we are simply making up our own novel, not attending to Dickens's performance in the Dickens theatre.

The point is that Lady Dedlock herself is putting on a performance here which is meant to be assessed with a pleasurable expertise. We see her first through the eyes of Mr. Tulkinghorn and we are invited to share his respect and admiration for the boldness, the power, the skill of her 'acquired presence'. We continue this attitude when we see what she does when she is alone: we are meant to applaud the grandeur and intensity of her 'style' of suffering and the grandeur and intensity of the emotions she is expressing. She is meant to be a wonderful creature, a great 'heroine'—her passion and her conflict are wonderful things to look at.

When he treats Lady Dedlock's motives, and Mr. Tulkinghorn's, Dickens's energy again is directed mainly towards the manipulation of the audience:

Lady Dedlock is always the same exhausted deity, surrounded by worshippers, and terribly liable to be bored to death, even while presiding at her own shrine. Mr. Tulkinghorn is always the same speechless repository of noble confidences: so oddly out of place, and yet so perfectly at home. They appear to take as little note of one another, as any two people, enclosed within the same walls, could. But whether each evermore watches and suspects the other, evermore mistrustful of some great reservation; whether each is evermore prepared at all points for the other, and never to be taken unawares; what each would give to know how much the other knows—all this is hidden, for the time, in their own hearts. (XII) (p. 166)

Observe that any serious concern for motive here is actively discouraged. Despite the artful teasing, there is no mystery, and the theatrical artist is telling us just what is in fact hidden in these hearts. But in the manner of his telling he leads us to the response he wants, for we are by far less concerned with what these two are thinking and feeling than with the *frisson* of mystery, the thrilled apprehension of hidden motives and plans.

Nor is Dickens ever afraid of a repeat performance. Within his theatrical style, he is extraordinarily inventive of new ways of making the same point:

Yet it may be that my Lady fears this Mr. Tulkinghorn, and that he knows it. It may be that he pursues her doggedly and steadily, with no touch of compunction, remorse, or pity. It may be that her beauty, and all the state and brilliancy surrounding her, only gives him the greater zest for what he is set upon, and makes him the more inflexible in it. Whether he be cold and cruel, whether immovable in what he has made his duty, whether absorbed in love of power, whether determined to have nothing hidden from him in ground where he has burrowed among secrets all his life, whether he in his heart despises the splendour of which he is a distant beam, whether he is always treasuring up slights and offences in the affability of his gorgeous clients—whether he be any of this, or all of this, it may be that my Lady had better have five thousand pairs of fashionable eyes upon her, in distrustful vigilance, than the two eyes of this rusty lawyer, with his wisp of neckcloth and his dull black breeches tied with ribbons at the knees. (XXIX) (p. 402)

This splendid array of possible motives figures merely as the *material* which the theatrical mystification-artist is manipulating for his desired effect. He leads us excitingly and excitedly *past* his exhibit of mysterious suggestions and brings these theatrical speculations to their appropriate fruition in another thrilling tableau; the fashionable lady improbably threatened by the rusty old lawyer. The loud and distinct irony of this image not only pleases both the narrator and the reader but also satisfies us as the appropriate goal of all the teasing mystification that preceded it. But this whole procedure—this trifling with the 'mystery' of human motivation only in order to work up our thrilled acceptance of a theatrical tableau—this amounts, by ordinary standards of serious art, to an exploitation of our moral stupidity. If we co-operate with it, it is because we are not for the moment, and Dickens almost never is, interested in moral intelligence as George Eliot would understand it.

When the murder of Tulkinghorn is discovered, however, and Bucket makes Lady Dedlock believe that he suspects her, there is some attention to Lady Dedlock's inner life which functions as the exception that proves the rule I have been demonstrating:

She has thrown herself upon the floor, and lies with her hair all wildly scattered, and her face buried in the cushions of a couch. She rises up, hurries to and fro, flings herself down again, and rocks and moans. The horror that is upon her, is unutterable. If she really were the murderess, it could hardly be, for the moment, more intense.

For as her murderous perspective, before the doing of the deed, however subtle the precautions for its commission, would have been closed up by a gigantic dilatation of the hateful figure, preventing her from seeing any consequences beyond it; and as those consequences would have rushed in, in an unimagined flood, the moment the figure was laid low—which always happens when a murder is done; so now she sees that when he used to be on the watch before her, and she used to think, 'if some mortal stroke would but fall on this old man and take him from my way!' it was but wishing that all he held against her in his hand might be flung to the winds, and chance-sown in many places. So, too, with the wicked relief she has felt in his death. What was his death but the key-stone of a gloomy arch removed, and now the arch begins to fall in a thousand fragments, each crushing and mangling piece-meal!

Thus, a terrible impression steals upon and overshadows her, that from this pursuer, living or dead—obdurate and imperturbable before her in his well-remembered shape, or not more obdurate or imperturbable in his coffin-bed—there is no escape but in death. Hunted, she flies. The complication of her shame, her dread, remorse, and misery, overwhelms her at its height; and even her strength of self-reliance is overturned and whirled away, like a leaf before a mighty wind. . . .

She veils and dresses quickly, leaves all her jewels and her money, listens, goes downstairs at a moment when the hall is empty, opens and shuts the great door; flutters away in the shrill frosty wind. (LV) (pp. 758–9)

The picture of Lady Dedlock in the first paragraph and the last is of a piece with the earlier external representations of her theatrical agony. But in the intervening paragraphs more 'serious' matters are undertaken, the degree of seriousness registered, interestingly, in the unusually difficult—not to say obscure—prose. Dickens is here, as he was not in her scenes with Mr. Tulkinghorn, engaged in promoting our understanding of Lady Dedlock's reasons for fleeing—the 'picture' of her fleeing (fluttering away in the shrill frosty wind) handsome as it is, is not enough. He is trying—with, of course, only indifferent success—to help us 'conceive' her 'centre of self', and the fact that he is doing so with this character in this situation defines the part played by 'the dramatization of the inner life' in the Dickens theatre. For Dickens's insight into Lady Dedlock's mind here represents a special act of the sympathetic imagination which is caused by Dickens's special interest in the psychology of guilt. What we hear about Lady Dedlock's inner life is by no means inconsistent with the rest of Dickens's characterization of her, but it is not in any way continuous with it, nor indeed is it specific to Lady Dedlock. 'Why should a person who is not guilty act like a guilty person'? is the question we almost hear Dickens asking, and his answer has general rather than specific relevance. The abnormal obscurity and near-pretentiousness of the prose points to an abnormal sense of the 'seriousness' of the occasion. And the next paragraph, with its excitingly vague melodrama ('the complication of her shame, her dread, remorse, and misery, overwhelms her at its height'—the emotional states are merely words, and not well-differentiated ones), returns to the fluently effective theatrical mode of the rest of the book.

This special interest in the psychology of guilt shows up again and again in Dickens's work, in *Martin Chuzzlewit*, in *Our Mutual Friend* and elsewhere, but nowhere with more beautiful or more informative results than in the early *Oliver Twist*, in the scene of Fagin's trial. Certainly most of Dickens's characterization of Fagin is crude enough, however boldly effective. But in the trial scene there occurs a brilliant passage of an irresistible truthfulness which amounts to clairvoyance:

He looked up into the gallery again. Some of the people were eating, and some fanning themselves with handkerchiefs; for the

crowded place was very hot. There was one young man sketching
his face in a little note-book. He wondered whether it was like, and
looked on when the artist broke his pencil-point, and made another
with his knife, as any idle spectator might have done.

In the same way, when he turned his eyes towards the judge, his
mind began to busy itself with the fashion of his dress, and what it
cost, and how he put it on. There was an old fat gentleman on the
bench, too, who had gone out, some half an hour before, and now
come back. He wondered within himself whether this man had
been to get his dinner, what he had had, and where he had had it;
and pursued this train of careless thought until some new object
caught his eye and roused another.

Not that, all this time, his mind was, for an instant, free from
one oppressive overwhelming sense of the grave that opened at
his feet; it was ever present to him, but in a vague and general
way, and he could not fix his thoughts upon it. Thus, even while he
trembled, and turned burning hot at the idea of a speedy death, he
fell to counting the iron spikes before him, and wondering how the
head of one had been broken off, and whether they would mend it
or leave it as it was. Then, he thought of all the horrors of the
gallows and the scaffold—and stopped to watch a man sprinkling
the floor to cool it—and then went on to think again. (LII) (p. 405)

Although apparently a straightforward investigation of the
inner life of a human being in an extreme emotional position,
this passage is odd because Dickens finds that no inner life,
properly speaking, is taking place. Moreover, so beautiful is
the passage, so right does it seem, that it amounts to a
momentary repudiation of the traditional assumptions and
practices of serious art. It occurs to us that, whereas George
Eliot might at this juncture have implicated us in a serious,
and convincing, inner drama of remorse and fear, Dickens's
guess about Fagin's state of mind seems at once more truthful
and more generous to Fagin. This, we feel, is the work of a
sympathetic imagination totally uninhibited by conventional
expectations and therefore uninterested in dominating reality
by those expectations. But the beauty of the passage, of course,
only emphasizes the rule to which it is the exception.

All Dickens's attempts to register the inner life are, in
one way or another, demonstrations by exception of the rule
that we do not ordinarily think of him as someone who very
often wondered what it was like to be another person. That it

was for the most part the inner life only of guilty persons that engaged his attention has not only the biographical signifi- cance that Edmund Wilson has demonstrated but another kind of significance as well; and these exceptions to the rule of Dickens's ordinary methods are nevertheless perfectly at home in the Dickens theatre. The late chapters of *Martin Chuzzlewit* in which the processes of Jonas Chuzzlewit's guilty conscious- ness are so closely followed do not, as they would in non- theatrical art, come to us as an extension of an habitual concern for the inner lives of human beings. They are on the contrary explicitly offered as something extraordinary, and it is, then, exactly as something extraordinary that the sympathetic imagination takes its place in the Dickens theatre. The guilt of Jonas Chuzzlewit is, indeed, rather too loud a 'feature'; one is irritated in these pages by the disproportion between the self-advertising emphasis of the virtuoso's voice and the relative paltriness and conventionality of the insights which that voice is offering. But even the spontaneous flash of insight about Fagin is pointed up as something extraordinary. 'How does the man on trial really feel'? We all but hear the question—and, it goes without saying, this is not in the least damaging to the entire success of the answer.

The Dickens theatre, then, is a mode of art in which only the most mysterious and out of the ordinary emotional states awaken, in both the artist and the audience, the attention of the sympathetic imagination. For Dickens's energetic and emphatic voice notifies us that *we* need not, in the face of such self-delighting 'work' on the part of the theatrical artist, do much work ourselves. We are at our ease, and one of the things we are easy about is the inner life of other people. But just as in everyday life extraordinary people or people in extra- ordinary conditions will arouse even the most torpid and unimaginative to a temporary act of imagination about the inner life, so in the Dickens theatre we are willing to take the imaginative leap that the passage about Fagin both embodies in itself and demands from us.

Nevertheless, it was not, I believe, laziness of imagination that was responsible for Dickens's lack of interest in the inner lives of others. As an experienced theatrical worker, he may have known about his public's laziness in these respects, but he did not share it, nor, of course, did he in the least exploit it in the spirit of the modern entertainment businessman who gives the public what it wants. Dickens's lack of interest in the inner life has nothing of the Philistine in it. Nor did he share the motive which Tolstoy attributes to Karenin in *Anna Karenina*:

> He began to think of [Anna], and of what she was thinking and feeling. For the first time he pictured vividly to himself her personal life, her ideas, her desires, and the idea that she could and should have a separate life of her own seemed to him so alarming that he made haste to dispel it. It was the chasm which he was afraid to peep into. To put himself in thought and feeling in another person's place was a spiritual exercize not natural to Alexey Alexandrovitch. He looked on this spiritual exercize as a harmful and dangerous abuse of fancy. (Part II, chap. VIII)

This spiritual exercise was unnatural to Dickens for directly antithetical reasons. It was, one imagines, the all-absorbing intensity of his own inner sense of life and freedom, the copiousness of his emotional responsiveness to other people, the strength and impetuosity of his love and hate—it was, in a word, the essential quality of his genius that kept him, as a rule, so strangely innocent of the spiritual exercise which we think of as natural to the serious dramatic artist.

Towards the end of his career, in *Little Dorrit* and *Our Mutual Friend*, Dickens made an earnest effort to master these interests which were so alien to his own nature and genius, and it is likely that he was at least partly motivated by his resentment against those critics who had persistently noted his 'implausibility', his habitual theatricality. The careers of Arthur Clennam, of Bella Wilfer, of Eugene Wrayburn, and others represent, then, another kind of exception to the rule I have been defining. To me these attempts were for the most part unsuccessful, and even when they can be called successful they cut but a poor figure in comparison with the work of novelists to whom these methods came naturally, and in comparison with Dickens's own work in his own natural style.

4

PERSONALITY AS PERFORMANCE

DICKENS is a performing artist, displaying his verbal skills in familiar modes and in a theatre created by the insistent and self-delighting rhetoric of his voice. His characters are performers too. Lady Dedlock gives performances of cold hauteur and self-command for, among others, Mr. Tulkinghorn, who provides the appropriately expert audience for her 'act'. When she is alone Lady Dedlock is no less a performer than when she is in public, though her style is a different one, that of operatic anguish and torment. In fact all of the typically Dickensian characters can best be thought of as 'performing' their own personalities or the emotions characteristic of their 'roles'. We can say of the descriptions, too, that they 'perform': a house, a room, a landscape in Dickens performs its nature in front of us. There is a perfect consonance between our response to the narrator of these novels and our response to the objects and characters he is rendering.

We ordinarily think of people and things in novels as being *expressive*: characters *express* and *enact* their natures. It is because of this that people in books are commonly understood to be different from people in real life. For E. M. Forster, the fact that people in art consist entirely of what is on the page is one of the things that makes art valuable:

In daily life we never understand each other, neither complete clairvoyance nor complete confessional exists. We know each other approximately, by external signs, and these serve well enough as a basis for society and even for intimacy. But people in a novel can be understood completely by the reader, if the novelist wishes; their inner as well as their outer life can be exposed. And this is why they often seem more definite than characters in history, or even our own friends; we have been told all about them that can be told; even if they are imperfect or unreal they do not contain any secrets, whereas our friends do and must, mutual secrecy being one of the conditions of life upon this globe.[1]

[1] *Aspects of the Novel* (New York, 1927), pp. 74–75.

It is also true that everything about a character in a novel is meaningful and expressive, or at least ought to be. How each of Anna Karenina's words and gestures qualifies our total sense of her is a subtle and delicate question, yet those who admire this novel highly are sure that this actually happens, though Anna is as far as possible from being a colourful character with pronounced characteristics, and we seldom feel invited by the novelist to ask the question 'What kind of a person is Anna Karenina'? In shorter books, and in books of novelists who do not work in Tolstoy's subtly expressive realistic mode, it is more obvious that each detail about each character is expressive of that character. Thus to speak of Dickens's characters as 'performing their own personalities' does not mean that every detail about each character is expressive of his nature, for that is the general rule in fiction.

We speak of people in our daily life as giving 'performances' and it is this use of the word that I have in mind. There are 'performers' whom we encounter with pleasure; we do not take them seriously, but this does not disturb us, for the question does not ordinarily even arise; we do not want or need to take them seriously. Dickens takes towards his mimicked people, and makes us take, a similar attitude. In this sense his characters are indeed real, but by the same token they are not what we expect to find in serious fiction.

There are two kinds of performing people in real life, about whom we have slightly different attitudes. There is the person whom we realize to be self-consciously and deliberately and wilfully playing a certain role and asking us to become an equally self-conscious and deliberate audience for his performance. This collaboration sets up a recognized 'theatre' and confers certain licences and prerogatives on both the collaborating parties. The performer is licensed to sue for our admiring attention and, if his suit is successful, to dominate the theatrical occasion; the audience is licensed to judge the skill and authority of the performance with extraordinary ruthlessness, and to reject the performance, if it wishes, with no hint of compunction. The parlour clown, the brilliant talker, the man in the know, the wise man, even on some occasions the holy man—all these are either applauded as professionals or scorned as amateurs or frauds. If they are applauded, their consciousness of an audience is inoffensive because the audience is happy to be an audience, whereas if they are rejected their consciousness of their audience is both offensive and foolish because they are playing to an empty house. Moreover, the audience in a successful theatrical collaboration somehow knows that the performer needs applause and is willing to work for it; a performer who is frank about this need is sometimes felt to be particularly endearing, sometimes merely over-eager; a performer who affects to scorn his audience can produce a pleasurable astringency in the theatrical occasion but on the other hand may seem merely dishonest. The poise of the collaboration between performer and audience is a delicate one. Pope's lines about Addison, for instance:

> Like Cato, give his little Senate laws,
> And sit attentive to his own applause—
> ('An Epistle to Dr. Arbuthnot,' ll. 209–10)

this is an outsider's view—powerfully destructive—of a theatrical occasion which might have felt quite different from the inside, the performer's attentiveness seeming a way of honouring the audience and covertly confessing his own need for their attention. It goes without saying, of course, that the audience in all such theatrical collaborations makes no contact with the inner life of the performer, with what is 'really happening' inside him, nor is this regrettable during the performance itself when the performance is successful. Nevertheless, even about successful performers, when we say, 'He gave one of his performances last night', we can be implying, 'I can't take him seriously as a human being, after all'; which is to say that, even though we have participated in several fairly successful theatrical collaborations with the performer without much worrying about his inner life, some insecurity in the poise of the theatrical collaboration has bred the suspicion that perhaps he has no inner life.

Because Dickens himself was this kind of performer, totally conscious of his audience, very few of his characters are allowed to be performers of the same kind: social lions are seldom receptive to the talents of their competitors. There are very few amiable literary representations of self-conscious perfor-mers. The instance of Falstaff comes to mind, and it is signi-ficant that nobody imagines Shakespeare himself to have been a theatrically brilliant or dominating personality in his own social life. Only this least single-minded, least wilful of artists could both anatomize and relish the supreme clown's relation-ship to his audience. In lesser hands the Pagliacci cliché often appears, or the treatment may be frankly hostile. The two representatives of this kind of social performer in Dickens's work were both derived from actual literary lions: Skimpole and Boythorn in *Bleak House*, who were modelled after Leigh Hunt and Walter Savage Landor respectively. But Skimpole, who is by far the more self-conscious of the two, is seen as an opportunist, a virtual con-man. Dickens wants us to become an admiring audience for Skimpole's fanciful clowning, but only to a certain extent. For the most part he skilfully keeps our feelings about Skimpole in a delicate poise of ambivalence, but this poise is crudely destroyed at the end of the book, when Dickens is winding up his own performance and settling the score:

As it so happened that I never saw Mr. Skimpole again, I may at once finish what I know of his history. A coolness arose between him and my guardian, based principally on the foregoing grounds, and on his having heartlessly disregarded my guardian's entreaties (as we afterwards learned from Ada) in reference to Richard. His being heavily in my guardian's debt, had nothing to do with their separation. He died some five years afterwards, and left a diary behind him, with letters and other materials towards his Life; which was published, and which showed him to have been a victim of a combination on the part of mankind against an amiable child. It was considered very pleasant reading, but I never read more of it myself than the sentence on which I chanced to light on opening the book. It was this. 'Jarndyce, in common with most other men I have known, is the Incarnation of Selfishness.' (LXI) (p. 831)

This detail about Mr. Skimpole has never convinced any reader. And, to borrow James's remark about Thackeray, we can legitimately accuse Dickens of jealousy.

The other kind of human behaviour which we call 'per-formance' is the one that Dickens continually represents in his most famous characterizations. There are people for whom we are an audience, without their seeming to be aware of it. They generate 'behaviour' in a copious and continuous flow, never showing the slightest concern about the effect they are making on other people. They are not completely unaware of other people: they will answer questions and react to the actions of others, they are not insanely solipsistic. But they do not listen to themselves, and we recognize that it is just for this reason that they are able to perform their personalities with an exceptional freedom of impulse which yields an exceptionally vivid distinctness and fullness of identity.

When we meet such people in our everyday life—and it will be granted that it is a common enough experience—we sometimes fear and hate them, and we are very often bored by them, but sometimes we take a conscious pride in becoming a willing and enjoying audience for their performances. Our pride testifies that this enjoyment seems to us a morally intelligent way of taking human beings and also that we are not always capable of it. The question is why we should feel this pride, since we are obviously not taking these people seriously: we are not judging their behaviour, nor are we trying to know them through the sympathetic imagination, or to share with them the experience of the moral life. This would seem to define our attitude towards them as an instance of moral stupidity. But it does not feel like stupidity. It is not at all like the kind of moral Philistinism that takes *its* kind of pride in not seeing why we have to be serious all the time. On the contrary, it is a remarkably sensitive attitude, particularly alert and responsive to speech and behaviour; and we recognize that it signals therefore a high degree of moral and emotional well-being and intelligence rather than the opposite. This is not to say, of course, that taking people seriously implies that things are not well with us; the question how to be morally intelligent about people will not admit of such simple oppositions. Taking people seriously surely arises from our strength, not from our weakness, but this other way of taking them does too. For when we become an audience for performing people, we are generously, out of our strength, exempting them from the moral obligation to take themselves, or us, seriously. Not because they have sued for such exemption, as with the

other sort of performers, the brilliant and conscious enter-
tainers, with whom we have a contractual relationship. Here
there is no contract; it is our own gratuitous act that builds
this theatre. And we are surely in the right to think such
generosity morally intelligent.

We practise this morally intelligent attitude towards
people regularly in the Dickens theatre. In any Dickens novel,
we are always conscious that the characters appearing before
us are performers of their identities, whether those identities
are 'good' or 'bad'; and Dickens's insistent rhetoric is always
directing us to see how distinctly, how fully, and how perfectly
—almost how 'professionally—his characters are performing
their natures. Within the Dickens theatre there are also many
smaller theatres in which we are invited to co-operate with
characters who are audiences for the performances of other
characters. In *Bleak House*, for instance, Bucket is called to
the bedside of Sir Leicester Dedlock, who has been struck into
speechlessness by Lady Dedlock's flight:

> Sir Leicester writes upon the slate. 'Full forgiveness. Find—'
> Mr. Bucket stops his hand.
> 'Sir Leicester Dedlock, Baronet, I'll find her. But my search
> must be begun out of hand. Not a minute must be lost.'
> With the quickness of thought, he follows Sir Leicester Dedlock's
> look towards a little box upon the table.
> 'Bring it here, Sir Leicester Dedlock, Baronet? Certainly. Open
> it with one of these here keys? Certainly. The littlest key? *To* be
> sure. Take the notes out? So I will. Count 'em. That's soon done.
> Twenty and thirty's fifty, and twenty's seventy, and fifty's one
> twenty and forty's one sixty. Take 'em for expenses? That I'll
> do, and render an account of course. Don't spare money? No, I
> won't.'
> The velocity and certainty of Mr. Bucket's interpretations on
> all these heads is little short of miraculous. Mrs. Rouncewell who
> holds the light, is giddy with the swiftness of his eyes and hands,
> as he starts up, furnished for his journey. (LVI) (p. 763)

That Mr. Bucket is giving a performance as a detective is
sufficiently obvious, but Dickens characteristically makes the
theatrical situation explicit in Mrs. Rouncewell's response.
But when Mr. Bucket begins his work, there is this amusing
passage:

His first step is to take himself to Lady Dedlock's rooms, and look all over them for any trifling indication that may help him. The rooms are in darkness now; and to see Mr. Bucket with a wax-light in his hand, holding it above his head, and taking a sharp mental inventory of the many delicate objects so curiously at variance with himself, would be to see a sight—which nobody *does* see, as he is particular to lock himself in. (LVI) (p. 764)

Here, in a nutshell, are the two kinds of performance of which I have been speaking: that of Dickens, the theatrical enter-tainer, visible before us (in the teasing last clause) as no 'creator of a self-developing organism' could ever allow himself to be; and that of Bucket, alone and unselfconscious, being himself, performing his own loud and distinct nature.

On the image of Bucket performing his nature in view of the audience which he has been careful to lock out, I will rest my case. Further exemplification of Dickens's central mode of rendering human behaviour and human nature is super-abundantly possible and completely unnecessary. The reader is invited to open any Dickens novel at random to see which character, which landscape, which house, which room is on that page performing its loud and distinct nature to which audience.

5

PERFORMING CHARACTERS IN NON-THEATRICAL ART

In what sense can Dickens's characters be said to 'act'? What mode of action can the theatrical artist contrive to organize his performances into large-scale structures?

Many of Dickens's most famous characters simply do not act. Mrs. Gamp, for instance, is connected with a plot by an arbitrary act of the theatrical artist, and her importance in *Martin Chuzzlewit* is widely recognized as having little to do with her plot function. She is interesting in her own right and the reader's relationship to her remains exactly what it was at her first appearance. Virginia Woolf said that whenever the plot in a Dickens novel burned low, he threw on another character. This affectionate ridicule of Dickens's conception of action adequately takes care of much of the early work.

It is generally recognized that the later Dickens novels are more carefully and more successfully organized than the earlier ones. But it is not a method of organization to which we are accustomed in non-theatrical art, and we can see more clearly its central principle if we examine how performing characters have been organized into large-scale structures in earlier works in English literature. For, although his theatrical mode of art is consistently maintained throughout his work and therefore is unique in our literature, Dickens, of course, did not invent it, nor did he invent the kind of characterization of which Mrs. Gamp and Micawber are the two most famous examples.

We know that Dickens played Captain Bobadil in several amateur productions of Jonson's *Every Man in his Humour*, and we know that he read Fielding, Smollett, and Sterne when he was a boy. But even without this knowledge there would be no mistaking the similarity between Sir Epicure Mammon,

Ursula the Pig Woman, Parson Adams, Tabitha Bramble, and my Uncle Toby on the one hand, and Pickwick, Sairey Gamp, Pecksniff, Micawber, and Uriah Heep on the other. Dickens derived his methods from the classics of English comedy. The success of his whole theatrical enterprise, indeed, depended on his audience's familiarity with his methods. Moreover, it is exactly my argument about the value of Dickens's work that it represents a mode of seeing people and dealing with them which is a permanent and valuable part of human experience and human potentiality.

In the classics of English comedy from which Dickens derived his own methods, characters who perform their nature without seeming to have an inner life are 'placed', usually for the purpose of hostile criticism of them, by contrasting them directly or indirectly with serious characters and with the serious way of taking people in general. The action in classic comedy is either an action of self-determination or self-discovery on the part of the serious people, or an action of moral and social judgement on the part of the narrator or of the audience. An infinite variety of forms and tones is possible here and English literature has produced a fair number, but the *normal* form is that of the satirical comedy which I have already described and of which the classic example is *The Way of the World*. If the tone in this normal form is amiable enough, the performing characters who cannot be taken seriously may yet be taken affectionately; from another perspective they may be cheerfully inspected with an urbane detachment, as if they were animals in a zoo; or they may even be envied, momentarily, as the lives of shepherds are envied in the pastoral convention. And yet, for all the amusement they afford, they will be firmly rejected as the appropriate companions or lovers of the serious people. Lady Wishfort, in *The Way of the World*, is given the freedom of the theatre for long and rich performances of her nature; she is granted considerable animal force and even inventiveness; but her sufferings constitute only a parody of inner life:

Well, friend, you are enough to reconcile me to the bad world, or else I would retire to deserts and solitudes; and feed harmless sheep by groves and purling streams. Dear Marwood, let us leave the world, and retire by ourselves and be shepherdesses. (v. iii)

Sir Willful Witwoud's bluff heartiness is played off against his half-brother's foppery and briefly honoured for its vigorous animal health; but we cannot take him seriously as a suitor for Millamant, not because of his country tastes and habits but because he lacks an inner life which Millamant could know and love. That these theatrical characters are enjoyed by the audience is a manifestation of Congreve's freedom of form and of spirit, for their essential inhumanity is most firmly and delicately established. The extravagance and entertaining richness of their performances does not throw the essentially moral criticism of the comedy out of balance. In works of lesser comic writers, to be sure, the theatrical charm of such performing characters can come to be an end in itself; the formal structure of moral and social criticism will be mechanically imitated in an opportunistic exploitation of accepted modes. These are the writers about whom we say that they can create colourful characters but cannot write plays.

Ben Jonson's satirical comedy works differently. Shaw called Jonson brutish, probably because he exhibits no *warmth* of sympathetic imagination; but despite his superficial commitment to the old 'humour' psychology, Jonson's humour characters are distinctly criticized against an alive and concretely realized standard of seriousness.

Jonson's favourite device is to implicate the audience itself, not by 'holding the mirror up to nature', but by pulling the rug out from under our feet. In *The Alchemist*, the fools—Sir Epicure Mammon, Tribulation Wholesome, and the rest—are easily held in contempt for their mechanical fixations, but we can enjoy them and their self-performances because they are being effectively cheated by Subtle, Face, and Doll; their imminent humiliation exempts us from any strong necessity to criticize them. With Subtle and his friends, though, we are in a different relationship because their success is felt to be merely temporary, and because they are cheating such notable fools. Face's master, Mr. Lovewit (we do not notice his name until it is too late), has fled to the country to escape the London plague, but we know he will return to put things right; meanwhile, thus exempted from scrupulous moral concern, we decidedly enjoy the skill and *brio* of the various performances by which Subtle, Face, and Doll cheat their victims. But when Lovewit returns, he proves to be unworthy of our confidence; for he 'loves wit', and is so delighted by Face's clever performance (and with the proceeds of the swindle, which Face turns over to him) that he consents to keep him on in his service. Subtle and Doll are left out in the cold, and so are we; our 'sense of justice' makes us criticize, in the response of Lovewit, an attitude which has been our own up to his return. Our embarrassed sense of moral confusion vividly enforces the necessity of self-examination.

In the sentimental comedy of Fielding and Sterne we find attitudes much closer to Dickens, yet there are important differences. Parson Adams and the eccentrics in *Tristram Shandy* are meant to be lovable and their performances are relished by the narrator. But in both works the value of such eccentric behaviour comes into existence through the narrator's contempt for merely conventional, and hypocritical, respectability and orderliness and rationality. The world in both books is one in which the mechanical sterility of conventional norms and disciplines had made 'generous' sentiment impossible; and it is a paradox in both works that only the eccentric fools manifest true human dignity and rational generosity. In Sterne there is a constant Punch and Judy flavour, with the 'world' of discipline and reason cast as the policeman who is continually flouted, teased, flirted with, and secretly depended on. Dr. Leavis speaks too primly of Sterne's 'nasty trifling'. For me, what keeps the book from being the masterpiece of freedom that it is often thought to be is the fact that the clown is too mechanically and too neurotically the antithesis of the policeman, that the policeman is in fact the real audience—and motivating energy—for the performance, and therefore that the performance remains 'naughty' and never achieves true freedom and generosity of spirit.

Fielding's was a more profound and serious disillusionment with conventional serious thinking and behaviour. The hero of *Tom Jones* is completely un-selfregarding, completely generous and outgoing in feeling, but he is also non-eccentric, the 'type' of the ordinary healthy man as hero. The book is too long, for such a hero cannot become involved in any very significant action as we have come to understand it. The machinery of the plot, so extravagantly praised by Coleridge, is tidy and smooth at best; its function is to provide occasions on which Tom can perform the attractive behaviour of the healthy, generous man. The drama—and the only significant action—of the novel arises out of the relationship between the hero and the narrator. The narrator's nature is exactly the opposite of Tom's: he is an image of seriousness gone sour and bitter. His way of taking people is for the most part a cheerfully cold misanthropic distrust, and the career of Tom is interesting mainly because it is reported to us by this very different voice. Such a narrator can with special authority praise the moral value of truly unselfconscious generosity, and there is moreover an impressive generosity in his being able to believe in a mode of being completely different from his own. But this generosity fails, and the novel fails, when the narrator puts his own authority behind Allworthy's recommendation that Tom acquire 'prudence', the virtue of seeming to others to be as good as you actually are. This advice is both nonsensical and jealous. Prudence cannot be added to Tom's free and unselfconscious generosity without destroying it. Nevertheless, the image of Tom's freedom remains a vivid one, and it is significant and morally interesting because it has come to us from the dramatic perspective of the narrator's voice, which is deeply schooled in the disciplines of self-awareness and self-criticism.

Jane Austen's work offers performing characters together with an explicit dramatic rendering of the problem created by such people in real life. In *Pride and Prejudice* there are two famous examples of characters who perform their own natures, Mr. Collins and Lady Catherine de Bourgh. These two characters have often been thought to be at odds with the tone and texture of the rest of the novel, and in truth the way we take them is not always finely adjusted to the way we take the other characters. Mr. Bennet is indirectly, and sometimes directly, criticized for being and wanting to be only an audience for people who perform their personalities. He seldom bothers to take even Elizabeth and Jane seriously; he claims to and intends to, but is unwilling to work at it. Though Elizabeth thinks of him, and is proud of him, as a gentleman (the word suggests primarily the good manners that come through self-awareness), his gentlemanly habits of discipline and duty have withered and soured into a consistent irony which is reminiscent of the tone of voice of the narrator in *Tom Jones*. He emerges from his library only to be an audience for the human comedy or to perform his irony before his wife (who is a satisfactory audience for him because she is eternally bewildered by his style) or his sensible daughters, from whom he expects admiration for his freedom and wit: 'I admire all my three sons-in-law highly,' said he. 'Wickham, perhaps, is my favourite; but I think I shall like *your* husband quite as well as Jane's.' (III. xvii) (LIX) (p. 379)[1] The splendid amplitude, the almost incredible consistency, of Mr. Collins's performances give him perhaps the keenest delight he enjoys in the whole novel:

'Much as I abominate writing, I would not give up Mr. Collins's correspondence for any consideration. Nay, when I read a letter of his, I cannot help giving him the preference even over Wickham, much as I value the impudence and hypocrisy of my son-in-law.' (III. xv) (LVII) (p. 364)

He invites Elizabeth to share his pleasure in Mr. Collins, and reads aloud the letter in which Mr. Collins reports the rumour that Darcy is in love with Elizabeth. 'But, Lizzy, you look as if you did not enjoy it. You are not going to be *Missish*, I hope, and pretend to be affronted at an idle report. For what do we live, but to make sport for our neighbours, and laugh at them in our turn?'(III. xv) (LVII) (p. 364)

Elizabeth pretends for the moment to be 'excessively diverted', but she has not actually been affronted and is not being 'missish' but merely showing, by her embarrassment, that she is engaged with life, with Mr. Darcy in particular, and that she 'lives for' interests quite different from her father's. Though she has before been able to share her father's detached comic view of the world, it is suggested that this attitude was attractive to her because of her limited circumstances: the lack of interesting and valuable people in the little country town, the folly and stupidity of her mother and three of her

---

[1] All quotations from Jane Austen are followed by three kinds of reference: in the first parenthesis to the chapter number in editions which divide the novels into volumes; in the second parenthesis to the chapter number in editions which do not; in the third parenthesis to the page number in the *Oxford Illustrated Jane Austen*, third edition

sisters. Yet her spirited commitment to traditional disciplines and duties is such that she can never regard her immediate family as an amusing exhibit; indeed, her comic view of the outside world seems to get a special impetus from the unrewarding labour of trying to take seriously people like her mother, who has no inner life at all, who has only the 'nerves' for which Mr. Bennet claims to have high respect. 'They are my old friends. I have heard you mention them with consideration these twenty years at least.' (I. i) (I) (p. 5) But by the time Mr. Bennet reads Mr. Collins's letter aloud, Elizabeth has entered a serious involvement with Darcy, a man towards whom earlier she had been an audience, and a very critical one. She has become incapable of her father's objectivity toward Mr. Collins's folly, and never resumes his mode of being merely an audience for the foolish performances of the world.

Instead she develops a new mode of comic laughter. Her new sister-in-law admires but is puzzled by her new freedom:

Georgiana had the highest opinion in the world of Elizabeth; though at first she often listened with an astonishment bordering on alarm, at her lively, sportive, manner of talking to her brother. He, who had always inspired in herself a respect which almost overcame her affection, she now saw the object of open pleasantry. Her mind received knowledge which had never before fallen in her way. By Elizabeth's instructions she began to comprehend that a woman may take liberties with her husband, which a brother will not always allow in a sister more than ten years younger than himself. (III. xix) (LXI) (pp. 387–8)

What makes Darcy an object of open pleasantry is his performance as the stiff man of legitimate pride and duty, and it is clear that Darcy allows Elizabeth to take liberties, which are certainly to some extent critical in intention, because they are not entirely critical: because she loves him, Elizabeth can by her laughter at his performances tell Darcy that she understands him and loves him exactly for what he is, but that she realizes his limitations too. She can take both attitudes towards Darcy—and he can enjoy this—without experiencing the 'tension of ambivalence', because this ebulliently optimistic novel is claiming that precisely these remarkable achievements are possible to people who love. Jane Austen is not one to make heavy weather of the mystery of love, but the happy marriage of Elizabeth and Darcy is a sufficiently profound instance of the mysterious unity that makes love possible. And what is unified here is highly germane to my theme; Elizabeth is able to conceive the centre of Darcy's self without losing the theatrical way of seeing him and without making that way seem trivial or dishonourable to either Darcy or her self. Indeed, her laughter invites Darcy to enjoy his own performances.

The theatrical characterizations of Mr. Collins and Lady Catherine are successful in so far as they function organically in the drama of Elizabeth's changing relationship to her world. But one feels occasionally a lapse of this organic functioning, when these grotesque characters seem to step outside the drama and to perform directly before us, as a Dickens character would; and we feel too, though in a much milder degree, that Jane Austen herself is beginning to perform before us as Dickens would, as a creator and manipulator of amusing and effectively colourful people. This is no very catastrophic failure and the novel as a whole remains a wonderful success; yet there is a discontinuity between the Mr. Collins who proposes to Elizabeth and the Mr. Collins who is accepted as Charlotte Lucas's husband; between the Lady Catherine before whom 'the party then gathered round the fire to hear [her] determine what weather they were to have on the morrow' (II. vi) (XXIX) (p. 166) and the Lady Catherine who is taken seriously by Darcy. When the narrator says, in a later scene at Rosings, that 'Mr. Darcy looked a little ashamed of his aunt's ill breeding, and made no answer' (II. viii) (XXXI) (p. 173), there is an awkward mixture of two different kinds of illusion; for we have freely *enjoyed* Lady Catherine's outrageous rudeness to Elizabeth and cannot easily take it as a fit object for moral or social criticism.

If we feel a certain awkwardness in this brilliant book, Jane Austen has only herself to thank, for it is from her own *Emma* that we derive the highest standards of delicacy and tact in these matters. It is extraordinary how numerous, and how subtly distinguished, are the modes of human relationship in this novel. Take, for instance, the scene in which Mr. Woodhouse welcomes his guests:

[Jane Fairfax's] attention was now claimed by Mr. Woodhouse, who being, according to his custom on such occasions, making the circle of his guests, and paying his particular compliments to the ladies, was ending with her—and with all his mildest urbanity, said,

'I am very sorry to hear, Miss Fairfax, of your being out this morning in the rain. Young ladies should take care of themselves.— Young ladies are delicate plants. They should take care of their health and their complexion. My dear, did you change your stockings?'

'Yes, sir, I did indeed; and I am very much obliged by your kind solicitude about me.'

'My dear Miss Fairfax, young ladies are very sure to be cared for.—I hope your good grandmamma and aunt are well. They are some of my very old friends. I wish my health allowed me to be a better neighbour. You do us a great deal of honour today, I am sure. My daughter and I are both highly sensible of your goodness, and have the greatest satisfaction in seeing you at Hartfield.'

The kind-hearted, polite old man might then sit down and feel that he had done his duty, and made every fair lady welcome and easy. (II. xvi) (XXXIV) (pp. 294–5)

The subtlety and finesse with which Mr. Woodhouse's behaviour is connected with the novel's serious concern with manners, morals, and the inner life is remarkable. Mr. Woodhouse is 'giving one of his performances' in at least two senses: he is deliberately acting a role, playing a part, that of the courteous host; he is also performing his nature with a completeness and consistency that reveals his lack of an inner life, or a self. We do not take him seriously in either performance but—at this particular moment—we enjoy and feel affection towards both. In both performances we take him as we would take a polite child, whom, although we do not hold him accountable for all his actions, we nevertheless praise for what he has learned so well and so dutifully and for his kind sentiments. He is licensed to question Jane Fairfax—elegant and accomplished and involved in a complex love affair—about her stockings because he is carefully, with sweet deliberateness, playing an accepted role as host and because he is in his odd way kind-hearted and concerned for the well-being of others (though with such total lack of imagination about their actual wants and needs that he generously persuades them not to

eat the scalloped oysters and cake which his generosity has
also provided). But his licence is, in a much more important
sense, derived not from his own work or identity, but from the
security and maturity of those around him. Their imaginative
concern for the inner lives of others and their own capacities
for self-criticism and self-effacement generously grant him his
licence. This generosity is clearly visible in Jane Fairfax's
response to his courtesy, in Emma's and Mr. Knightley's
consistent solicitude about his welfare, and in the narrator's
affectionately clear-headed description of his self-satisfaction
at the end of the passage I have quoted. It is missing in Mrs.
Elton's way of taking him:

In this style she ran on; never thoroughly stopped by any thing
till Mr. Woodhouse came into the room; her vanity had then a
change of object, and Emma heard her saying in the same half-
whisper to Jane,
'Here comes this dear old beau of mine, I protest!—Only think
of his gallantry in coming away before the other men!—what a
dear creature he is;—I assure you I like him excessively. I admire
all that quaint, old-fashioned politeness; it is much more to my
taste than modern ease; modern ease often disgusts me. But this
good old Mr. Woodhouse, I wish you had heard his gallant speeches
to me at dinner. Oh! I assure you I began to think my caro sposa
would be absolutely jealous.' (II. xvii) (xxxv) (p. 302)

Mrs. Elton's response to Mr. Woodhouse is a coarse parody of
Jane Fairfax's. Blinded by vanity, she responds in a way that
violates common decency. With Jane Austen, power comes
through precision: when Mrs. Elton uses the words 'gallantry'
and 'jealousy' about Mr. Woodhouse's childlike sexlessness,
her insensitivity has the impact of actual obscenity, with the
result that despite the narrow range of feeling so consistently
maintained in the whole novel she is very intensely condemned
and with the full co-operation of the reader.
    As for Mrs. Elton's performances in themselves, they are
so finely adjusted to the serious dramatic illusion of the whole
work that we can think of them as performances only when we
have left the illusion behind and are indulging in fond remini-
scence. While we are reading *Emma* we seldom if ever depart
from the social perspective in which Mrs. Elton is almost in-
tolerable. Our view of her is more inclusive than that of any

of the characters in the novel, yet we remain engaged in the web of interrelationships which comprises the dramatic illusion. But when Mrs. Pardiggle, in *Bleak House*, comes into the room 'like cold weather' and begins her monologue, the dramatic illusion of a social situation has been only very sketchily suggested and is only intermittently maintained: Mrs. Pardiggle steps immediately to the front of the stage of the Dickens theatre and performs her nature directly to an audience which retains no strong sense of Esther's response to her while she is talking. Even in the brickmaker's house, where more attention is paid to Mrs. Pardiggle's effect on others, the illusion of the internal pressure within the social situation is only brought into being by direct reminders from the narrator. We need no such reminders when we are attending to the self-developing illusion in Jane Austen's novel. Therefore, in the speech of Mrs. Elton's I have quoted, theatrical pleasure in Mrs. Elton's performance of her own nature is made impossible by the fact that our attention is engaged in other matters: our knowledge of the actual identity of Mr. Woodhouse, our memory of Jane's response to his courtesy, our image of the state of mind in which both Jane and Emma are receiving Mrs. Elton's flow of talk. In comparison with this complexity, sensitivity, and continuity of dramatic illusion, our response to Mr. Collins and Lady Catherine in *Pride and Prejudice* is often a theatrical response to a theatrical performance which, in the context of the generally non-theatrical mode of the novel, seems a cruder thing than what surrounds it, and therefore a flaw. But in Dickens the theatrical mode is the norm and when Mrs. Pardiggle comes to the front of the stage of the Dickens theatre, no significant interruption of the illusion has taken place.

The dramatic illusion in *Emma* is by no means due only to Jane Austen's realistic methods, her verisimilitude, which recent Dickens critics are pleased to hold in contempt. Our concrete sense of a living pressure within an illusion is an inevitable effect of self-development in a work of art and it happens in Shakespeare's poetic art as often as in realistic art. In the heath scenes in Act III of *King Lear* there is, to be sure, no very nicely observed and continuous social decorum in language or behaviour, what with the various disguises and the various degrees and forms of insanity in play; Edgar and Kent are playing roles and nobody is listening to anybody else with any consistency. But, while it would certainly be a grossly 'realistic' misreading to speculate about what Edgar is really feeling, our sense of the pressure of inner activity within Lear himself is consistently maintained. The 'pattern of imagery' does not, as some critics seem to believe, come to the front of the stage and work directly on us: a dramatic illusion is maintained here as consistently as in Emma Wood-house's drawing-room, though certainly it is not in the same realistic mode.

If Mr. Collins interrupts the dramatic illusion by his theatri-cality, it is a moot question whether Jane Austen's charac-terization of Miss Bates in *Emma* does not err in the opposite direction, that of imitative form. Mrs. Elton's vanity is rendered with a richly inventive exactness of ear which makes her every appearance pleasurable (though not in the theatrical sense), but some readers have found Miss Bates as boring as Emma found her. I myself do not find her boring, though it would take a delicate and difficult analysis, and probably considerable eloquence, to convince those who do. Yet no one would question the fact that Jane Austen in this instance is quite explicitly aiming at a powerful feeling of internal pressure within the illusion itself; she is never merely creating an amusingly grotesque character. Miss Bates is a social prob-lem, for her routine is too tiresome and too pitiful to be en-joyed as a performance by any of her neighbours, and she is too kind-hearted to be insulted. Another hard fact is that, unlike Mr. Woodhouse, she has no scalloped oysters to offer. All in all, she would be a subject for unpromisingly drab verisimilitude—Dutch realism at its stalest—were it not that Jane Austen's precision and justice make powerful dramatic capital of her. 'How to take Miss Bates' has become a very resonant and fruitful question by the end of the novel.

Emma herself mimics Miss Bates in an extremely interesting passage—she is discussing with Mrs. Weston the possibility that Mr. Knightley might marry Jane Fairfax:

'If it would be good to her, I am sure it would be evil to himself; a very shameful and degrading connection. How would he bear to have Miss Bates belonging to him?—To have her haunting the

Abbey, and thanking him all day long for his great kindness in marrying Jane?—"So very kind and obliging!—But he always had been such a very kind neighbour!" And then fly off, through half a sentence, to her mother's old petticoat. "Not that it was such a very old petticoat either—for still it would last a great while—and, indeed, she must thankfully say that their petticoats were all very strong." '

'For shame, Emma! Do not mimic her. You divert me against my conscience.' (II. viii) (XXVI) (p. 225)

In this passage, the human habit of mimicry is examined in a way which will help us place Dickens's theatrical art. Mrs. Weston's reproof seems sensible and respectable within the context of the novel, but the narrator's view is more liberal and more complex. For it is Emma who is the mimic here, and the passage raises the question why Mr. Knightley loves Emma, while merely respecting Jane Fairfax, and why Jane Austen chose as her heroine this young woman whom she was sure nobody but herself would like.

We cannot help relating her mimicry of Miss Bates to the fact that Emma herself is always putting on performances and is always conscious of the style of others. She is mocked continually for these habits and interests. Here is her reaction to Robert Martin, whose attractions for Harriet she wants to discourage:

'He is very plain, undoubtedly—remarkably plain:—but that is nothing, compared with his entire want of gentility. I had no right to expect much, and I did not expect much; but I had no idea that he could be so very clownish, so totally without air. I had imagined him, I confess, a degree or two nearer gentility.'

'To be sure,' said Harriet, in a mortified voice, 'he is not so genteel as real gentlemen.' (I. iv) (IV) (p. 32)

Such behaviour, such language, is an index of Jane Austen's boldness; for it would seem impossible to take the person who is putting on this ludicrous act seriously, were it not for the fact that the narrator very clearly wants us to. And in our gradual discovery of how and why to take Emma seriously lies part of the essential drama of the novel. Emma puts on another of her performances when she praises Mr. Knightley for coming to the Coles's party in his carriage, 'like a gentleman'. (II. viii) (XXVI) (p. 213) Mr. Knightley ridicules her attitude, and the reader is sure Mrs. Weston is right when she guesses that Mr. Knightley used his carriage only to accommodate Miss Fairfax and Miss Bates; Emma is blinded to reality by her own preoccupation with style. Yet ' "Nonsensical girl!" was his reply, but not at all in anger.' The reader believes that Mr. Knightley is in love with Emma, and that he is sexually attracted to her just because of that quality in her which is the source of her ridiculous and pretentious performances. It is Emma's spontaneity, generosity, the force and vigour of her animal spirits that Mr. Knightley loves, and these qualities are nowhere more visible than in her various pretentious routines. In comparison, Jane Fairfax 'has a fault', as Mr. Knightley says himself: 'she has not the open temper which a man would wish for in a wife'. (II. xv) (XXXIII) (p. 288) Mr. Knightley's view of Emma is not unlike Fielding's view of Tom Jones. Nor is it unlike the view which those who are deeply committed to serious art find themselves taking towards Dickens's generous and spontaneous performances.

Jane Austen is an optimistic comic moralist, however, and she believes in the marriage of—shall we say—seriousness and generosity. In comparison, Fielding's attitude seems like a pessimistic yearning for a pastoral generosity which can never be known. Mr. Knightley has taken Emma seriously all along and he is justified in doing so by the fact that Emma discovers herself. After spending most of her wonderful energy in performing various roles and in manipulating the action of her friends, she suddenly discovers herself in an action—she discovers that she herself can experience the feelings which she had earlier only seen as the theatrical behaviour of others, and she takes charge of her own destiny, acting for and from herself:

A few minutes were sufficient for making her acquainted with her own heart. A mind like her's, once opening to suspicion, made rapid progress. She touched—she admitted—she acknowledged the whole truth. Why was it so much worse that Harriet should be in love with Mr. Knightley, than with Frank Churchill? Why was the evil so dreadfully increased by Harriet's having some hope of a return? It darted through her, with the speed of an arrow, that Mr. Knightley must marry no one but herself! (III. xi) (XLVII) (pp. 407–8)

From this point on, Emma takes herself seriously in every sense of the phrase: she achieves a just, if limited, self-criticism without losing or dishonouring her healthy egotism. When Mr. Knightley declares his love, Jane Austen is careful to point out that

as to any of that heroism of sentiment which might have prompted her to entreat him to transfer his affection from herself to Harriet, as infinitely the most worthy of the two—or even the more simple sublimity of resolving to refuse him at once and for ever, without vouchsafing any motive, because he could not marry them both, Emma had it not. She felt for Harriet, with pain and with contrition; but no flight of generosity run mad, opposing all that could be probable or reasonable, entered her brain. (III. xiii) (XLIX) (p. 431)

Once having discovered her self, the temptation to another kind of performance which would deny that self does not arise.

Emma's final self-discovery is achieved through the chain of encounters with reality which makes up the plot of the novel. The most important of these is also a self-discovery, the result of Mr. Knightley's strong reproof of her rude behaviour to Miss Bates. Mr. Knightley expresses anger towards Emma twice in the course of the novel, and on both occasions his anger leads him to an explicit articulation of his code of 'taking people seriously'. On the first occasion, his anger is directed specifically against Frank Churchill, whom he has not yet met, because he sees that Emma is in love with her idea of Churchill and because it is a bad idea. Emma's idea of Frank Churchill is, appropriately, a fantasy image of the consummate social performer:

'My idea of him is, that he can adapt his conversation to the taste of every body, and has the power as well as the wish of being universally agreeable. To you, he will talk of farming; to me, of drawing or music; and so on to every body, having that general information on all subjects which will enable him to follow the lead, or take the lead, just as propriety may require, and to speak extremely well on each; that is my idea of him.'

'And mine,' said Mr. Knightley warmly, 'is, that if he turn out any thing like it, he will be the most insufferable fellow breathing! What! at three-and-twenty to be the king of his company—the great man—the practised politician, who is to read every body's character, and make every body's talents conduce to the display of his own superiority; to be dispensing his flatteries around, that he may make all appear like fools compared with himself! My dear Emma, your own good sense could not endure such a puppy when it came to the point.' (I. xviii) (XVIII) (p. 150)

Emma answers that Knightley turns 'everything to evil', and in truth he has taken a seriously moral view of a way of life which Emma has been imagining with innocent relish as an extension of her own pleasures in performing social roles. Earlier in the quarrel Mr. Knightley has enunciated the standards against which Emma's image of Frank is judged in the novel as a whole:

'No, Emma, your amiable young man can be amiable only in French, not in English. He may be very 'aimable,' have very good manners, and be very agreeable; but he can have no English delicacy towards the feelings of other people: nothing really amiable about him.' (I. xviii) (XVIII) (p. 149)

Emma thinks Mr. Knightley's prejudice is unworthy of his 'real liberality' of mind. She retains her fantasy image of Frank and proceeds to conduct an entirely theatrical love-affair with him, with spurious self-examinations, sublime renunciations—the whole works. And it is while she is engaged in a sophisticated theatrical flirtation with Frank Churchill at Box Hill that she insults Miss Bates. The situation is very exactly rendered. Emma is 'gay and thoughtless [not] from any real felicity; it was rather because she felt less happy than she had expected.' Her role-playing is carrying her far enough from her own self to make her genuinely uneasy; in another sense, her 'self' is in the process of being born. In the little theatre constructed by Frank (whom Emma had imagined as 'the king of his company'), Emma is ironically cast as 'the queen of her company':

'Ladies and gentlemen, I am ordered by Miss Woodhouse (who, wherever she is, presides,) to say, that she desires to know what you are all thinking of.' (III. vii) (XLIII) (p. 369)

As E. M. Forster says, how this woman can write! For Emma is at the farthest possible remove from being able to imagine the inner life of anyone in the scene. She outrages even the courtesy which she had heretofore practised, out of a learned duty, to her father and her friends; it is with 'mock ceremony' that she insults Miss Bates.

When Mr. Knightley reproves her, he not only pays attention to Miss Bates's 'feelings' but by the complexity of his image of those feelings renders a convincing image of Miss Bates's inner life. This is surprising, for we too had been all but unaware that she had one.

'You, whom she had known from an infant, whom she had seen grow up from a period when her notice was an honour, to have you now, in thoughtless spirits, and the pride of the moment, laugh at her, humble her—and before her niece, too—and before others, many of whom (certainly *some*) would be entirely guided by *your* treatment of her.' (III. vii) (XLIII) (p. 375)

But 'a mind like [Emma's], once opening to suspicion, made rapid progress'. The spontaneous, generous energy, which had formerly produced the spiritedness of her performances, now produces genuine and deep remorse, 'and Emma felt the tears running down her cheeks almost all the way home, without being at any trouble to check them, extraordinary as they were'.

Here, then, is the wonderful finesse with which Jane Austen involves the mimicking and role-performing Emma in a genuine dramatic action which amounts to a moral conversion. As we actually experience the novel, we *enjoy* Emma's performances as the signs of her vitality, her energy, her generosity, her 'great expectations'. Her mimicry of Miss Bates is diverting because it expresses an energetic, joyous rebellion against a dutifully learned courtesy, and if dutiful learning were all that the world afforded in this direction Emma's rebellion would be preferable to it. But the impulse to mimicry is outgrown, as it were, when more interesting employments for the human spirit begin to be within her reach.

6

ACTION AND STRUCTURE IN
THE DICKENS THEATRE

To return to Dickens from the completely dramatic action of
Emma is to come not to a cruder version of Jane Austen's
methods but to a theatre in which an entirely different mode of
illusion and moral awareness is practised. The difference between Dickens's theatrical art and the use of theatrical methods
of characterization in English classic comedy is simply this:
that there is in Dickens's work no counterpart to the serious
action in classical comedy. By serious action I mean, first, the
most obvious kind: the drama of Elizabeth Bennet's and
Emma Woodhouse's self-discovery and of their falling in love.
I mean also the less obvious kind: the drama provided by the
tension between the theatrical view of human beings and the
other, serious view, which I have called 'taking them seriously'.
For Dickens, taking people theatrically is the only way, and
his books are exclusively concerned with it.

A more accurate way of saying this, of course, is that taking
people theatrically is the only way that engaged his genius. All
his early novels are organized by means of plots which apparently involve love-affairs and self-discoveries and all the
other traditional modes of dramatic action, but were it not for
the fashionable new readings of Dickens as a symbolic artist
these plots would still be acknowledged, as a matter of course,
as inert and without imaginative life. For that is what they are.

The reason is simple and the phenomenon familiar to
everybody. The action in the early novels is performed by
the least interesting members of Dickens's theatrical company,
performers so uninteresting that it sometimes seems only the
contractual commitments of the management that keeps them
on the stage. Actors on the payroll must earn their money,
and it is a convention that a full evening in the theatre must
include a story. The Marx Brothers' movies, except for *Duck*

Soup and *Monkey Business*, always wasted time and money over stories which, one suspected, bored even the performers. This apparently necessary tedium was occasionally lightened by the appearance of a tenor as the *jeune premier* or of a soprano as the *ingénue*, but even the best songs seemed only a ritualistic interruption of what the audience really came to see. Dickens himself was sensitive to the absurdity of inert theatrical conventions, as in the description of Mr. Wopsle's Hamlet in *Great Expectations*:

> I believe it is well known in a constitutional country that Mr. Wopsle could not possibly have returned the skull, after moralizing over it, without dusting his fingers on a white napkin taken from his breast; but even that innocent and indispensable action did not pass without the comment 'Wai - ter!' (XXXI) (p. 240)

But in the improvisatory haste and urgency of his early novels, Dickens mimicked conventional plots because it was expected that a novel should contain a plot. And it is not surprising that his performances of the regular, pretty features and the nice clothes of conventional lovers did not engage his highest creative gifts or even his interest.

The action in the early works seems to have been ordered ready-made from the literary or in some instances theatrical market-place. Dickens's use of the conventional material of the crime-novel in *Oliver Twist*, of stage melodrama in *Nicholas Nickleby*, has often been demonstrated. In some instances, he mounted this imported material on his own stage with no apparent personal involvement: all is the merest, and usually the crudest, stage-management. No moderately sophisticated reader has ever given any but the most perfunctory attention to Nicholas Nickleby's love life or young Martin Chuzzlewit's redemption. The importations from the crime-novel shop did get some personal attention from Dickens, however. The criminal careers of Fagin, Bill Sykes, Jonas Chuzzlewit, and the others are followed with distinct excitement on the part of the narrator and some thrilling moments for the reader are achieved. But except for a very few passages like the clairvoyant penetration into Fagin's mind at the trial, the narrator's excitement yields nothing intellectually or morally more dignified than the comfortable reader's thrilled fascination with crime and violence. We feel the force of the narrator's obsessive interest, but if we perhaps find in ourselves a similar interest the rapport so established is a far different thing from that participation in a self-developing organism of fiction which is created by action as we ordinarily understand it: with Dickens it is a kind of complicity. Dickens's criminals may seem pretty mild and even healthy in comparison with the horrors to which the twentieth century has made us accustomed, but our complicity with him in these matters is, judged by the standards of high art, by no means innocent. And the same can be said of the kind of attention Dickens lavished on his suffering children, Oliver Twist and Little Nell and the others. These early plots are not 'significant action'.

Dostoevski's testimony is hardly relevant. When he read these early novels with excitement and found them valuable, his mind as his novels demonstrate was busy transmuting the obsession with crime which he shared with Dickens into the intense, imaginative realization of the inner life which came to him as naturally as breathing. But it rarely came to Dickens at all.

Vivid registration of inner suffering or inner guilt, and intense sympathy for such inner feelings, is often confused with the kind of dramatization of the inner life which I am claiming Dickens to have been incapable of. One of Tolstoy's supreme statements may clear this up once and for all. It is a passage in which we see Tolstoy encountering the reality of experience for the millionth time and beginning again to forge the conscience of his race. He was working in a campaign of organized welfare when the epiphany occurred:

After some hesitation, however, I entered the gate. As soon as I did so I noticed an abominable stench. The yard was horribly filthy. I turned a corner, and at that moment, upstairs to the left, heard the clatter of feet running on the wooden gallery, first along the boards of the balcony and then down the steps of the staircase. A lean woman in a faded pink dress, with turned-up sleeves and with boots on her stockingless feet, ran out first. Following her came a shock-headed man in a red shirt and very wide trousers that looked like a petticoat, and with goloshes on his feet. At the bottom of the stairs the man seized the woman: 'You won't get away!' said he, laughing. 'Listen to the squint-eyed devil!' began the woman, evidently flattered by his pursuit, but she caught sight of me and shouted angrily: 'Who do you want?' As I did not want anybody I grew confused and went away. There was nothing remarkable about all this; but this incident . . . suddenly showed me quite a new side of the affair I was engaged on. I had set out to benefit these people by the help of the rich; and here for the first time I realized that all these unfortunates whom I wished to benefit, besides the hours they spend suffering from hunger and cold and waiting for a night's lodging, have also time to devote to something else. There is the rest of the twenty-four hours every day, and there is a whole life, about which I never thought. Here, for the first time, I understood that all these people, besides needing food and shelter, must also pass twenty-four hours each day, which they, like the rest of us, have to live. I understood that they must be angry, and dull, and must pluck up courage, and mourn, and make merry. . . . And when I understood that each of these thousand people was a human being with a past: and with passions, temptations, and errors, and thoughts and questions, like my own, and was such a man as myself—then the thing I had undertaken suddenly appeared so difficult that I realized my impotence.[1]

Tolstoy's fanatical self-criticism has detected himself in the morally stupid error of unimaginative pity, but in most of Dickens's work such pity represents his furthest imaginative reach. What is wrong with pity, for Tolstoy, is that it forces an identity, a role, on a human being and therefore denies him freedom. But all the objects of pity in Dickens are performers of their pitiable identity: indeed, Dickens's energy is quite openly directed to manœuvring them into their performances. And he is also, at the same time, manœuvring us into our appropriate receptivity as an audience for the performance. One could sympathize with a Tolstoy-like contempt for this whole procedure, were it not for the curious fact that generosity comes in, as it were, at the back door. For if the objects of pity are forced into their role and made to perform their pitiful natures with no thought that they 'have twenty-four hours a day to pass', they are at the same time given an unexampled freedom *in that role*. They are given materials of the utmost copiousness to work with and their performances are received with an almost superhuman amplitude of responsiveness. I call attention, as only one

---

[1] *What Then Must We Do?*, tr. Aylmer Maude (London, 1925), pp. 27–29.

example and that not the most familiar, to the extraordinary chapter describing the party at school which little Paul Dombey attends shortly before his death. This chapter (XIV) is a huge and most deliberately contrived testimonial to Paul's charm, sweetness, and pathos; the occasions on which people express their affection for him seem, as we read, almost infinite in number, and a considerable poetry is achieved merely by the outrageous dimensions of the scene. But it is of course exactly in this area that the habits of our moral tradition force into our consciousness something like the self-criticism which Tolstoy experienced, and then the weird generosity of the sentiments may strengthen our irritation about the moral stupidity of the whole procedure. But the generosity is there.

A more instructive example of Dickens's commitment to theatrical methods even when expressing his deepest sympathies occurs in *Bleak House*. Esther and Ada, who have accompanied Mrs. Pardiggle on her 'visiting' rounds, are offended by her methods of 'dealing with' the brickmaker and his family:

> Ada and I were very uncomfortable. We both felt intrusive and out of place; and we both thought that Mrs. Pardiggle would have got on infinitely better, if she had not had such a mechanical way of taking possession of people. . . . We both felt painfully sensible that between us and these people there was an iron barrier, which could not be removed by our new friend. By whom, or how, it could be removed, we did not know; but we knew that. (VIII) (pp. 107-8)

This—particularly the word 'mechanical'—looks promising from the perspective of Tolstoy's criticism. But 'mechanical' really means cold and unfeeling, and the barrier is in fact removed by pity, though in an interestingly complicated way. When Ada is holding the brickmaker's wife's baby, it dies.

> Such compassion, such gentleness, as that with which she bent down weeping, and put her hand upon the mother's, might have softened any mother's heart that ever beat. The woman at first gazed at her in astonishment, and then burst into tears. (VIII) (p. 109)

When Ada and Esther try to comfort the mother, she only weeps. But another poor woman enters, goes straight up to the mother, says, 'Jenny! Jenny!' and the mother falls into her embrace.

I thought it very touching to see these two women, coarse and shabby and beaten, so united; to see what they could be to one another; to see how they felt for one another; how the heart of each to each was softened by the hard trials of their lives. I think the best side of such people is almost hidden from us. What the poor are to the poor is little known, excepting to themselves and GOD. (VIII) (p. 109)

After Mrs. Pardiggle has left, Ada and Esther return to the brickmaker's house and find that the mother is asleep and that her friend has laid out the body of the dead baby: 'and on my handkerchief, which still covered the poor baby, a little bunch of sweet herbs had been laid by the same rough scarred hands, so lightly, so tenderly!' (VIII) (p. 110) Dickens continues to suggest that no true communication is possible between the classes, for when Ada and Esther praise the mother's friend as 'a good woman', she is surprised at the word. Yet this lack of communication is really quite unimportant in the face of the obvious claim that Ada and Esther have achieved a right understanding of the 'scene' through pity. For it has been a scene. A sensitive reader might justly observe that the child's life has been sacrificed in the interests of 'theatre'—certainly the child's death is the kind of fortuitous coincidence that serious writers try to avoid. All these characters must be regarded as giving performances of their identities. And Ada, in responding with appropriate pity to these performances, is herself admired for her performance as the Virgin Mary: 'I raised my handkerchief to look upon the tiny sleeper underneath, and seemed to see a halo shine around the child through Ada's drooping hair as her pity bent her head.' (VIII) (p. 111)

The action of the early novels, when there is any at all, consists of manœuvring performing theatrical characters into various arrangements, in order to provide new and different occasions for thrilling or affecting performances. It is theatrical action. And much of what goes on in the middle and late novels is also theatrical action.

Dickens's leading motive and consuming interest in the early period was in his own performances before his newly discovered public. The earliest newspaper and magazine sketches still sound, at their best, like auditions; at their worst they are depressingly eager merely to *exist* as professional writing, to be effective, to make an impression. Very soon after the beginning of *The Pickwick Papers* the wonderful sound of professional assurance is heard and the invention expands and flowers with self-delight under the warm sun of a known public's affection. What has been achieved is, in the flattest sense of the word, humorous writing, in the vein of exaggerated burlesque, but in this one style and tone the special Dickensian copiousness and freedom of invention is already fully operating. Now begins the professional business of expanding the repertory, of deepening and broadening the humorous style already achieved and beloved, and of contriving new occasions for its use. In *Martin Chuzzlewit* and *Dombey and Son*, the experienced professional begins to take some interest in the large-scale organization of his material, by no means very successfully. Thematic consistency is attempted: *Martin Chuzzlewit* is organized on the theme of hypocrisy and greed, *Dombey and Son* on the theme of pride. Moreover, the action of both books depends upon a basic change of attitude on the part of a leading character: both young Martin and old Dombey are softened and made less selfish by painful experience and by love. Engineering these metamorphoses wastes a lot of energy and the resulting serious pages are laboriously tedious; but there is plenty of energy available, and the minor characters in both these books are brilliantly vivid.

From one point of view, this early career is a beautiful thing to contemplate. The basic operation is a pure projection of will, but this takes the form of doing, performing, acting— never of self-revelation or vanity. The great entertainer claims attention and love for what he does, not for what he is, with the result that wonderful work is done, immense quantities of energy are expended. (I am taking for granted the superlative quality of the talent.) And all this work has the self-delighting spontaneity of play. Dickens's ambition is to encompass the world through mimicry; not by dominating the world, owning it, and depriving it of its free life, but by copying and thus experiencing its life in his own actions. The generosity and spontaneity of this spirit everyone has recognized. Dickens entirely lacked the impulse to 'do dirt on life', to destroy something because he wanted to see it dead (though he had, one grants, plenty of the 'impulse to kill'). Dickens *knows* the world through mimicking it, and to his youthful eyes the life in the world is as infinite as he feels his own vitality to be: he can mimic everything and there is everything to be mimicked. He can make contact only with what can be mimicked, but it is also true, and this is the most important point about his early career, that mimicry is *sufficient* contact with the world as he saw it. Communication is unnecessary.

From another point of view, however, this early career is not so completely attractive or successful. Since Dickens's impulse is completely outgoing, none of the advantages of self-criticism is available to him, and we encounter repeatedly a callow unawareness of his limitations. This leads on occasion to an undignified and nervous dependence on the goodwill of his public. More often it leads to deliberate and self-delighting ineptitudes, crudities, banalities, sheer vacuities such as are to be found in the work of no other great writer. Nevertheless, these gross faults of taste are really negligible because the theatrical situation is always so clear: since we are so comfortably aware that we are being an audience for his performances, we are comfortably cheerful about rejecting his failures without irritation. And I think every admirer of Dickens is glad that he never acquired the sort of self-knowledge that turns so many of our present-day comedians into cautious entrepreneurs and their routines into a commodity instead of a gift. That Dickens retained his innocence throughout his entire career is registered in the fact that he perhaps actually killed himself by working too hard for applause.

When self-knowledge came to Dickens, it took a form which has little to do with what we ordinarily understand by the term. *David Copperfield* is generally agreed to mark the mid-point in Dickens's career, even though in its methods and substance it belongs decidedly to the early half. It is common knowledge that this novel uses as some of its material certain of Dickens's own experiences, and there is general agreement too that the differences in method and tone between the early novels and the later ones are in some way connected with

Dickens's 'coming to terms with himself'. But we can discover the nature of this process only by examining the evidence in the novels themselves and making a speculative hypothesis about Dickens's own inner happenings, for even his 'revelations' to Forster were hopelessly reticent.

The fact that Dickens never really developed a fictional mode suitable for self-examination suggests that what took place within him was not really self-examination at all. My guess is that there had been taking place a gradual breakdown in the process of mimicry I have described above. Mimicking the performances going on in his world gradually began to produce a less and less vivid sense of living in Dickens himself and a less vivid sense of contact with the world outside—this may have been caused merely by growing older and by being successful. Gradually there developed a sense of discrepancy between Dickens's inner images of true vitality and true contact with other people and what the world seemed to offer in these respects. The writing of *David Copperfield*, which can be described as mimicry of his own experience, amounted then to a testing of that experience, with disappointing results. For although *David Copperfield* puts on stage some of Dickens's richest and most vivid performing characters (Uriah Heep's villainy is as inexhaustible and as irresistible as Pecksniff's), and although David is promised both life and love in his marriage with Agnes (though few readers have found this ending very interesting or more than perfunctorily convincing), although, in short, Dickens's former attitudes saw him through the actual composition of *David Copperfield*, everything that happened afterwards shows that an important change had taken place. And with *Bleak House* begins the great campaign of indignant criticism of the world for failing to embody his own images of living and loving. The theatrical method remains basic to the new art, which has changed its tone and its methods of organization but not its essential direction. The performance continues; mimicry is still the essential artistic and moral process; self-examination, and the imaginative understanding of the centre of self of others, to which self-examination is the only path, have never been discovered, much less practised. Instead, celebration has turned to accusation.

To this change in Dickens's view of the world, the moral and philosophic answer is easy enough to articulate. 'You are a mimic and you see in human behaviour only what can be mimicked: physical appearance (face, build, posture, clothes) and habitual physical and verbal movements. You see people this way because you, a professional mimic, are always interested in building effective routines. But people really are like this, and you observe accurately; people who say you exaggerate have simply, for one reason or another, good or bad, closed their eyes and ears to this part of the world which you see so clearly.

'You have discovered that these routines, the more you look at them and the more clearly you see them, are no longer as interesting as they once were. There are still plenty of them to be discovered—the number is infinite—but this has become less important than the fact that the routines themselves are beginning to seem mechanical, lifeless, determined, unfree. You *feel* alive, inside of you; you know exactly what being alive feels like. But it seems that no one else does. Everywhere you see mechanical routines of behaviour instead of anything that matches the sense of life and freedom you have within you. Everybody is dead: those recurrent twitches and speeches are a parody of life, not the real thing. This is loathesome enough in itself. But worse is the fact that the free inner life within you yearns for a living contact with the free life of another person, whereas all you can make contact with are mechanical routines. You have loved and pitied and hated particular people before, particular routines, but that has come to be not enough.

'You are experiencing a classic dilemma: you have, as it were, made your kind of discovery of determinism and you cannot account convincingly for your own sense of freedom. The traditional solution to this dilemma is through introspection and self-criticism. It is unlikely that you are the only free person in the world, and therefore it is likely that many people feel the way you do. You must put yourself in their place and realize that to other people you, too, seem nothing but a mechanical routine of habits, a performing fool or clown or monster. Thus converted to a new perspective, you will begin to get a vision of the free sense of life within other people, and you will then perhaps be able to make contact with that life. Such contact will always be a limited and faltering thing in comparison with the fullness and vividness of your actual sensuous vision and you will find that your conscience, in this respect, needs continual recreating.'

I have phrased my answer to Dickens's dilemma in direct discourse because one tends to feel a warm personal attachment to the manager of the Dickens theatre. If this also makes my answer seem condescending, that too is not inadvertent— for it dramatizes what seems to me an inevitable reaction to Dickens's solution. Indeed, a straightforward statement of his solution may be found by some readers unworthy of serious attention, yet the solution provides precisely that 'social vision' which makes him a great and inspired social prophet.

The conversion never took place. Instead, Dickens developed a view of the world as almost totally in the grip of a gigantic conspiracy which takes myriad forms but of which the sole effect is to thwart and stifle human freedom and the free contact between free spirits. This view is saved from the charge of paranoia and lent a kind of generosity and grandeur by Dickens's ambiguity as to whether it is a deliberate and intentional conspiracy. Conspiracy seems the wrong word, in so far as those in control of the conspiracy are often presented as having inherited their functions from the past, or as being decent people in private life, or underlings in a hierarchy of power, or inept or half-hearted in their role; and these people in control are always represented as being themselves dehumanized and deprived of freedom by their functions. But they deserve to be called conspirators because for the most part they work hard and deliberately at their function, and regard themselves as worthy of respect and honour because of it. They all reap material advantages at the same time, and are insensitive to the suffering they cause.

Whether or not we use the word conspiracy to describe this immense blight which, in Dickens's view, has fallen over the world, it will be agreed that the blight involves three factors: first, a universality of mechanical, systematized behaviour; second, a class of people who willingly give themselves over to this systematic behaviour, to the System, and therefore

H

acquire power over the lives of others which they dignify with the name of duty or respectability or charity or law; and third, the unwilling victims of the System. The victims are driven into mechanical routines of behaviour, but are pitied because their compulsive tics and obsessive eccentricities are unquestionably involuntary and are therefore evidence of the pressure of the System on their lives. Among the rulers of the System in these later books, to name only the most obvious, are the lawyers and the members of the 'fashionable' world in *Bleak House*, the utilitarian schoolmasters and the mill-owners in *Hard Times*, the Puritans, the jailers, Mrs. General, and the members of the Circumlocution Office in *Little Dorrit*, Mrs. Wilfer and Mr. Podsnap in *Our Mutual Friend*. Typical victims are Miss Flite and Prince Turveydrop in *Bleak House*, Maggy and Affery in *Little Dorrit*, Mr. Wilfer and the dolls' dressmaker in *Our Mutual Friend*.

Dickens quite frankly argues for the validity of his new view of the world in four of the novels which follow *David Copperfield*: *Bleak House*, *Hard Times*, *Little Dorrit*, and *Our Mutual Friend*. He argues often with the greatest persuasiveness: what he thought he saw before him was really there. But it is also true that this insight was the result of his peculiar perspective, of his fundamental identity as a mimic, a theatrical performer of life. It is not then surprising that theatrical methods turn out to be exactly the right ones for demonstrating the validity of that view. Moreover, the most successful of the four novels are those in which the argumentative intention is most overt and the burden of the argument least complex. Dickens's purpose in *Bleak House* is to demonstrate that the whole world is penetrated, stifled, and terrorized by a huge network of interconnecting systems: the structure of the novel embodies this vision by offering a satisfyingly large number of examples of systematized characters, and by contriving many and pointed interrelations between them. *Hard Times* is a logical refutation of the Utilitarian definition of human nature and of the Utilitarian mechanics for the production of human happiness: the structure of this novel is accordingly that of a 'moral fable' (to use Dr. Leavis's term), a pointed cautionary tale. These two novels are triumphs of convincing theatrical rhetoric by virtue of the extraordinary

energy of Dickens's richest invention and the brilliant simplicity of his themes, which is thoroughly in consonance with
his odd perspective on life. In neither novel is the success
of the whole structure damaged by the generally recognized
failure of individual elements: an experienced habitué of the
Dickens theatre can casually reject the sentimentalities connected with Esther Summerson and Stephen Blackpool without believing that this rejection in the least endangers the
success of the books as wholes.

In *Little Dorrit* and *Our Mutual Friend*, an attack on System
is again theatrically rendered, and often (in particular in *Little
Dorrit*) with great success. But in these novels Dickens chose
to combine loud and simple denunciations of System with an
attempt to focus on and to render dramatically the spiritual
progress by which certain individuals, who are deeply implicated in System, nevertheless emerge from its blight into some
small kind of freedom and happiness. Arthur Clennam's sick
will is healed by the love of Little Dorrit, and Bella Wilfer's
hard-hearted pursuit of money is softened into love by Mr.
Boffin's monitory impersonation of money-madness. In these
novels, then, Dickens honourably but unwisely attempted the
drama of human choice and change. Unwisely, for even when
Clennam's inner spiritual state is fairly convincingly described,
there is a disturbing discordance between this element of the
novel and the brilliant theatrical mimicries and denunciations
which surround it. The process through which Clennam's sick
will is healed is a theatrical manipulation tricked out to look
like drama, and Bella Wilfer's change of heart is tediously
conventional. One simply regrets that Dickens should have
spent his waning energies in attempting a mode of art so alien
to his genius. His rendering of the drama of the inner life
suffers, even at its best, from inevitable comparison with the
work of novelists to whom this mode of representing human
beings came naturally. But the best is rare, and for the most
part we are embarrassed by a disastrous mixture of modes:
again and again Dickens seems simply unable to keep himself from working up lurid theatrical routines out of material
which would seem to call for a more self-effacing method. *Our
Mutual Friend*, furthermore, exhibits a decided loss of inventive energy.

Great Expectations stands apart from these four novels by virtue of Dickens's temporary loss of interest in his attack on System. This novel theatrically impersonates the voice of a man who has learned how to live in a systematized world, but who is not for the moment interested in mounting a rhetorical attack on it. But *Great Expectations* stands apart from the other late novels by virtue of another characteristic which makes it an altogether unique literary phenomenon. The life story of Pip is in perfect accordance with the traditional language of pride, love, and duty by means of which it is explicitly moralized. But this story also speaks quite different meanings in and of itself, which are not the same as the explicit meanings and which were not, one imagines, available to the conscious part of Dickens's mind. This odd state of affairs produced, in *Great Expectations,* a beautiful and successful work of art.

PART II

THE WORLD OF SYSTEM

7

BLEAK HOUSE

CRITICS used to take it for granted that Dickens was a reformer, a man with a message. It is a prime example of the continuing Dickens problem that recent criticism has felt it necessary to abandon these obviously appropriate descriptions of Dickens's intentions in the mature novels. The new Dickens is a visionary symbolist, whom it would be undignified to think of as a man with a message. But in theatrical art there is nothing undignified—or surprising—in the fact that the virtuoso public entertainer should appear on his stage as a man with a message and should use his familiar contrivances, always so loudly directed to manipulating his audience's feelings, as equally loud rhetorical devices for arguing a message. And this is exactly what takes place in *Bleak House*.

Any novel comes to us as the record of a voice commenting directly or indirectly on a scene which it is also enacting. Non-theatrical art seeks to create what Edmund Wilson called a 'self-developing organism' of language: and the non-theatrical novelist will thus try to make us believe that the scene being enacted is really there, that the novelist and the reader are observing a piece of the physical world which is really in front of them. Because most novels are novels of manners, reflecting the modes of living and of expression which people in a certain society actually use, this self-developing illusion of reality will normally take the form of plausibility, of verisimilitude. In *Emma*, for instance, our sense that the author is *inventing* her characters, and directing our attention deliberately to certain meanings, begins and ends with her choice of heroine. Once Emma Woodhouse has been chosen as the centre of interest, everything else must and does seem to follow naturally, with no sense of particular purpose on the author's part. We meet no one whom Emma would not meet in the course of her everyday activity, and we meet everybody she would meet. One of Jane Austen's concerns is how Emma deals with particularly interesting and important people (Frank Churchill and Jane Fairfax), but she is even more interested in how Emma deals with the uninteresting and unimportant people, like Miss Bates, who make up her everyday life. Yet the creator of a self-developing illusion of reality must be careful not to seem to thrust Miss Bates into contact with Emma. For then the novel would seem to be testing Emma, instead of merely observing her, and the validity of the illusion would be destroyed.

The difference between *Emma* and *Middlemarch* in this respect is merely one of scope: we observe not just one person, but many, yet Jane Austen's rules apply with each of these many characters. One of the great scenes of *Middlemarch*, about which the author has many points to make quite directly when it happens, is the scene in which Dorothea comforts Rosamund Lydgate. It is a scene which occurs late in the novel because, by the laws of verisimilitude, it could not have happened naturally before. Mr. Brooke, early in the novel, invited Mr. Vincy to dinner, but he did not invite Mrs. Vincy or Rosamund, who come from a class which he does not choose his nieces to be acquainted with. And even later, when Dorothea is an independent widow, she does not really visit Rosamund before this great scene: it is only a deliberate act on Dorothea's part that brings the two together, and this deliberate act is significant of a large change of purpose in Dorothea's life.

In *Middlemarch*, George Eliot focuses on one particular centre of interest for a considerable period of time before she switches to another; and of course all her characters live in the same little provincial community. In *Anna Karenina*, Tolstoy shifts his attention more rapidly and over larger gaps of time and place, but he too is concerned with an illusion of reality. We begin by watching Oblonsky and following him about wherever he goes; when he meets Levin we switch trails and follow Levin, who visits the Tscherbatskys, in whose company we meet Vronsky and follow him for a while; when Vronsky goes to meet his mother at the railway station, we meet Anna, whom we then follow for a long time. After this closely linked beginning, we are able without losing the illusion of reality to switch our attention among all these people.

How different Dickens's purposes and methods are from those of non-theatrical art can be seen in the simple fact that Dickens exactly inverts Tolstoy's linking device. He links his characters with one another at the end rather than at the beginning, with of course a correspondingly inverted effect. When Lady Dedlock encounters the brickmaker's wife late in *Bleak House*, we are conscious that a point and purpose is being expressed by the *unlikely* juxtaposition of the two. No one in the book ever seems to meet anyone else just because it would be natural for this to happen. For Dickens is not really interested in how people live their lives, day to day, minute by minute: he is not a patient observer and he does not ask us to be. He asks us to see what he mimics, but because we consciously observe the process of mimicry, in and for itself, we consequently do not believe that what we see is quietly taking place before us, in actuality, as we tend to in non-theatrical art. This is perfectly acceptable, because we are believing something else; we are believing the points and messages for which the mimicry provides the vivid rhetorical exemplification.

S. J. Perelman (certainly not the equal of Dickens, but a remarkable verbal talent in a mode not entirely dissimilar) sets one of his comic sketches in a Schrafft's restaurant, and stations there some 'world-famed illustrators' who are 'limning the brilliant scene with swift strokes'.[1] One trouble with Dickens is that it is hard to avoid language like this when you try to define his style. In the opening pages of *Bleak House* we hear the voice of an artist, and what that artist is doing, as we quite consciously and pleasurably remark to ourselves, is limning a brilliant scene with swift strokes. The intention is just as explicit as Perelman's words suggest. Furthermore, we do indeed 'see' the Megalosaurus and the horses and the dogs and the ancient Greenwich pensioners and the wrathful skipper and the shivering little 'prentice boy on the deck'; and seeing is believing. But if by the standards of non-theatrical art we are enabled, even compelled, to say that we do not believe in that wrathful skipper, we mean that we do not take a certain attitude towards him: we do not observe, study, contemplate

[1] 'A Pox on You, Mine Goodly Host', *The Best of S. J. Perelman* (New York, 1947), p. 100.

that skipper in order to understand who he is and what he is like and to make up our minds about him. We have by no means the kind of perspective on him that would enable us to take these attitudes. Instead we get Dickens's point about him, which in this instance hardly goes further than what could be paraphrased thus: this is a vivid description of London, this is an inclusive description of London, London is a great and busy city and we are going to see it all. We are, then, not primarily observing a scene and learning from what we see; we are following the skill and the concerns and the will of the artist himself. This artist has, as a describer, a series of limited purposes, which we get the point of immediately; and we are therefore not surprised to find that he has other and larger purposes which we accordingly also get the point of immediately:

> The raw afternoon is rawest, and the dense fog is densest, and the muddy streets are muddiest, near that leaden-headed old obstruction, appropriate ornament for the threshold of a leaden-headed old corporation: Temple Bar. And hard by Temple Bar, in Lincoln's Inn Hall, at the very heart of the fog, sits the Lord High Chancellor in his High Court of Chancery.
> Never can there come fog too thick, never can there come mud and mire too deep, to assort with the groping and floundering condition which this High Court of Chancery, most pestilent of hoary sinners, holds, this day, in the sight of heaven and earth. (1) (p. 2)

We have arrived at our destination: an institution, but more significantly a vehement denunciation of that institution. We have not arrived in a natural, plausible illusion of a real tour of London: we have been brought here because the artist wants to make a point about this institution, and we gather from the force of his language that this is to be a very important point. Before we have actually *seen* the institution, strictly speaking, Dickens is already attacking it; and what he goes on to show us about it we can only take as proof and evidence for the point he has already made.

His point is correspondingly easy to see and to paraphrase: the High Court of Chancery is utterly cut off from relationships to humanity, and is rather a self-perpetuating machine, an apparatus, a ritual, a *system* of Justice, than a group of human beings working together naturally to achieve natural human purposes. But real human beings are governed by this institution, which therefore is powerful and dangerous. On the other hand, the ritual going on is ridiculous and silly, too; it is entertainingly inhuman. Therefore in one sense we do not believe in its power: we do not enter the illusion that we ourselves are implicated, engaged, or theatened by the danger because we are not studying it, contemplating it, trying to make up our minds about it. We have been shown it, triumphantly and self-confidently, by someone who hates it and wants it destroyed but does not fear it, for he has indeed complete verbal and rhetorical power over it. Rhetorical power is the power we actually experience in this theatrical art, and we co-operate with it because it speaks openly and infectiously to us and for us. The result is that, far from feeling that we have only made a beginning on a long process of patient observation of human behaviour, we are on the contrary already convinced and satisfied.

Thus there is no surprise when the artist does not in his next chapter immediately follow up the action he would seem to have begun in the first chapter: we are not, we do not have to be, engaged in the scene of the first chapter, because we already perfectly understand its significance. The events, in other words, were not in themselves the beginning of an action: rather we have heard a voice beginning an action of persuasion of which the scene in Chancery was but one exhibit. In the next chapter we are given a new exhibit: 'It is but a glimpse of the world of fashion that we want on this same miry afternoon. It is not so unlike the Court of Chancery, but that we may pass from the one scene to the other, as the crow flies.' (II) (p. 8) Why do we want a glimpse? Because we are building up a case, of which the world of fashion is also an instance. It is as another betrayal of normal human instincts that Dickens is giving us a glimpse of the aristocracy. And again we confirm the artist's point with the same certainty and confidence with which it was made.

The third chapter may surprise us momentarily, because we are suddenly listening to the first-person narrative of Esther Summerson. E. M. Forster argues[1] that this shift in point of view is successful because it 'bounces' us into

[1] *Aspects of the Novel* (New York, 1927), pp. 119–20.

acceptance, meaning, I take it, that the device has enough self-confidence and energy to make us go along with it blindly. A better explanation is that we are not at all blindly accepting anything; we see immediately the purpose of Dickens's new device. After a few sentences which define the new mask, in very broad terms, as modest, shy, and rather pathetic, it becomes clear that Esther is pathetic because she has been raised in an environment dominated by another system, that of Calvinistic guilt-consciousness and harsh discipline. After the loud pur-posefulness of the first two chapters, two exhibits in the theatrical artist's vehement case against systematization, we are not baffled to find ourselves hearing the autobiography of a victim of systematization: such tactics are perfectly familiar ones. Moreover, it is still the theatrical artist's voice and purpose that we are hearing, which is to say that we are not surprised to find our belief in the existence of Esther Summerson to be a very limited kind of belief. 'Esther Summerson' is an extremely thin verbal mask over the powerful, assured, self-confident, and energetic voice of the theatrical artist himself. For the most part this mask consists of little self-doubting phrases implying a diffident attitude towards the people and situations which the theatrical artist's strong voice and invention are making brilliantly vivid and pointedly significant. Most readers are irritated by Esther Summerson, and perhaps every reader regrets that Dickens, because he chose this device so early in the book and for so important a place in his whole argumentative structure, was forced then to speak so much of his strongest and most confident invention through the mask of Esther's diffidence. But only a self-bewildering reader will have missed the point of the device, and, in the beginning of the novel at least, the device works very efficiently to strengthen the authority of the artist's case: 'Even Esther sees—and says—what is wrong about this' is what Dickens wants us to feel and what we usually do feel.

Esther Summerson, then, is not only a victim of systemati-zation but an audience within the book for the artist's case against systematization. She meets the other characters in the same way we met the lawyers in the first chapter and the world of fashion in the second: not to become engaged with their lives, outer or inner, but to get the point about them.

And, except for its diffidence and timidity, her response to the people she meets is the same as ours.

. . . . .

Dickens's attack on System consists for the most part of a gallery of exhibits of human behaviour. He constructs this gallery by a remarkable capitalization on his early methods of characterization. In the Dickens theatre we are always an audience for the people, the landscapes, the houses, we meet; in *Bleak House* Dickens has made us into a special kind of audience, one that instantly tries to see what relationship each new person, each new house, each new landscape, has to the great case against System. And no one has any trouble seeing these relationships. Mrs. Jellyby, for instance, is the overlord of a tiny system of organized benevolence, whom Mr. Jarndyce sent Esther, Ada, and Richard to visit 'on purpose'—he says so explicitly. (VI)(p. 63) What did they learn, and how did they learn it? Not a moment is lost in answering these questions: not a detail connected with the name Jellyby but serves as a piece of evidence for Dickens's, and in this case also Mr. Jarndyce's, attack on System. The Jellybys live 'in a narrow street of high houses, like an oblong cistern to hold the fog. There was a confused little crowd of people, principally children, gathered about the house at which we stopped, which had a tarnished brass plate on the door, with the inscription, JELLYBY.' (IV) (p. 35) Every detail here is a judgement, and the judgement is emphatic and simple. The narrowness of the street speaks instantly of a lack of freedom, and attacks that condition. A street should not be a cistern to hold the fog, and if Mrs. Jellyby chooses to live on this street it means that she likes fog. In the first chapter we saw the Lord High Chancellor sitting at the centre of the fog; Mrs. Jellyby is then like him. Crowds of people should not be confused, children should not be in crowds, a brass plate should not be tarnished. Because we are in the Dickens theatre, listening to Dickens's attack on System, we translate every detail into a judgement with a rapidity which makes the judgements very simple ones.

The sense of confusion, constriction, and neglect is brought to an immediate focus by the fact that the little crowd is watching Peepy Jellyby, who has caught his head in the area railings. The various responses to Peepy's predicament are also immediately translated into judgements. Esther is sympathetic, but Mr. Guppy tells her that this sort of occurrence is too commonplace to be worried about: she is advised to be careful about herself. The milkman and the beadle are inefficiently trying to extricate Peepy: they are well-intentioned but caring for little children is not their 'natural' role. Esther is a natural young woman; natural women know how to take care of children; Esther suggests the proper method of releasing Peepy and it works.

When Esther finds out that, contrary to her deduction, Peepy's mother is not at home, the little scene is complete and its emblematic nature clear. The child is in trouble because it is being tended by the wrong people, by servants, milkmen, beadles, instead of by its mother. Mothers can keep their children's heads out of area railings, and this is their natural function. When natural functions are working naturally, all goes well. When not, the result is dirt, confusion, loss of freedom, the well-intentioned (or ill-intentioned) interference of incompetent public servants or of System itself.

The rest of this first glimpse of the Jellybys amplifies the disorder and also focuses the explanation for it more exactly. Mrs. Jellyby has displaced her attention from the correct objects of her responsibility, her children and her husband and her housekeeping, to the operation of a system of benevolence, an abstract, distorted, impersonal substitute for her natural instinct to take care of people. She loses contact not only with her children but with all human individuals, and thinks only in terms of numbers and groups: 'We hope by this time next year to have from a hundred and fifty to two hundred healthy families cultivating coffee and educating the natives of Borrioboola-Gha, on the left bank of the Niger.' (IV) (p. 37) The only single human beings she really notices are those like herself, similarly dehumanized, whose sole emotion is anxiety 'for the welfare of their species all over the country'. These people she calls 'private individuals' to distinguish them from 'public bodies'. (IV) (p. 37)

The relationship between Mrs. Jellyby and Chancery is clear: both are initially motivated by a genuine human interest—benevolence and justice respectively—but both have lost sight of the single human being and are concerned with the operation of a System. And the actual workings of both systems concern, not even 'public bodies' and 'plaintiffs', but material objects, paraphernalia. In Chancery, the 'maces, or petty-bags, or privy-purses' (i) (p. 3) deal mainly with 'bills, cross-bills, answers, rejoinders, injunctions, affidavits, issues, references to masters, masters' reports, mountains of costly nonsense'. (i) (p. 2) These are parodied in the contents of Krook's warehouse: 'quantities of dirty bottles: blacking bottles, medicine bottles, ginger-beer and soda-water bottles, pickle bottles, wine bottles, ink bottles . . . heaps of old crackled parchment scrolls, and discoloured and dog's-eared law-papers . . . rusty keys, of which there must have been hundreds huddled together as old iron.' (v) (pp. 49–50) In both instances, the tools for the furthering of human interests are prized in themselves, not for what they can do for human beings. Krook merely collects these tools: 'Everything seemed to be bought, and nothing to be sold there.' (v) (p. 49) Chancery is more foolish and more dangerous because it seems to carry on a kind of action with the tools, but the tools make contact only with other tools—bills speak only to cross-bills, references to masters are answered by masters' reports. In Mrs. Jellyby's system, even the two hundred healthy families on the left bank of the Niger are shadowy and unreal in comparison with the actual paraphernalia of Mrs. Jellyby's enormous 'correspondence', the 'litter' of papers with which her room, and her life, is entirely filled. 'Correspondence' ought to represent clarity of communication between single human beings but figures instead as litter and dirt. The ink with which this correspondence is written only dirties Caddy Jellyby. But although Caddy Jellyby looks discontented and sulky, Mrs. Jellyby is not aware that she is deep in dirt, but sits 'serene' in her system, as the Lord High Chancellor sits 'with a foggy glory round his head, softly fenced in with crimson cloth and curtains'. (i) (p. 2)

The Law is more dangerous than Mrs. Jellyby's system. Mr. Gridley 'can by no means be made to understand that the Chancellor is legally ignorant of his existence after making it desolate for a quarter of a century', (i) (pp. 3–4) and the Lord High Chancellor has simply forgotten, softly fenced in with crimson cloth and curtains as he is, that the chief party in the court's favourite comic case, Jarndyce and Jarndyce, has

committed suicide. He has to be reminded of this fact in the
foggy talk that passes for human communication in Chancery:
' Begludship's pardon—victim of rash action—brains. ' (1)
(p. 6) But although Mrs. Jellyby thinks her children are
'naughty' when they only want a little attention, nevertheless
the children do exist and they do call themselves to her attention. (Mr. Jellyby, however, has been reduced to a cipher.)
Caddy Jellyby, indeed, emerges from the litter and dirt to a
more natural life—we will examine her more carefully later.
There is something perhaps even positive in the fact that part
of the 'litter' in Mrs. Jellyby's household is actual dirt. This
system has not been perfected to its ultimate inhumanity:
the sinister interaction of one tool with another. There is no
dirt, one fancies, in Mrs. Pardiggle's household, and the five
little Pardiggles are already, although unwillingly, engaged in
the charitable distribution of their allowances. The Smallweed
family and the Vholes family are horrid parodies of family
life, guaranteeing the sterility of the household instead of
contradicting it. There are only adult children in the Smallweed house, genuine childishness arriving only in the form
of senility. And Mr. Vholes's remarkable statement, 'I both
have, and am, a father,' (XXXIX) (p. 553) is pure process:
the systematic exactness of the syntax takes all hope of living
human impulse out of these family relations, reducing the
elements of the sentence, and the sexual act, to the correctly
functioning parts of a machine. But there is some hope of life
in Mrs. Jellyby's system.

Mrs. Jellyby, once presented, never changes. When she
reappears from time to time, she is engaged as always in her
correspondence, serene, untidy, mildly displeased with her
naughty children, but tolerant of their unilluminated state.
We never learn anything new about her; she fits E. M. Forster's
category of 'flat' characters perfectly in that she reappears
entire, with all her clothes, her gestures, her speech, intact.
She does not change, she does not grow, she never engages in
any dramatic action, she has no centre of self and therefore we
do not engage with her. When she reappears there is little
pretence of verisimilitude in Dickens's bringing her back:
Esther is sent to visit her again 'on purpose', though this
time it is Dickens's, not Mr. Jarndyce's purpose: to give the

audience a repeat performance of an interesting and amusing and instructive theatrical routine. And in this respect she is quite like Dickens's earlier characters.

But there is one significant difference between Dickens's methods in *Bleak House* and his methods earlier. Since every detail about Mrs. Jellyby is now meaningful in moral, judgemental terms, every characterization is offered to us for immediate judgement and condemnation, and therefore her lack of inner life, her inability to change, her inability to engage in any action is also offered to us for condemnation. When Caddy Jellyby tells her that she is going to be married, Mrs. Jellyby is offered an opportunity to engage in a human action; the fact that she does not take the opportunity is the final confirmation of her systematized existence, her inability to meet experience, and this inability is very firmly brought to our attention and condemned.

The majority of the characters in *Bleak House*, who make up the majority of the exhibits in the great case against System, are, like Mrs. Jellyby, systematized. Whether they are rulers or victims, Dickens makes us see that they never change, that they are not truly alive, that they are subordinated entirely to routine. Dickens views these systematized people with varying degrees of condemnation, with horror in some cases, with amused tolerance in others. Taken together, they very richly embody a powerful demonstration and denunciation of the world of System.

This world, the 'world of *Bleak House*', is not a world we live in—more accurately, not a world we have the illusion of living in, as we have the illusion of living in the world of novels as diverse in method and tone as *Emma* or *The Trial* or *Resurrection* or *The Sound and the Fury*. The world of *Bleak House* is a theatrical performance rendered by a theatrical artist who is proving a case. Accordingly, the standards by which we judge it are those by which we judge an argument: we do not ask, then, 'Is it real'? but 'Is it convincing'?

The sheer number of the systematized beings in *Bleak House* is large enough to give a convincing sense that a whole world is being examined; and their variety is a convincing representation of the variety we expect to encounter in the world. There are, for instance, the several representatives of the system of Law: Mr. Tulkinghorn, Conversation Kenge, Mr. Guppy, Mr. Vholes; and then several others who either serve or parody the Law: Mr. Krook, Mr. Snagsby, Coavinses, the Smallweeds. The number of these is large enough to make the insidious power of the Law believable. And the differences between them and our different responses to them are vivid and pointed enough to make the case seem a fair one: we seem to have looked at all sides of the argument. This is true of all the other systems in the book.

Granted this quantity and variety of the dehumanized beings, no organic and progressive interaction between them will be necessary to show this world in action. These mechanical people are by definition incapable of knowing each other as individuals, of engaging with each other's minds, even of adapting their behaviour to each other. Some recognitions take place: Mrs. Pardiggle honours Mrs. Jellyby (though she criticizes her too), the Law respects Philanthropy and Fashion and is respected by them in turn, Mr. Skimpole conspires with Mr. Vholes. And the victims reach out ineffectually to each other: Mr. Snagsby to Jo and Guster, the brickmakers' wives to Jo, Jo to Nemo, Caddy to her father. But these poignant gestures are always furtive and guilty, and they are as nearly mute as articulate human behaviour can be. Indeed, since the instruments of articulate human behaviour have all been thoroughly systematized, these little moments of communication between victims of the System are close to being merely instinctive, and it is as such that Dickens approves of them. In opposition to all this, most of the articulate conversations we hear in *Bleak House* manifest a decided lack of communication.

The System in action, then, comes to us for the most part as a richly varied series of encounters between people who cannot talk with each other and who therefore can only perform their own natures in antiphonal duet with each other. Dickens has invented a remarkable number of these duets and there is a remarkable variety in them. For only one instance, consider the meeting between Mr. Skimpole and Coavinses early in the novel, an encounter between an apparent victim who is really a parasitic ruler of the System and an official representative of the System who is really a pathetic victim. The failure to communicate is complete, but as we watch this encounter we sense that we are watching evidence for a case which is being very richly and subtly argued, with plenty of attention to the exceptions. Or consider the entire 'life' of Snagsby. Mr. Snagsby's manner never changes: apologetic and loyal subservience to System linked with furtive, embarrassed benevolence, his periphrastic language filled with the deference towards his overlords he knows he is expected to feel and which he almost entirely does feel, though he cannot understand why things do not work out for happiness when he obeys all the rules. We see him first in his own proper, local, and domestic slavery to Mrs. Snagsby. Then in his professional slavery to Mr. Tulkinghorn. Then in half-hearted, unintentionally rebellious subservience to Mr. Chadband, then skilfully bullied into silence by the ambiguous Bucket. We see him with beadles and policemen, with Guster and Mr. Guppy, with Mademoiselle Hortense, with Allan Woodcourt, finally with Esther. Always he is the same and we never learn anything more about him than we found out at his first introduction; but the number and the variety of situations in which he appears keep him interesting.

In the last analysis what makes this curious kind of action believable, as the action of a believable world, is that such writing calls for a gift which Dickens possessed in abundance. We never tire of unchanging, undeveloping, unacting Mr. Snagsby because of the inexhaustible inventiveness with which Dickens reimpersonates his original conception whenever the occasion asks him to. This is perhaps Dickens's most important single creative talent; certainly it is a talent without which the copiousness of his theatrical art would be impossible. But it is a beautiful and valuable talent, as well as a practical one. For it makes it possible for Dickens to enact, in his own performances in his own theatre, exactly the fundamental energy and generosity of instinctual life from which his attack on System derives. I cannot quote an adequate example of Dickens's amazing inventiveness in this respect, since the whole point is that this invention carries him successfully through every single appearance of Snagsby. But here is one important element of the impersonation of Mr. Snagsby in its first appearance and in a repeat performance:

But these vague whisperings may arise from Mr. Snagsby's being, in his way, rather a meditative and poetical man; loving to walk in Staple Inn in the summer time, and to observe how countrified the sparrows and the leaves are; also to lounge about the Rolls Yard of a Sunday afternoon, and to remark (if in good spirits) that there were old times once, and that you'd find a stone coffin or two, now, under that chapel, he'll be bound, if you was to dig for it. He solaces his imagination, too, by thinking of the many Chancellors and Vices, and Masters of the Rolls, who are deceased; and he gets such a flavour of the country out of telling the two 'prentices how he *has* heard say that a brook 'as clear as crystial' once ran right down the middle of Holborn, when Turnstile really was a turnstile, leading slap away into the meadows—gets such a flavour of the country out of this, that he never wants to go there (x) (p. 130)

He has more leisure for musing in Staple Inn and in the Rolls Yard, during the long vacation, than at other seasons; and he says to the two 'prentices, what a thing it is in such hot weather to think that you live in an island, with the sea a-rolling and a-bowling right round you. (xix) (p. 266)

The repeat performance adds nothing new to our understanding of Snagsby; the remarkable thing is how exactly it says what the earlier example said, and yet how delicately particularized an image of Snagsby is rendered by both examples. Mr. Snagsby is dreaming of freedom, and the dream is pathetically timid, touchingly undemanding of life. The point is made so affectionately and with such precision in the image of the lost Holborn spring that it would seem all but impossible for Dickens to say the same thing with different material without producing a merely mechanical variation. But the repeat performance is even more poignant than the first.

Dickens's image of the world of System depends on this basic talent of his theatrical art not only for its argumentative success but for its moral beauty and value. I have spoken often of Dickens's overt purposes in *Bleak House* as argumentative, and so they are, very loudly and insistently so. The question arises, and not only for the oversensitive modern mind, whether there is not something rather unlovely in the contrived rhetoric of this loud, insistent, vehement voice which is so eager to denounce what it hates and to convince us by this denunciation. If we sense purposeful contrivances and manipulations on every page of *Bleak House*, what prevents us from getting an overpowering, overriding impression of the human

will in action? Why do these loud points and purposes not
come to seem an imposition on us, a tyranny over us which is
at least as oppressive as the tyranny of Chancery?

For contrivance is surely observable in the two passages
about Mr. Snagsby which I have quoted. The theatrical artist
is clearly enough working to plan here too, the plan being to
reimpersonate one of his own exhibits. It is just as clear that
he proceeds with the most knowing consciousness of what his
plan requires of him; he has to make up another image of
Snagsby's timid dream of freedom. The simple fact is that he
can really do this; the central and wonderful truth about
Dickens, which silences our criticism, is that he can perform
his own plan with a spontaneous energy of invention which
entirely burns away the atmosphere of mechanically insensitive
wilfulness. The planning remains perfectly obvious, but there
is new life available to the artist at every moment as he
performs his plans. Dickens's theatrical impersonation of the
world of System is as alive as its subject is dead. And, in
the Dickens theatre, this means that we believe he is telling the
truth.

What the world of System lacks, of course, is the complexity
that goes with drama. It is as flat as its inhabitants, and this
is inevitable and right. A mechanical being cannot embody
any very complex meaning and cannot be the vehicle for any
very complex judgement. Mrs. Jellyby, Mr. Snagsby, and the
rest of the mechanized characters are assessed with accuracy
and often with subtlety, and with a great range of feeling and
tone. Dickens has clearly demonstrated why we cannot take
these characters seriously as morally active human beings with
inner lives. But this means that the moral judgements
embodied by these characters and their world are not complex
moral judgements. Dickens's attitude towards this world is
a serious one, in the sense that it is impassioned and urgent and
compelling. But his judgement is that it cannot for a moment
be accepted as a possible way of life for human beings. It is a mistake from first to last for human beings to enter into System,
for System is absolutely hostile to everything that makes
them human. System, then, is not *criticized* as a complex moral
phenomenon, but single-mindedly denounced and rejected.

．　．　．　．　．

In describing this actionless world of System, I have, as the reader will have realized, ignored some important elements in *Bleak House*. There are, in fact, some actions in the novel which yield a more complex view of human nature than the simple denunciation of System. Caddy Jellyby marries Prince Turveydrop; Rosa, Lady Dedlock's maid, marries Watt Rouncewell; Richard Carstone marries Ada; Esther marries Allan Woodcourt—here are four images of the free continuing of human life. How does System make room for them? Dickens also organizes and gives forward movement to much of the novel by focusing on Lady Dedlock's guilty secret and the various mysterious investigations of it, both comic and sinister, which occupy so many of the characters in this world of System. What does this whole process tell us about System?

Caddy Jellyby's act of life is one of Dickens's triumphs of invention and of tone. Mrs. Jellyby introduces Caddy to her visitors as 'my eldest daughter, who is my amanuensis', and the solemn systematic word contrasts pointedly with the actual girl:

But what principally struck us was a jaded, and unhealthy-looking, though by no means plain girl, at the writing-table, who sat biting the feather of her pen, and staring at us. I suppose nobody ever was in such a state of ink. And, from her tumbled hair to her pretty feet, which were disfigured with frayed and broken satin slippers trodden down at heel, she really seemed to have no article of dress upon her, from a pin upwards, that was in its proper condition or its right place. (IV) (p. 37)

When Caddy comes sulkily to Esther's room the same night she has come for help towards being a natural young woman. She looks enviously at the sleeping Ada: 'But knows a quantity, I suppose? Can dance, and play music, and sing? She can talk French, I suppose, and do geography, and globes, and needlework, and everything?' (IV) (p. 44). This is the neglected and deprived girl's fantasy image of natural womanliness: what Esther teaches Caddy is plain sewing. But Caddy has pretty feet and wears satin slippers, and her own independent motion towards natural life takes the form of going to dancing school. This is fully meaningful—Esther does not scold her for it—because the Jellyby children have not been allowed to play without being called naughty by their mother, and because Caddy in fact ends up working at dancing. This progress is viewed with a delicate and perfectly controlled irony by Dickens. Caddy really succeeds only in entering yet another system, that of organized grace and 'deportment', and her new master, old Mr. Turveydrop, is a more demanding one than Mrs. Jellyby. Yet in this odd profession she does work which seems to us real and good, because it is motivated by love for her little husband with a dog's name, Prince Turvey-drop (who was actually named after the Prince Regent). Caddy herself expresses a half-aware ironic view of the conditions of her life which comes close to real insight. Here is her first account of the little dancing-apprentices:

The notion of the apprentices was still so odd to me, that I asked Caddy if there were many of them?
'Four,' said Caddy. 'One in-door, and three out. They are very good children; only when they get together they *will* play—children-like—instead of attending to their work. So the little boy you saw just now waltzes by himself in the empty kitchen, and we distribute the others over the house as well as we can.' (xxxviii) (p. 537)

This sounds just enough like Mrs. Jellyby's view of children to show that Caddy is still implicated in System, but the point is charmingly made and Caddy is affectionate towards the children and annoyed with them only because she wants to do her own job well. And then there is a clearer realization: 'when I put up the window, and see them standing on the door-step with their little pumps under their arms, I am actually reminded of the Sweeps.' (xxxviii) (p. 538) Here Caddy gets the funny pathos about the dancing-apprentices across to the reader and to herself.

Caddy's womanly instincts are purely maternal, towards Peepy, towards her father, and towards her husband, whom she calls her darling child:

I curtseyed to a little blue-eyed fair man of youthful appearance, with flaxen hair parted in the middle, and curling at the ends all round his head. He had a little fiddle, which we used to call at school a kit, under his left arm, and its little bow in the same hand. His little dancing shoes were particularly diminutive, and he had a little innocent, feminine manner, which not only appealed to me in an amiable way, but made this singular effect upon me: that I received the impression that he was like his mother, and that his mother had not been much considered or well used. (XIV) (pp. 189–90)

The child of this marriage is rather pointedly symbolic, but Dickens's delicacy of touch carries the day:

such a tiny old-faced mite, with a countenance that seemed to be scarcely anything but cap-border, and a little lean, long-fingered hand, always clenched under its chin. It would lie in this attitude all day, with its bright specks of eyes open, wondering (as I used to imagine) how it came to be so small and weak. Whenever it was moved it cried; but at all other times it was so patient, that the sole desire of its life appeared to be, to lie quiet, and think. It had curious little dark veins in its face, and curious little dark marks under its eyes, like faint remembrances of poor Caddy's inky days; and altogether, to those who were not used to it, it was quite a piteous little sight. (L) (p. 680)

The theatricality of Dickens's art makes it possible for us to consent to 'read' the meaning of this symbolic child (who turns out to be deaf and dumb) as straightforwardly and simply as it was invented. Herein lies the advantage of Dickens's obvious rhetorical intentions. For in non-theatrical, non-rhetorical fiction, where there is a consistent dramatic pressure within the scene, we could not contemplate a symbolic figure like this one with anything like the mild pathos which is possible in the Dickens theatre. Consider our feelings about Benjy in Faulkner's *The Sound and the Fury*, who is surely as meaningful—and as intentional—a symbol of bad blood as Caddy's baby. We are not, for Benjy, the sympathetic and pitying audience that we are for the patient hopelessness of Dickens's symbolic figure. With Benjy, we are engaged in a dramatic situation, we participate in the intensities of feeling directly, we *live with him* in an illusion of reality. And, in fact, we watch Benjy dribble and drool and weep, nor are we insulated from disgust by anything like Dickens's theatrical presence, performing these painful things before us. Accordingly, we experience a painfully (and beautifully) intense *complexity* of attitude towards Benjy, which in turn is the necessary preparation for our intense feeling of admiration and love for Dilsey.

If we were similarly engaged in a dramatic scene when we encounter Caddy's husband and her baby, we would experience a feeling of horror at the distortion and emotional poverty of Caddy's new life. There is no horror engendered by Dickens's performance of his exhibit and Dickens knows how to arouse horror when he wants to, though, of course, again a theatrical horror. It is pathos Dickens is after in the present instance, and that is what he achieves. The fact that it is a rather comfortable and easy pathos is a necessary result of Dickens's theatrical art and its conditions; we are in the extremely public intimacy of a theatre, we are not in an illusion of reality, we are not being led to experience imaginatively what Caddy's life is really like. We are in contact with the voice of a theatrical performer, obedient to that voice, assured by that voice. And we feel ourselves to have been watching a very touchingly sad and delicate exhibition of the limitations of life within System.

What is true of Caddy's baby is true of all the symbolic figures in *Bleak House*, and indeed in all of Dickens's work with the exception of *Great Expectations*. I am an enthusiastic admirer of Dickens's symbolic methods: he is usually in complete control of them and brilliantly inventive in performing them. But his symbols are part of his theatrical mode, and they function quite differently from symbols in non-theatrical art. In non-theatrical art a symbol is valuable because it can be implicated in a complex dramatic action and can therefore serve as the focus for a complex of attitudes towards a theme of which the symbol is also the objectification. Moreover, because the theme is thus genuinely objectified and genuinely implicated in a dramatic action, the attitudes towards it can be expressed with the unparaphrasable subtlety and precision, above all with the ambiguity, which non-symbolic art cannot achieve except by discursive analysis. A conveniently obvious instance is the cherry orchard in Chekhov's play, which expresses the rich complexity and ambiguity of Chekhov's attitude towards the passing of an old order. As the various characters discuss the cherry orchard, argue about it, make decisions about it and act on them, contemplate it, or even ignore it, all these attitudes towards the old order come together in a rich and living unity which would be difficult to achieve without the use of symbolic methods. We become engaged with all the characters in the play, we have the illusion of living with them, and they in turn are engaged with the symbolic object, they live with it; and in this way the object itself comes to be extraordinarily resonant, subtly and complexly expressive.

Except in *Great Expectations*, this never happens in Dickens's use of symbols. Mrs. Jellyby is a symbolic figure, but we do not live with her. We observe her as an exhibit. What she means is vividly embodied, but it is very simple too, and our attitude towards her is correspondingly simple. This is true of the fog in London, the rain in Lincolnshire, of all the landscapes and houses and rooms—each one symbolic—in which the people in the novel are exhibited to us. None of these symbols is the vehicle for complex meaning like Chekhov's cherry orchard. Consider the description of Bleak House itself:

It was one of those delightfully irregular houses where you go up and down steps out of one room into another, and where you come upon more rooms when you think you have seen all there are, and where there is a bountiful provision of little halls and passages, and where you find still older cottage-rooms in unexpected places, with lattice windows and green growth pressing through them. Mine, which we entered first, was of this kind, with an up-and-down roof, that had more corners in it than I ever counted afterwards, and a chimney (there was a wood-fire on the hearth) paved all around with pure white tiles, in every one of which a bright miniature of the fire was blazing. Out of this room, you went down two steps, into a charming little sitting-room, looking down upon a flower-garden, which room was henceforth to belong to Ada and me. Out of this you went up three steps, into Ada's bed-room, which had a fine broad window, commanding a beautiful view (we saw a great expanse of darkness lying underneath the stars), to which there was a hollow window-seat, in which, with a spring-lock, three dear Adas might have been lost at once. Out of this room, you passed into a little gallery, with which the other best rooms (only two) communicated, and so, by a little staircase of shallow steps, with a number of corner stairs in it, considering its length, down into the hall. But if, instead of going out at Ada's door, you came back into my room, and went out at the door by which you had entered it, and turned up a few crooked steps that branched off in an unexpected manner from the stairs, you lost yourself in passages, with mangles in them, and three-cornered tables, and a Native-Hindoo chair, which was also a sofa, a box, and a bedstead, and looked in every form something between a bamboo skeleton and a great bird-cage, and had been brought from India nobody knew by whom or when. From these, you came on Richard's room, which was part library, part sitting-room, part bed-room, and seemed indeed a comfortable compound of many rooms. Out of that, you went straight, with a little interval of passage, to the plain room where Mr. Jarndyce slept, all the year round, with his window open, his bedstead without any furniture standing in the middle of the floor for more air, and his cold-bath gaping for him in a smaller room adjoining. Out of that, you came into another passage, where there were back-stairs, and where you could hear the horses being rubbed down, outside the stable, and being told to Hold up and Get over, as they slipped about very much on the uneven stones. Or you might, if you came out at another door (every room had at least two doors), go straight down to the hall again by half-a-dozen steps and a low archway, wondering how you got back there, or had ever got out of it. (vi) (pp. 65–66)

This house is obviously a symbol: one immediately proceeds to interpreting it. But it does not speak for itself: we are conscious that the theatrical artist is speaking his purposes through the symbol. (This consciousness is buttressed by the fact that Mr. Jarndyce is also showing his house to the young people 'for a purpose'.) The artist has several purposes in mind, not exactly contradictory but definitely different ones, and his procedure is simply to add another room for each purpose. Dickens wants the house to speak about Mr. Jarndyce's kind solicitude for Esther and Ada, so he makes it the kind of house which these two young girls can find charming and delightful. Because Mr. Jarndyce himself is charmingly and delightfully eccentric, the quaintness of Bleak House is not altogether inappropriate for him. But it is somewhat inappropriate: it is too feminine, too much of a cosy retreat, for a man with supposedly serious moral purposes and an active philanthropic life. A special room, expressive of manly freedom and serious activity, is accordingly added for Mr. Jarndyce. Mr. Jarndyce is hopeful that Richard will settle down to serious work too, but he is still only a boy: Dickens contrives a suitable room for him too. It is clear that Dickens wants the whole house to be expressive of the domestic virtues and at the same time of freedom and life within the domestic virtues, for Mr. Jarndyce builds an exact replica of Bleak House for Esther and Allan Woodcourt. The house does serve well enough for this purpose, though

its feminine charm somewhat gets in the way. The symbol
achieves what it sets out to achieve and the reader gets the
point throughout.

Yet the house is surely a complicated contraption rather
than a complex unified object. It is not a house which the
reader lives in or with, nor are we invited really to imagine
Mr. Jarndyce living in this house. If we did try to imagine him
doing so, we might ask whether the arrangement of furniture
in his own room was the result of a deliberate rebellion against
the cosy encircling warmth of the rest of the house. But we
do not ask such questions in the Dickens theatre. When Mr.
Jarndyce is discovered to have moments of raging pessimism
about System, Dickens invents a special little room—the
Growlery—for him to growl in: 'in part a little library of books
and papers, and in part quite a little museum of his boots and
shoes, and hat-boxes'. (VIII) (p. 94) This little 'museum' seems
a half-hearted attempt to make the Growlery into a real room
that someone might actually live in, but no such attempt is
strictly necessary.

When we learn of the proposed marriage between Rosa,
Lady Dedlock's maid, and Watt Rouncewell, we meet for the
first time John Rouncewell the Ironmaster, who completes a
group of three symbolic figures who together embody a rather
complex view of the aristocracy. Again Dickens has several
points to make and again he adds, so to speak, special rooms
to take care of each of them.

At the beginning of the second chapter, Dickens tells us
that the world of fashion is 'not so unlike' the Court of
Chancery, and Chancery alliterates with Chesney Wold, the
seat of the Dedlocks in Lincolnshire.

> Both the world of fashion and the Court of Chancery are things
> of precedent and usage; oversleeping Rip Van Winkles, who have
> played at strange games through a deal of thundery weather;
> sleeping beauties, whom the Knight will wake one day, when all
> the stopped spits in the kitchen shall begin to turn prodigiously!
> (II) (p. 8)

But the first chapter by no means led us to think of Chancery
as a sleeping beauty: we take these fanciful remarks, and
particularly the tenderly mocking tone in them, to apply only

to the world of fashion, the system of aristocracy. And Dickens makes important distinctions between these two systems.

Much of the time, to be sure, Sir Leicester Dedlock is a ridiculous pompous snob whom Dickens hounds with all the tender irony of Trabb's boy. But in the first description there is another, more ambiguous attitude expressed:

> Sir Leicester Dedlock is only a baronet, but there is no mightier baronet than he. His family is as old as the hills, and infinitely more respectable. He has a general opinion that the world might get on without hills, but would be done up without Dedlocks. He would on the whole admit Nature to be a good idea (a little low, perhaps, when not enclosed with a park-fence), but an idea dependent for its execution on your great county families. He is a gentleman of strict conscience, disdainful of all littleness and meanness, and ready, on the shortest notice, to die any death you may please to mention rather than give occasion for the least impeachment of his integrity. He is an honourable, obstinate, truthful, high-spirited, intensely prejudiced, perfectly unreasonable man. (II) (p. 9)

First the hearty impudence of the professional humorist. But the last two sentences express a more ambiguous attitude towards the aristocratic system, and the remarkable epithets in the last sentence are not merely a list but an almost dramatic act of engagement with the complexity of the aristocratic system itself. Such dramatic complexity is of course by no means maintained in the book as a whole. Our view of Sir Leicester shifts between these two attitudes as easily as it does in this first introduction.

A higher degree of tension is maintained in Dickens's representation of the Rouncewell family, a cluster of symbolic figures ingeniously extrapolating Dickens's ambivalence about the aristocracy. Mrs. Rouncewell is, at first glance, a systematized being:

> It has rained so hard and rained so long, down in Lincolnshire, that Mrs. Rouncewell, the old housekeeper at Chesney Wold, has several times taken off her spectacles and cleaned them, to make certain that the drops were not upon the glasses. Mrs. Rouncewell might have been sufficiently assured by hearing the rain, but that she is rather deaf, which nothing will induce her to believe. She is a fine old lady, handsome, stately, wonderfully neat, and has such a back and such a stomacher, that if her stays should turn out when

she dies to have been a broad old-fashioned family fire-grate, no-body who knows her would have cause to be surprised. (VII) (pp. 82–83)

Her absolute stiffness, her propriety, her refusal to recognize her deafness, all these make her exactly the sort of house-keeper Sir Leicester would like.

He has a great liking for Mrs. Rouncewell; he says she is a most respectable, creditable woman. He always shakes hands with her, when he comes down to Chesney Wold, and when he goes away; and if he were very ill, or if he were knocked down by accident, or run over, or placed in any situation expressive of a Dedlock at a disadvantage, he would say if he could speak, 'Leave me, and send Mrs. Rouncewell here!' feeling his dignity, at such a pass, safer with her than with anybody else. (VII) (p. 83)

He is right; his trust is justified not only by her correct appearance but by her correct opinions. She is fond of her Ironmaster son 'but has a plaintive feeling towards him—much as if he were a very honourable soldier, who had gone over to the enemy'. (VII) (p. 85) She praises Rosa for her modesty: 'It is a fine quality in a young woman. And scarcer', says Mrs. Rouncewell, expanding her stomacher to its utmost limits, 'than it formerly was!' (VII) (p. 85) When she tells the story of Sir Morbury Dedlock, who sided with King Charles, 'the blessed martyr', her sympathies are entirely on the side of the aristocracy. And 'she regards a ghost as one of the privileges of the upper classes'. (VII) (p. 89)

Yet what in Sir Leicester is pompous and foolish, in Mrs. Rouncewell is attractive and genuinely dignified, though distinctly old-fashioned too. She is not subservient but loyal. Her 'gracious severity of deportment' as she shows visitors around Chesney Wold is not, like Mr. Turveydrop's, a foolish imitation of aristocratic stiffness but an expression of honest pride in a job well done. Dickens's fancy about her stays and the fire-grate is not mockery but an amused respect for her endurance and self-control; the homeliness of the fire-grate seems to speak of her essential honesty. Were Sir Leicester to refuse to recognize that he was growing deaf, he would be refusing to recognize that he was a human being like the rest of us. With Mrs. Rouncewell, exactly the opposite is true: who wants to face the fact that he is getting old and out of things and no longer capable of honest work? All this is focused in a fine image of the aliveness of Mrs. Rouncewell's loyalty: 'the whole house reposes on her mind. She can open it on occasion, and be busy and fluttered; but it is shut-up now, and lies on the breadth of Mrs. Rouncewell's iron-bound bosom, in a majestic sleep.' (VII) (p. 83) Mrs. Rouncewell, who began her service in the stillroom, shows us that the aristocratic system is still an adequate object of loyalty, because there is still meaningful work to be done within its limits. This is confirmed by the fact that she is surrounded by youth and life and is the source of life. 'Mrs. Rouncewell has known trouble. She has had two sons, of whom the younger ran wild, and went for a soldier, and never came back.' (VII) (p. 84) The other son troubled her too, because he became John Rouncewell, the Ironmaster. But when we first see her, she is in affectionate converse with John's son, Watt; and though she is uncomprehendingly regretful that Rosa, her pet, is going to marry Watt and leave service, she shows sympathy with this young love and hope.

The aristocratic system is not hostile to life, but it can no longer really support and nourish life. Mr. George, who ran wild and went for a soldier, shows this most clearly, for he manifests the heroic loyalty and spiritedness that reveals the best in aristocracy: if the system were still really alive, he would serve it. But although Dickens calls Sir Leicester 'high-spirited', the only remnant of this heroic quality is his chivalric service to Lady Dedlock, for whom he opens coach doors from Paris to Lincolnshire with an antique devotion which reflects a sincere and intense idealization of experience in terms of the aristocratic code. Yet Dickens is quick to point out that the chief value of this fine old ritual is to bring a moment of glamour into the lives of inn-keepers. Sir Leicester is no adequate lord and master for Mr. George's genuine high spirits.

The way in which Mr. George gets entangled in the System shows what happens to genuinely alive heroic ideals and behaviour in the new institutionalized world. For whereas Sir Leicester has placed most of his heroic interests in the hands of the sinister Tulkinghorn, Mr. George expresses his

high-spirited ideals in his everyday behaviour, and ends up
in the clutches of Mr. Smallweed and in jail. The duets between
Mr. Smallweed and Mr. George are powerful images of the
heroic ideals of loyalty trapped in the cash nexus. But when
Mr. George goes to prison, Dickens gets somewhat out of his
depth, or at least into an area of feeling inappropriate to the
theatrical mode. Imprisoned on suspicion of having murdered
Mr. Tulkinghorn, Mr. George, with nothing to lose but his life,
again 'runs wild': he trusts his own virtues, and escapes from
the Law as he had wanted to escape from Mr. Smallweed and
as he actually did escape from Chesney Wold. He refuses legal
aid and trusts to his honour to get him through, without
recourse to any intermediary system, which he would feel to
be corrupting. He becomes a martyr, a heroic fool.

'But, my good fellow, even an innocent man must take ordinary
precautions to defend himself.'

'Certainly, sir. And I have done so. I have stated to the magis-
trates, "Gentlemen, I am as innocent of this charge as yourselves;
what has been stated against me in the way of facts, is perfectly
true; I know no more about it." I intend to continue stating that,
sir. What more can I do? It's the truth.'

'But the mere truth won't do,' rejoined my guardian.

'Won't it, indeed, sir? Rather a bad look-out for me!' Mr.
George good-humouredly observed. (LII) (p. 704)

Jarndyce is forced to recommend the aid of lawyers; he
explains, 'a little at a loss', that his chief distrust is of Equity.
But Mr. George answers in an off-hand manner, 'I am not
acquainted with those shades of names myself, but in a general
way I object to the breed.' (LII) (p. 705) His position is im-
pregnable and it is, of course, the position of the whole novel
on the subject of the Law. Dickens's consistency about Mr.
George embarrasses not only Mr. Jarndyce but himself.

When Esther and Mr. Jarndyce leave Mr. George's cell,
Esther says that she hopes to find him 'more reasonable' when
she sees him again. 'More grateful, Miss Summerson, you
can't find me,' he returned. (LII) (p. 709) A significant rebuke:
all of Mr. George's virtues are implied in the word 'grateful'
and the same could be said about the virtues which *Bleak
House* as a whole praises. If the word 'reasonable' means
anything in *Bleak House*, it can mean only one of two things:

either it is simply a cant word used as a weapon by the systematizing people; or, if it can be thought to be a good word, it can only refer to behaviour which will preserve and further *freedom*. Mr. George's view, that having anything to do with a lawyer endangers one's freedom—though it may save one's life, of course—is absolutely confirmed by all of Dickens's exhibits. Yet Esther tries again, in a curiously evasive exhortation: 'And let me entreat you to consider that the clearing up of this mystery, and the discovery of the real perpetrator of this deed, may be of the last importance to others besides yourself.' (LII) (p. 709) This seems simply dishonest: Bucket is on the job already, and Mr. George's decision to hire a lawyer can do nothing important towards solving the mystery. When Mrs. Bagnet scolds Mr. George for his 'folly', her main argument is that Mr. George is wanting in due respect to the 'ladies and gentlemen' who are trying to persuade him. This is actually unpleasant from the mouth of the good Major's wife. The fact is that Dickens has painted himself into a corner and is showing, in these desperate off-key tactics, that he only half realizes it.

On the other hand, the reader is in no fear that Mr. George will have to pay the price for his heroism. Dickens's tactics have assured us that the true murderer will be apprehended by the remarkable Bucket. When Dickens is setting the stage for a death scene, the sacrificial victim is publicly groomed for the role long in advance: consider the whole treatment of Jo, the Tough Subject. Moreover, Dickens has ready to hand a theatrical trick for effecting Mr. George's release from his, and Dickens's, 'dilemma'. Mrs. Rouncewell is brought to the prison, there is an affecting reunion between the handsome old lady and her soldier son, and Mr. George's sense of honour bows to his filial tenderness. Such are the strategies of theatrical art when the highest energy of invention is temporarily lacking. Nor does Dickens's awkwardness about Mr. George's 'folly' infect the book as a whole, or even the complex view of the aristocracy as a whole. It is only for a moment that, as the whole enterprise falters, we catch a glimpse of the limitations of theatrical art and of the view of System which that art is arguing.

Another such glimpse is to be caught in the treatment of John Rouncewell. When Mr. Rouncewell speaks to Sir Leicester

and Lady Dedlock about Rosa, he is a sympathetic figure. He
speaks, to be sure, of certain plans and projects in an orderly
and business-like way, but these plans concern one single
human being, and they seem genuinely to have Rosa's well-
being in mind. But the strongest reason for our sympathy with
Mr. Rouncewell is a theatrical one: Dickens instructs us to find
the Ironmaster a sensible man and a good man by making
Sir Leicester pompously haughty about the very idea of Mr.
Rouncewell:

> 'He is called, I believe—an—Ironmaster.' Sir Leicester says it
> slowly, and with gravity and doubt, as not being sure but that he
> is called a Lead-mistress; or that the right word may be some other
> word expressive of some other relationship to some other metal.
> (XXVIII) (p. 393)

It is the Ironmaster who has the genuine dignity in this interchange with Sir Leicester. The first description of Rouncewell
shows us what the right kind of reasonable, responsible man of
affairs looks like:

> He is a little over fifty perhaps, of a good figure, like his mother;
> and has a clear voice, a broad forehead from which his dark hair has
> retired, and a shrewd, though open face. He is a responsible-looking
> gentleman dressed in black, portly enough, but strong and active.
> Has a perfectly natural and easy air, and is not in the least embar-
> rassed by the great presence into which he comes. (XXVIII) (p. 393)

Dickens's purposes are clear: to make Rouncewell truly an
orderly businessman without making him one of the systematized mechanical beings which the book is denouncing. And
we are brought to feel a good measure of respect for this
Ironmaster, though significantly enough we are not particularly
interested in him for himself—we mainly like the way he takes
Sir Leicester down a peg or two.

When Dickens comes to deal with the Ironmaster's 'relationship with metals' he shows how perfunctory his interest in and
admiration for this responsible man really is.

> Her second son . . . took, when he was a schoolboy, to construct-
> ing steam-engines out of saucepans, and setting birds to draw their
> own water, with the least possible amount of labour; so assisting
> them with artful contrivance of hydraulic pressure, that a thirsty

canary had only, in a literal sense, to put his shoulder to the wheel, and the job was done. (VII) (p. 84)

Dickens's conception of the Ironmaster's work really goes no further than this charming image. After Mr. George has been reunited with his mother, he visits his brother in the North country and is offered a job in the iron-works. He refuses, of course, and returns to Chesney Wold and loyal service to the broken Sir Leicester. We understand and accept this choice, but the fact is that he has not been offered a meaningful alternative to the aristocratic system's version of 'work'. Here is what Mr. George sees in the iron country:

> He comes to a gateway in the brick wall, looks in, and sees a great perplexity of iron lying about, in every stage, and in a vast variety of shapes; in bars, in wedges, in sheets; in tanks, in boilers, in axles, in wheels, in cogs, in cranks, in rails; twisted and wrenched into eccentric and perverse forms, as separate parts of machinery; mountains of it broken up, and rusty in its age; distant furnaces of it glowing and bubbling in its youth; bright fireworks of it showering about, under the blows of the steam hammer; red-hot iron, white-hot iron, cold-black iron; an iron taste, an iron smell, and a Babel of iron sounds. (LXIII) (p. 846)

And here is the Ironmaster's office:

> He is left alone with the gentleman in the office, who sits at a table with account-books before him, and some sheets of paper, blotted with hosts of figures and drawings of cunning shapes. It is a bare office, with bare windows, looking on the iron view below. Tumbled together on the table are some pieces of iron, purposely broken to be tested, at various periods of their service, in various capacities. There is iron-dust on everything; and the smoke is seen, through the windows, rolling heavily out of the tall chimneys, to mingle with the smoke from a vaporous Babylon of other chimneys. (LXIII) (pp. 846–7)

We cannot think that Dickens wanted these descriptions to mean that the Ironmaster's work is a sterile manipulation of paraphernalia, like Mrs. Jellyby's 'correspondence' with its litter, or the procedures of the maces and petty bags with bills and cross-bills of Chancery, or the empty bottles of Mr. Krook's warehouse. Yet, taken seriously, this is what the descriptions say. It is Dickens's fundamental identity as a mimic that has

painted him into a corner this time. When he comes to an iron-
foundry all he can do with it is to impersonate it, to make it
perform itself before us. He cannot, in the simplest sense,
understand the work being done, and he is not interested in or
capable of trying to imagine what the work feels like from the
inside. It is not enough to say that these descriptions are
rendered from the point of view of Mr. George and therefore
represent *his* incapacity to come to terms with this kind of
work. What one feels is Dickens's own helplessness. The
descriptions have plenty of theatrical self-confidence and are
indeed effective, but the assurance of the manner cannot hide
Dickens's basic uncertainty about what he is describing. Is the
iron-foundry deplorable or interesting or—as some of the details suggest—amusing and charming?

The secondary reasons for Dickens's confusion are easy to
understand. Dickens hated the northern mills and thought
them appallingly inhuman, and he had good reasons. On the
other hand, he had assigned himself Mr. Rouncewell as a
sympathetic, 'responsible' man, and he had plausible reasons
for deciding that Mrs. Rouncewell's industrious son might well
become one of the Northern mill owners. Then again, his most
important immediate purpose is to send Mr. George back to
Chesney Wold and to make this seem convincing. But theatrical
art is happiest when it is handling one purpose at a time.
Complex attitudes are likely to dull the brilliance of the
performance, even when they are well in hand.

But one hardly imagines Dickens to have had a clear sense
of his own ambivalence about Mr. Rouncewell, because the
primary reason for that ambivalence is his own virtual incapacity, as Orwell's essay has shown, to render a convincing
image of meaningful work of any kind. Certainly in *Bleak House*
there is no such image apart from Mrs. Rouncewell's service.
All of politics is meaningless and false. The Bagnets, who seem
responsible people, are musicians, and in this marginal
profession Mr. Bagnet occupies an even odder corner, as a
bassoonist. Mrs. Bagnet is supposedly a good cook, but only,
and incessantly, washes greens. Professor Dingo, one of Mrs.
Badger's former husbands, is a comic geologist:

'People objected to Professor Dingo, when we were staying in
the North of Devon, after our marriage,' said Mrs. Badger, 'that he

disfigured some of the houses and other buildings, by chipping off fragments of those edifices with his little geological hammer. But the Professor replied, that he knew of no building, save the Temple of Science. The principle is the same, I think?'

'Precisely the same,' said Mr. Badger. 'Finely expressed! The Professor made the same remark, Miss Summerson, in his last illness; when (his mind wandering) he insisted on keeping his little hammer under the pillow, and chipping at the countenances of the attendants. The ruling passion!' (XVII) (p. 230)

Esther and Mr. Jarndyce worry about Richard's lack of application to the various professions he chooses in turn, and the book says much in favour of solid work, patience, and perseverance. But nothing of this is shown except in comic or eccentric terms. Even Allan Woodcourt appears only as a heroic saviour of lives after a shipwreck or as a peripatetic Good Samaritan; he seems to have no office and no steady work. Every occupation in the book is turned into a grotesque tic, a compulsion. Despite the official denunciation of life ruled by paraphernalia, every occupation, however approved, is ruled by its instruments: we see Charley, the loyal little maid, 'folding up everything she could lay her hands on', (XXIII) (p. 335), and Phil Quod 'seems to do and undo everything that can be done and undone about a gun'. (XXVI) (p. 368)

All this derives from Dickens's habits and inclinations as a theatrical artist and, to this reader at least, it amounts to a valuable and significant testimony about work, a testimony which perhaps only Dickens could have given. As he inspects his world with his extraordinary eye and his extraordinary certainty about his own inner sense of life, he reports that most people are dominated by their tools, are losing their freedom by enacting systematic mechanical processes, which to a free eye are undistinguishable from compulsive tics. Who can deny this report? And what thinking person has never questioned the value of this loss of freedom? From this perspective, Dickens's incapacity for imagining meaningful work from the inside figures simply as an incapacity to die.

But since part of Dickens's official theme in *Bleak House* is the opposition of a bad kind of work to a good kind, his incapacity to imagine the good kind is disadvantageous, to say

the least. He seems to have heard about responsible, reasonable, patient work and he seems to have sincerely believed
in its value. And I for one very much respect him for this
sincerity which went against the grain of his deeper sincerity,
though he should not perhaps entirely escape the charge of
merely believing in what was respectable. If we choose not to
make this charge, it is because we hardly imagine Dickens to
have taken his own writing as 'work': the evidence is that the
act of composition was for him often closer to play, or even to
an hallucinative trance, than to anything requiring patience
or perseverance. We must respect him, then, for realizing that
for most people work was more mechanical, more 'like work',
than it was for him. But, as he praises the people who clothe,
feed, and house the world, he must do this arbitrarily,
theoretically, because his mode of vision turns even these life-
furthering occupations into compulsive systems.

.   .   .   .   .

The Rouncewells show Dickens's procedures for rendering
a complex moral attitude towards one of the world's systems,
and the moments of confusion about the Rouncewells show the
limitations of such procedures and of his insight. These limitations are exhibited even more clearly and damagingly in
Dickens's mode of rendering his chief characters, Mr. Jarndyce,
Richard and Ada, Lady Dedlock and Esther Summerson.

The trouble with Mr. Jarndyce, Richard and Ada, as with
many of Dickens's leading characters, is that in their role of
leading characters they must perform somewhat too frequently. Mr. Jarndyce is partly a comic eccentric, of the
sympathetic kind, with his Growlery and his East Wind; he
is also a Squire Allworthy figure of wise and good counsel.
These two identities are linked together as casually as the
correspondingly differing rooms in Bleak House. But in
neither role is Mr. Jarndyce allowed fully to enjoy the copiousness of Dickens's invention, and we never make imaginative
contact with his inner life as it engages in a dramatic action.
The result is that Mr. Jarndyce never comes to be a person,
or a meaning, in whom we take much interest.

Richard and Ada are crushed by System in a process which
Dickens follows fairly closely. The process is not a dramatic
action but pure victimization, and it is purely pathetic in

consequence. It is no surprise that Dickens should have been able to produce nothing beyond a fairly perfunctory pathos here: these two characters must keep their dignity as *jeune premier* and *ingénue*, must remain romantically pretty and innocent throughout their sufferings, and therefore can never be granted the vividness of the more violently twisted, eccentric victims of System. Richard, it is true, develops some suspicions about Mr. Jarndyce which, in non-theatrical art, might raise a significant question about the quietism which Dickens seems to be praising in the figure of Mr. Jarndyce:

'Come, sister, come,' said Richard, a little more gaily, 'you will be fair with me at all events. If I have the misfortune to be under that influence, so has he. If it has a little twisted me, it may have a little twisted him, too. I don't say that he is not an honourable man, out of all this complication and uncertainty; I am sure he is. But it taints everybody. You know it taints everybody. You have heard him say so fifty times. Then why should *he* escape?'

'Because,' said I, 'his is an uncommon character, and he has resolutely kept himself outside the circle, Richard.'

'Oh, because and because,' replied Richard in his vivacious way. 'I am not sure, my dear girl, but that it may be wise and specious to preserve that outward indifference. It may cause some other parties interested to become lax about their interests; and people may die off, and points may drag themselves out of memory, and many things may smoothly happen that are convenient enough.'

I was so touched with pity for Richard, that I could not reproach him any more, even by a look. I remembered my guardian's gentleness towards his errors, and with what perfect freedom from resentment he had spoken of them. (XXXVII) (p. 525)

This is skilfully done. It is plausible enough that Richard might have developed these suspicions, but Esther's response confirms what we are already perfectly sure of, that this view of Mr. Jarndyce is simply an 'error'. For Dickens has not attempted anything like a disinterested moral scrutiny of Mr. Jarndyce's position about Jarndyce and Jarndyce, a scrutiny of which Richard's suspicions might, in another sort of novel, be a perverse parody. Dickens's point here is simply that Richard has become systematized himself, against his better nature—he has entered into a kind of thinking about people's actions which is twisted and distorted. His salvation will come

only through a return to right feeling, in particular through the
tenderness and clarity appropriate to a death-bed scene. None
of Richard's 'errors' is allowed the dignity of being made to
seem worth following in detail, as the twisted distortions of an
inner life in conflict; pity rules out the possibility, and the
necessity, of reproach. But the possibility of taking Richard
seriously as a moral being is ruled out too: he is merely a
victim, and he takes rather a long time dying.

Lady Dedlock is meant to be a more impressive figure than
Richard and Ada, and she is, but in the end we cannot take her
any more seriously than the two young people or Mr. Jarndyce.
Yet we feel that we should be able to, for she is no simple
victim, but a passionate and wilful woman in conflict with
herself. Too little of this inner conflict is truly rendered, however, and we are conscious of having been exploited by the
theatrical artist, as we are never conscious of being exploited
by his treatment of Richard's victimization, despite—or
rather, because of—the explicit pathetic intention. Richard's
career is all theatre: Lady Dedlock's career, we might say,
pretends to be drama, and ends up as melodrama.

The reason for Mr. Tulkinghorn's implacable pursuit of Lady
Dedlock is, in one superb passage, powerfully enough articu-
lated to make the relationship between these two characters
one of Dickens's most impressive denunciations of System.
Mr. Tulkinghorn has, throughout his investigations, admired
Lady Dedlock as a worthy opponent, and when he finally
shows his hand he does so with a forthrightness which he
means to be complimentary:

'There is another point of view', he continues, 'in which the case
presents itself. Sir Leicester is devoted to you almost to infatuation.
He might not be able to overcome that infatuation, even knowing
what we know. I am putting an extreme case, but it might be so.
If so, it were better that he knew nothing. Better for common
sense, better for him, better for me. I must take all this into
account, and it combines to render a decision very difficult.'

She stands looking out at the same stars without a word. They
are beginning to pale, and she looks as if their coldness froze her.

'My experience teaches me,' says Mr. Tulkinghorn, who has by
this time got his hands in his pockets, and is going on in his
business consideration of the matter, like a machine, 'My experience
teaches me, Lady Dedlock, that most of the people I know would

do far better to leave marriage alone. It is at the bottom of three-fourths of their troubles. So I thought when Sir Leicester married, and so I always have thought since. No more about that. I must now be guided by circumstances. In the meanwhile I must beg you to keep your counsel, and I will keep mine.' (XLI) (p. 580)

Sir Leicester thinks that Mr. Tulkinghorn is his 'legal steward' but this passage confirms our suspicion that Mr. Tulkinghorn serves only the System itself. Human beings make 'trouble' for the System, and in no way do they make more trouble than by their habit of keeping life going, by marrying and breeding new life. Individual human life, indeed, *is* trouble: it is what System tries to discourage. Lady Dedlock's secret sin of the past is not for Mr. Tulkinghorn a matter for moral judgement: it is simply a sign of free life which might interfere with the smooth operation of the System, and therefore something over which Mr. Tulkinghorn must gain control. If Lady Dedlock's imperturbable hauteur had continued unchanged, Mr. Tulkinghorn would have been willing to keep the secret to himself. For the feelings, the rights, the very life of Sir Leicester have no bearing on the 'case': the actual human being who goes by the name of Sir Leicester Dedlock is subject to 'infatuation', and is not sufficiently systematized to be trusted; he is, in fact, just as dangerous and troublesome as Lady Dedlock. Mrs. Rouncewell gives her loyalty to Sir Leicester himself, but Sir Leicester is mistaken in thinking that Mr. Tulkinghorn does the same.

'When I speak of Sir Leicester being the sole consideration, he and the family credit are one. Sir Leicester and the baronetcy, Sir Leicester and Chesney Wold, Sir Leicester and his ancestors and his patrimony;' Mr. Tulkinghorn very dry here; 'are, I need not say to you, Lady Dedlock, inseparable.' (XLI) (p. 579)

In Mr. Tulkinghorn's business-like tone, 'like a machine', we hear the accents of System itself. In his patient explication of his thinking, as he tries to arrive at a 'decision', we hear the true action of System in process. And it is as a passionate opposition to this hideous version of reasonable thinking and planning and deciding that we are convinced by Dickens's praise of the senses and the basic instincts.

Mr. Tulkinghorn's tone can be described as a sincere compliment to Lady Dedlock, in so far as it assumes her to be as self-controlled and as contemptuous of the trouble caused by human emotions as Mr. Tulkinghorn himself. He expects her to follow his thinking and to accept it as 'common sense', because she has apparently brought her own emotions into complete systematization. But Dickens has not helped us to 'understand' Lady Dedlock's superb impersonation of aristocratic hauteur; he has merely got us excited about it.

My Lady Dedlock (who is childless), looking out in the early twilight from her boudoir at a keeper's lodge, and seeing the light of a fire upon the latticed panes, and smoke rising from the chimney, and a child, chased by a woman, running out into the rain to meet the shining figure of a wrapped-up man coming through the gate, has been put quite out of temper. My Lady Dedlock says she has been 'bored to death.' (II) (p. 9)

Lady Dedlock is clearly disturbed, rather than bored, by this beautifully luminous glimpse of domestic happiness, and Dickens's loud mystifications very soon begin to suggest that Lady Dedlock is Esther Summerson's mother. Knowing this, we are at liberty to imagine the state of Lady Dedlock's inner life to be whatever seems most interesting and exciting, for Dickens has chosen never to render that inner life itself, except in the curious passage which I have discussed in an earlier chapter. We are admitted into Lady Dedlock's inner life only when she is caught up in a hysterical seizure of guilt and shame. But the theme of the whole novel is the relationship between freedom and system, and Lady Dedlock's sense of guilt, while plausible, provides no illumination of that theme.

About this very important character, then, we are offered very little beyond her theatrical gestures of pseudo-aristocratic pride and her inner guilt. Towards this merely theatrical conflict we are led by Dickens to feel, first mystification and excitement, then—following Esther's lead—uncomplicated pity. Why is this insufficient and, indeed, rather offensive?

The answer, I think, is that Lady Dedlock's 'sin' is out of scale emotionally with the rest of the novel and that Dickens's treatment of it lacks not only true dramatic inwardness but candour. The world of *Bleak House* is for the most part a world in which System threatens creature comforts and domestic happiness. In this world, I, for one, am ready to co-operate with the invitation Dickens extends at the death of Jo, the

Tough Subject: 'Dead, your Majesty. Dead, my lords and gentlemen. Dead, Right Reverends and Wrong Reverends of every order. Dead, men and women, born with Heavenly compassion in your hearts. And dying thus around us every day.' (XLVII) (p. 649) But, despite Jarndyce and Jarndyce, despite Mr. Tulkinghorn, despite all the devices by which Dickens suggests that Lady Dedlock's fate is entwined with that of Jo, the Brickmaker's wife, and every other victim in the novel, Lady Dedlock's death is not the moral equivalent of Jo's.

Lady Dedlock is the woman taken in adultery—the identification is made very early in the book, before the facts of her secret sin are known. Esther is telling of her childhood and of her godmother:

It must have been two years afterwards, and I was almost fourteen, when one dreadful night my godmother and I sat at the fireside. I was reading aloud, and she was listening. I had come down at nine o'clock, as I always did, to read the Bible to her; and was reading, from St. John, how our Saviour stooped down, writing with his finger in the dust, when they brought the sinful woman to him.

'So when they continued asking him, he lifted up himself and said unto them, He that is without sin among you, let him first cast a stone at her!'

I was stopped by my godmother's rising, putting her hand to her head, and crying out, in an awful voice, from quite another part of the book: 'Watch ye therefore! lest coming suddenly he find you sleeping. And what I say unto you, I say unto all, Watch!' (III) (p. 19)

It is one thing that Dickens should ask for Christian charity towards his woman taken in adultery and should condemn her sister's self-righteousness; it is quite another that he should mystify and tease us about her life and her feelings, working us up into pleasurably vague fascination and excitement about her secret shame, only to fall at the climax into tasteful reticences and second-rate operatic emotionalities. Surely the Christian fear of self-righteousness is a more mysterious and problematical element in morality than Dickens's methods suggest. Moreover these methods themselves amount to a queer kind of self-righteousness. The facility of Dickens's theatrical manipulations in this instance

seems to stem from, and certainly appeals to, moral com-
placencies which are at a far remove from the spirit of the
Gospels. St. John baldly identifies the sinful woman by naming
her sin, and this is sufficient; no attempt is made to work up
our feelings about this woman. But Dickens is interested in
doing exactly this, and consequently his failure to enter Lady
Dedlock's inner life imaginatively is a failure to grant her
moral dignity. Forgiving, pitying, and loving Lady Dedlock
should have cost her creator more, and should cost the reader
more. Mrs. Pardiggle is accused of 'doing Charity by wholesale,
and of dealing in it to a large extent': the accusation is confirmed by the *cold* briskness with which she goes through the
'revolving duties' of her day. But Dickens can also be accused
of doing charity by wholesale in his treatment of Lady Dedlock,
for in spite of his ready and copious *warmth* of feeling his attitude is as arbitrary, wilful, and unsympathetic towards the
human individual as that of the cold Mrs. Pardiggle towards
the brickmakers.

The scene in which Lady Dedlock reveals her identity to
Esther Summerson, and asks her illegitimate child for forgiveness, is surely the nadir of imaginative inventiveness in the
whole novel. It is at first glance surprising that Dickens, so
extraordinarily gifted in verbal mimicry, could not have
contrived language at least more splendid, if not more mean-
ingfully dramatic, than the interchanges in this scene. But
inventiveness was inhibited by a crude moral purpose. Here
is Esther's answer to her mother's plea for forgiveness:

I raised my mother up, praying and beseeching her not to stoop
before me in such affliction and humiliation. I did so, in broken
incoherent words; for, besides the trouble I was in, it frightened
me to see her at *my* feet. I told her—or I tried to tell her—that if it
were for me, her child, under any circumstances to take upon me
to forgive her, I did it, and had done it, many, many years. I told
her that my heart overflowed with love for her; that it was
natural love, which nothing in the past had changed, or could
change. That it was not for me, then resting for the first time on my
mother's bosom, to take her to account for having given me life;
but that my duty was to bless her and receive her, though the
whole world turned from her, and that I only asked her leave to
do it. (xxxvi) (pp. 509–10)

To the candid view, this is as systematic as anything in the whole novel. Despite Dickens's little ventriloquistic devices for suggesting Esther's diffident humility, she, and Dickens, are lecturing no less fluently and systematically than Mrs. Pardiggle. Even by theatrical standards, Esther's feelings are completely unrealized in the language, with the result that her flat assertions of a love which is both 'natural' and 'overflowing' would seem pharasaical if they, and the whole scene, did not impress us instead as completely empty. And, of course, one reason for this is not only that what Lady Dedlock confesses must be suitable for the chaste ear of Esther, but that both of the protagonists in this scene reflect Dickens's deep lack of interest in the moral imagination.

To conclude this study of *Bleak House* with Esther Summerson is perhaps to exaggerate her importance. No one has ever thought Esther a success as a realized character. Indeed, her fate with Dickens's readers will serve in itself as a definition of the theatrical mode of art, for she has been both actively detested and quietly ignored. She is, one acknowledges, the heroine of *Bleak House*, yet the mode of *Bleak House* is such that the whole treatment of its heroine can be recognized as a clumsy mistake which does not damage the book as a whole. The unity of a work of theatrical art is of a very odd kind.

Actually, as I have tried to show, Dickens's use of Esther's voice and point of view is for the most part an obvious, and an obviously successful, theatrical contrivance. The brilliant, self-confident theatrical artist's views of the system are justified when they are shared by modest Esther, who only 'believes' and 'thinks' and 'dares say' that Mrs. Jellyby might be thought to be neglecting her children, or that Mrs. Pardiggle 'seemed to come in like cold weather'. When Dickens decided to give Esther a life of her own, he may simply have found himself trapped into maintaining the decorum of his theatrical contrivance. And I, too, am able to think of *Bleak House* 'as a whole' without remembering how disastrously unsuccessful, irritating, and repelling its heroine actually is. Yet she does mean something about Dickens's vision of life, and that meaning must be examined.

Esther Summerson is a familiar Dickensian image of the good woman, and it has been widely recognized (and the fact

has been most inadvisedly exploited by one school of modern
Dickens apologists) that this image was fairly generally shared
by Dickens's contemporaries. But there is a special consonance
between Dickens's artistic method and his image of the good
little woman, and a special significance in the fact that he
performed this image so often and with such cloying intensity.
What bothers us about Esther is that she is empty. She has no
convincing inner life, but that is less important than the fact
that she has no will, no sense of ego, hardly an identity at all.
Mr. Micawber has no inner life but we do not notice it. The
fact that Mrs. Jellyby has no inner life is distinctly brought to
our attention, to be condemned, and we go along with the
judgement. But with Esther and her whole tribe, the fact that
she has no will, no desires, no ego, is not only the whole burden
of Dickens's characterization but is also strongly praised and
celebrated. What Esther is praised for lacking is of course
exactly what Dickens himself enjoyed in abundance. Force of
will, force of appetite, intensity of sensuous responsiveness—
these, one imagines, amounted to Dickens's mode of 'knowing
himself', they gave him his sense of identity and his pride as
an artist and a man. But good women were different from himself—the truth about Esther is just so simple. Esther must
demonstrate in her every action that she is a good woman, and
this means that her nature must be the direct negation of what
made Dickens feel like a man. Dickens's pride in his talents,
to speak only of this one element in his sense of masculine
identity, is audible on every page of his work. Esther is
explicitly denied the pleasure of pride: 'I am always being
praised and I never understand why' is her keynote. The
effect is almost stupefyingly cloying, but it is a perfectly
logical result of Dickens's artistic method of mimicry.

Dickens's celebration of the will-less and desireless good
woman is, in *Bleak House* as in many of the novels, combined
with a fascinated and regretful rejection of an opposite image.
Lady Dedlock has a very strong self in Dickens's terms, she
has pride and will and appetite, and even the ghost of an inner
life. But Lady Dedlock is taken hardly more seriously than is
Esther, and when the two appear together it is not in the least
surprising that they have nothing to say to each other, and
that their scene together has no life of any kind in it. These

two women make no significant contact with each other
because the impulses in Dickens's mind which gave rise to them
were not at this time in his career in a meaningful relationship with each other. That Lady Dedlock is Esther's mother
might look like such a relationship, and it is indeed the kind
of 'symbolic relationship' which has been taken by many
modern Dickens critics as a licence to speak of original sin
and other exciting topics. But whatever a psychoanalytic perspective might guess about the structure of Dickens's private
fantasies which produced this 'connexion', the truth remains
that the connexion is a mechanical element of plot which is
not brought to *expression* in *Bleak House*, neither to dramatic
expression nor even to theatrical expression.

In the face of this depressing chronicle of failure it nevertheless remains oddly true that Esther Summerson and Lady
Dedlock are adequately connected with each other because
they are both connected with Dickens's great and simple
argument. They are both endangered by the mechanical
inhumanity of System, and it is because their careers are
after all but two more exhibits in Dickens's case against
System that his failure to dramatize them does not drag the
whole novel down into failure and confusion. If *Bleak House*
at any moment seemed to be a serious complex dramatization
of the process whereby human beings lose their freedom by
submitting to an orderly systematization of their impulses, it
would matter a great deal that we encounter only a theatrical
mimicry of Lady Dedlock's victimization and Esther Summerson's equally incomprehensible escape from it. But *Bleak House*
is interested in denunciation, not drama, and the unique
energy and resourcefulness of Dickens's rhetoric, the generosity
of his invention, the 'act of life' in that wonderful voice itself
—these not only ratify Dickens's case against System but
establish and make valid the remarkable simplicity of the case.
The experienced audience in the Dickens theatre will be fully
aware of that simplicity, and will therefore be insured against
any important confusion or dissatisfaction at Dickens's failure
to achieve dramatic complexity when the opportunity might
seem to have presented itself. All this, of course, is not to say
that failure is anything but failure.

8

HARD TIMES

In *Hard Times* Dickens continues the attack on System with undiminished vigour but with no significant advance in the direction of dramatic complexity. There is, however, a new economy of structure and a new sharpness of focus.

In turning his attention to the Utilitarian algebra Dickens discovered a new and dangerous instance of his theme and a new method of dealing with it. Utilitarianism, he saw, led to a special kind of personal and institutional inflexibility, one splendidly suited to his ventriloquistic mimicry, as the opening pages of *Hard Times* testify. But Utilitarianism also argued for a rationally systematic definition of human nature and prescribed a systematic mechanics for the production of social well-being and individual human happiness. Dickens, to put it simply, felt a triumphant conviction that he had spotted the fallacy in the Utilitarian reasoning and that he could argue effectively against it. Hence the difference in structural method between *Bleak House* and *Hard Times*.

Bleak House, Little Dorrit, and *Our Mutual Friend* are in many respects clumsily organized works which include—or at least allow room for—a lot of free-wheeling 'abundance' of life; nevertheless, both the complicated plotting and the additive principle of organization are really consonant with Dickens's themes and insights in these books. In *Bleak House* there has to be lots of Law in evidence, there have to be many lawyers and they have to appear in many and surprising places, for the theme is exactly this, that the sinister power of Chancery is operative everywhere in society, that it is inescapable, that it blights the lives even of people of whose existence it is officially unaware. The unity and economy of *Hard Times*, on the other hand (not to mention its relative shortness), is due to the fact that the novel is a *logical refutation* of the Utilitarian definition of human nature and of the whole Utilitarian system.

Dickens's refutation proceeds by showing that the Utilitarian algebra misrepresents human nature by denying the importance of and even the existence of powerful human impulses and needs. The system of education founded on this definition of human nature will therefore fail *even in its own terms*, since denial of impulses will lead to the repression and eventually to the distortion of those impulses. The result will be social evil, individual human unhappiness, and crime, pronounced enough to be visible even to the eyes of the most convinced Utilitarian.

Dickens's Utilitarian is Thomas Gradgrind of Coketown, a man committed to his calculus of human emotions because he is unaware of his own normal human impulses and needs. The action of the novel accordingly consists of Gradgrind's discovery of these parts of himself, as a result of which his system is confuted. His two children, Tom and Louisa, have been bred on 'facts' and disciplined against 'fancy'; they have not been allowed to play; they have been discouraged from using the word 'love' (which is a 'misplaced expression' even in a discussion about Louisa's marriage to Bounderby) and from taking love into their 'accounting' of their own motives and interests. They end up in misery and crime. When Mr. Gradgrind (whose perfectly real love for them had, as Dr. Leavis points out,[1] been invisible to him because it had been brought together 'in an illusory oneness' with his pride in his system) discovers their condition, he at the same time discovers in himself both an intense concern for them as human beings and a total incapacity to help them in any practical way. They are helped in the end by two representatives of a travelling circus, Sleary's Horse-riding, a way of life which Gradgrind had earlier despised as 'wasteful' and from which he had shielded his children. It is Sissy Jupe who nurses Louisa back into some degree of emotional health, and Mr. Sleary who engineers Tom's escape from justice. Neither of these two non-Utilitarians regard loving help as a commodity which it is their duty to buy in the cheapest and sell in the dearest market: their 'services' are freely rendered out of spontaneous fellow-feeling for suffering people, and these services are in the highest degree 'practical': Gradgrind's system is thus confuted.

[1] *The Great Tradition* (London, 1948), p. 240.

I have left out of consideration Stephen Blackpool the
good workman and Slackbridge the Union agitator, who form
a separate story line which has been generally condemned as
fairly thin and crude in itself and not very well adjusted to the
central fable. But my outline is faithful to the most significant
qualities in the novel: the clear, strong, and rapid forward
movement, the succinct rendition of episode and character,
above all the emphasis with which logical refutation is
announced as Dickens's object and the success with which it
is accomplished. The success of Dickens's refutation justifies
the triumphant confidence with which it is made, as Dr. Leavis
has very solidly demonstrated.

Yet Ruskin's reservations about this success are worth
considering:

> Allowing for his manner of telling them, the things he tells us are
> always true. I wish that he could think it right to limit his brilliant
> exaggeration to works written only for public amusement; and
> when he takes up a subject of high national importance, such as
> that which he handled in *Hard Times*, that he would use severer
> and more accurate analysis. The usefulness of that work (to my
> mind, in several respects, the greatest he has written) is with many
> persons seriously diminished because Mr. Bounderby is a dramatic
> monster, instead of a characteristic example of a worldly master;
> and Stephen Blackpool a dramatic perfection, instead of a
> characteristic example of an honest workman. But let us not lose
> the use of Dickens's wit and insight, because he chooses to speak
> in a circle of stage fire. He is entirely right in his main drift and
> purpose in every book he has written; and all of them, but
> especially *Hard Times*, should be studied with close and earnest
> care by persons interested in social questions.[1]

Granted what is irrelevant and even unpleasant here, the sense
that Ruskin is wishing his brilliant ally had more respectable
literary manners—nevertheless Ruskin's qualified praise is a
candid reflection of the Dickens problem. His standards are not
merely 'respectable'; they are the normal standards by which
we judge serious works of art, and Ruskin is surely right in
saying that it is Dickens's theatricality which most offends
against them.

---

[1] *Unto This Last, Complete Works*, Library Edition (London, 1903–10),
xvii, 31 n.

When Ruskin calls Bounderby 'a dramatic monster, instead of a characteristic example of a worldly master', he is not making an unsophisticated demand for realism, or for a verisimilitude statistically measurable. He is making a demand for justice. When he wishes that Dickens had used 'a severer and more accurate analysis', he means that he wishes Dickens had been severer towards Dickens. He wants Dickens's 'wit and insight' to be fully 'useful'; this can happen only if Dickens's attack on Bounderby seems to his readers fair and just; and justice comes through self-discipline, self-demand, self-severity. The brilliant exaggeration of Dickens's portrait of Mr. Bounderby will damage his case not only for those contemptible readers whose bad faith will allow them to take Dickens's exaggeration as a sign that he is prejudiced. It will also damage the case in the eyes of those readers of good faith and good will who are committed to the kinds of intellectual self-discipline which we are accustomed to find in serious works of art.

Dr. Leavis does not deal specifically with Ruskin's views on *Hard Times*, but his essay is at least to some extent an answer to Ruskin's kind of objection. This answer depends on a definition of Dickens as the symbolic poet of the novel, and it is the best statement of this position I have encountered because unlike so much of Dickens criticism it is not naïvely over-excited by the word 'symbol'. Dr. Leavis's view is that Dickens's art in *Hard Times* is a 'highly conventional art' which is managed with great flexibility and tact, so that many different fictional modes are reconciled with each other in a coherent unity.

To the question how the reconciling is done . . . the answer can be given by pointing to the astonishing and irresistible richness of life that characterizes the book everywhere. It meets us everywhere, unstrained and natural, in the prose. Out of such prose a great variety of presentations can arise congenially with equal vividness. There they are, unquestionably 'real'. It goes back to an extraordinary energy of perception and registration in Dickens. 'When people say that Dickens exaggerates', says Mr. Santayana, 'it seems to me that they can have no eyes and no ears. They probably have only *notions* of what things and people are; they accept them conventionally, at their diplomatic value.' Settling down as we read to an implicit recognition of this truth, we don't readily and confidently apply any criterion we suppose ourselves to hold for distinguishing varieties of relation between what Dickens gives us and a normal 'real'. His flexibility is that of a richly poetic art of the word. He doesn't write 'poetic prose'; he writes with a poetic force of evocation, registering with the responsiveness of a genius of verbal expression what he so sharply sees and feels. In fact, by texture, imaginative mode, symbolic method, and the resulting concentration, *Hard Times* affects us as belonging with formally poetic works.[1]

Most of Dr. Leavis's specific claims seem to me justified, and they are made with his characteristic clarity and force; yet the whole argument, and the whole tenor of the essay in general, adds up to an implicit overvaluation of the depth and imaginative range of Dickens's achievement in *Hard Times*. The qualities listed in the last sentence of the passage are those we find in, for instance, *Measure for Measure*, of which Dr. Leavis has also written an authoritative defence. And *Hard Times* does exhibit a certain version of these qualities, in the sense that it shows a very great master's flexibility and tact in the manipulation of non-realistic, formal, conventional *devices* and stylizations. The difference between the two works, however, is of the greatest importance, and Dr. Leavis does not seem interested in it, though it can be described fairly in his own terms. There is, for instance, his illuminating classification of *Hard Times* as a 'moral fable': 'I need say no more by way of defining the moral fable than that in it the intention is peculiarly insistent, so that the representative significance of everything in the fable— character, episode, and so on—is immediately apparent as we read.'[2] (This is a fine account of that central quality in Dickens's art which I call 'theatrical'.) Moreover, Dr. Leavis rightly describes the dramatic climax of the novel as the moment in which Gradgrind's system is confuted. Now *Measure for Measure* is surely one of Shakespeare's most intentional and pointed works; it is also unrealistic, formal, and conventional in method; yet no one would be happy to call it a 'moral fable', or to call what happens to Angelo and Isabella a confutation or refutation of their respective

[1] *The Great Tradition* (London, 1948), p. 234.   [2] P. 227.

'systems'. Shakespeare's is a symbolic work not only im-
measurably denser and deeper in texture and moral relevance
than *Hard Times*, but composed in an entirely different spirit.
Thus for Dr. Leavis's word 'concentration' I would substitute
the word 'clarity'; what is brought to a wonderfully satisfactory conclusion in Gradgrind's self-discovery is an altogether less complex, less deeply, and richly significant thing
than what the Duke draws together in his Act V theatricals.

The overthrow of Bounderby, who was for Ruskin a
'dramatic monster' and who is certainly a prime instance of
Dickens's brilliant exaggeration, is a simple enough business,
everyone will agree: the Bully of humility is proved to be a
simple liar. Dickens's methods here are the traditional ones
which we are familiar with from, for instance, Fielding's
account of the overthrow of Thwackum and Square in *Tom
Jones*, or from similar instances in Jonson's comedies and
elsewhere. But it took no miracle of flexibility on Dickens's
part to 'reconcile' this kind of characterization with the
central fable of his novel, for the completely successful
rendering of Gradgrind's self-discovery is not notably more
complex or more inward than the rendering of Bounderby.
In a non-theatrical novel we might not be so easily satisfied
that Bounderby is the bosom-friend of Gradgrind, who comes
to us defined as a man of good will. We might be dissatisfied,
not as Dr. Leavis seems to suggest because we should stupidly
think such a relationship unlikely in real life—we believe
easily enough that real life Gradgrinds were sympathetic with
real life Bounderbys—but because we would want to understand this relationship more deeply than we do. But in *Hard
Times* it becomes 'immediately apparent as we read' that
Gradgrind's relationship to Bounderby means that he is the
victim of his own system, which hides his own instincts from
himself. When we see that Gradgrind is more demanding of
Louisa than he is of Sissy—and therefore hurts her more—we
see what it means just as promptly: his love for his daughter
makes him want to be proud of her. When we watch Gradgrind approaching his daughter with Bounderby's proposal,
we do in a certain sense ask, 'But how can Gradgrind want
his beloved Louisa to marry this despicable coarse Bully of
humility?' But this is, in the most exact sense, a rhetorical

question; it is not a serious question. We ask it only in order
to dramatize its answer, which is already firmly in our grasp:
'How, indeed? What a victim this man is of his own system!'
The scene is characteristically rich in invention: Dickens
amplifies his single point with a fine variety of devices. When
Gradgrind is momentarily nonplussed by Louisa's rational
calmness (a brilliant yet obvious stroke), again in a certain
sense we ask, 'But why is he surprised to find that his system
has succeeded so well?' Again the answer is immediately
apparent: 'He is surprised because he really does have good
instincts; he knows there is something wrong with this
marriage, that Louisa ought to have to be persuaded by
rational arguments, just as he has had to persuade himself by
rational arguments. But he can't face this fact yet.'

Here, then, is Gradgrind: a man of good instincts victimized
by his own system. The fable is very simple. As in *Bleak House*
the system was not criticized but instead powerfully indicted,
so in *Hard Times* Gradgrind's system is not criticized but
simply repudiated. It is dangerous nonsense, and it is made to
seem so by means of an argument which leads us to dismiss it
out of hand. We are never led into a dramatic engagement
with the conflict within Gradgrind's mind, for the Utilitarian
calculus *in itself* is not made to seem the expression of any of
the significant interests or needs of this man. It is, of course,
his system, and he has an ego-investment in it; but in itself
it is pure error, pure folly. Correspondingly, what the system
leaves out is presented by means of devices which lead to
simple and warm approval. In short, Dickens's imaginative
mode and symbolic methods do not function as devices for
the critical exploration of a way of thinking or for the dramatization of a complex conflict of human interest. They function
as the theatrical virtuoso's mode of execution of his powerfully
simple refutation of the Utilitarian algebra.

A simple scenario, an extraordinarily rich verbal execution
of that scenario. That this should be an accurate description
of *Hard Times* is merely another demonstration that there is
a Dickens problem.

Dr. Leavis, I suspect, overestimates *Hard Times* not only
because it expresses something like his own contemptuous
dismissal of Benthamism, but for a better reason. When it

is he who calls Dickens a 'genius of verbal expression', the
phrase (ordinary enough in itself and unlikely to be questioned
by any critic) comes to us with a special impact. For Dr.
Leavis's moral severity is inseparable from, and vindicated
by, another characteristic which has achieved much less
notoriety—his unusually pure and intense responsiveness to
the *medium* of verbal expression. There is a devastating sentence in an essay in *The Common Pursuit* called 'The Logic of
Christian Discrimination': 'One might, after looking through
the book, start by asking why Mr. Every has devoted so much
time to poetry, and to creative literature in general, since (I
hope I may be forgiven for saying) he shows no compelling
interest in it, and no aptitude for its study.'[1] In the general
view, Dr. Leavis writes like this either out of sheer bad manners or out of a perverse pleasure in manufacturing a nasty
atmosphere for literary debate. My view is that one winces
sympathetically for Mr. Every because the insult has so unquestionable an authority behind it. It goes without saying,
perhaps, that Dr. Leavis, on every page of his criticism, shows
a compelling interest in the medium of verbal expression and
a responsiveness to what it achieves; but what goes without saying in this particular case is nevertheless what gives
authority to the whole critical enterprise. Nobody *need* have a
compelling interest in 'verbal expression', but insight about
works of literary art will only come from those who do. The
great virtue of Dr. Leavis's essay on *Hard Times* is that it is
written by a critic who has such an interest and that it points
to the qualities in Dickens which make him a genius of verbal
expression. (Dr. Leavis often prefers to point rather than to
analyse, and his achievement in this particular essay again
justifies his method.) This direct attention to Dickens's
language makes the essay one of the best pieces of Dickens
criticism in print. Yet it is, I believe, Dr. Leavis's intense
responsiveness to Dickens's mastery of the medium which
leads him to overestimate the complexity and the breadth
and depth of reference in *Hard Times*.

The overestimation is partly an inadvertent result of
certain powerful words which Dr. Leavis uses to describe
and praise Dickens's prose. Here, for instance, is Dickens's

[1] (London, 1952), p. 248.

first presentation of Sissy Jupe, together with Dr. Leavis's commentary on it:

'The square finger, moving here and there, lighted suddenly on Bitzer, perhaps because he had chanced to sit in the same ray of sunlight which, darting in at one of the bare windows of the intensely whitewashed room, irradiated Sissy. For, the boys and girls sat on the face of the inclined plane in two compact bodies, divided up the centre by a narrow interval; and Sissy, being at the corner of a row on the sunny side, came in for the beginning of a sunbeam, of which Bitzer, being at the corner of a row on the other side, a few rows in advance, caught the end. But, whereas the girl was so dark-eyed and dark-haired, that she seemed to receive a deeper and more lustrous colour from the sun, when it shone upon her, the boy was so light-eyed and light-haired that the selfsame rays appeared to draw out of him what little colour he ever possessed. His cold eyes would hardly have been eyes, but for the short ends of lashes which, by bringing them into immediate contrast with something paler than themselves, expressed their form. His short-cropped hair might have been a mere continuation of the sandy freckles on his forehead and face. His skin was so unwholesomely deficient in the natural tinge, that he looked as though, if he were cut, he would bleed white.' (II) (pp. 4–5)

There is no need to insist on the force—representative of Dickens's art in general in *Hard Times*—with which the moral and spiritual differences are rendered here in terms of sensation, so that the symbolic intention emerges out of metaphor and the vivid evocation of the concrete. What may, perhaps, be emphasized is that Sissy stands for vitality as well as goodness—they are seen, in fact, as one; she is generous, impulsive life, finding self-fulfilment in self-forgetfulness—all that is the antithesis of calculating self-interest. There is an essentially Laurentian suggestion about the way in which 'the dark-eyed and dark-haired' girl, contrasting with Bitzer, seemed to receive a 'deeper and more lustrous colour from the sun', so opposing the life that is lived freely and richly from the deep instinctive and emotional springs to the thin-blooded, quasi-mechanical product of Gradgrindery.[1]

Here the telling word is 'Laurentian', but this passage exhibits also the qualities about which Dr. Leavis uses the word 'Shakesperian':

in ease and range there is surely no greater master of English except Shakespeare. This comes back to saying that Dickens is a great

[1] Pp. 230–1.

poet: his endless resource in felicitously varied expression is an extraordinary responsiveness to life. His senses are charged with emotional energy, and his intelligence plays and flashes in the quickest and sharpest perception.[1]

The words 'life' and 'emotional energy' remind one again of Dr. Leavis's views on Lawrence, so that the identification is very firmly made: Shakespeare, Dickens, Lawrence. Now the specific evidence is convincing enough—it is the unacknowledged general implications that get out of hand.

Dickens's metaphorical presentation of Sissy Jupe is a 'flash' of intelligence and insight in another sense too: it flares brilliantly and then goes out. It is hard to see why Dr. Leavis is not interested in this. It is one thing to praise *Hard Times* for its economy; it is another to fail to acknowledge how momentary the Laurentian suggestion in this passage about Sissy Jupe really is. We hear nothing more of Sissy Jupe's dark eyes and dark hair which 'seemed to receive a deeper and more lustrous colour from the sun'. Though Bitzer is 'colourless' or 'light' at every reappearance, this suggestion is rarely brought to imaginative life after the beginning; but the more important point is that Sissy is *never* again vividly seen in these or indeed in *any* vivid 'terms of sensation'. This is surprising in itself: Dickens is famous, even notorious, for his habit of reimpersonating his characters over and over again in the same terms. It seems an exaggeration, then, to single out for crucial quotation a description of a character which is not in fact made anything of later by this highly repetitive artist. More important, however, is that the disappearance of this metaphor poses the question of the difference between Lawrence's characteristic symbolic and structural habits and Dickens's, a difference so great as to make the word Laurentian in Dr. Leavis's usage extremely questionable.

In *Women in Love*, Gerald Critch's blondness begins as a flash of insight in terms of sensation, as Gudrun observes him at the wedding. But one would think that the whole point about Lawrence's methods is that the concrete physical identity of Gerald is symbolic in the sense that it serves as an instrument for the continuous large-scale, complex, and

[1] P. 246.

cumulative exploration of Gerald Critch's nature. As it is viewed from different perspectives (often in conflict with each other) and as it enters mutually illuminating comparisons and contrasts with other physical identities (in, for instance, 'Gladiatorial')—and only because all this *does* happen— Gerald's blondness comes to serve as the symbolic instrument for a large and complex criticism of what Gerald represents. The immediate flash of insight is, doubtless, a *sine qua non*: but the large complex continuities are also what we mean when we use the word 'Laurentian'. Dr. Leavis skirts the issue I am raising by speaking of Dickens's effect as a Laurentian 'suggestion'. But the issue persists.

Dickens forgot about Sissy Jupe's lustrous dark eyes and dark hair for a good reason—good in terms of the Dickens theatre. What he had in mind as Sissy's further career could not be conveniently adjusted to the earlier, vivid registration of her 'vital impulse'. Dr. Leavis regards the whole characterization as an unqualified success:

A general description of her part in the fable might suggest the worst, but actually she has nothing in common with Little Nell: she shares in the strength of the Horse-riding. She is wholly convincing in the function Dickens assigns to her. The working of her influence in the Utilitarian home is conveyed with a fine tact, and we do really feel her as a growing potency.[1]

This is too strong. Sissy does indeed have something in common with Little Nell, though naturally much more in common with the heroines of the other novels of the fifties: with Esther Summerson and Little Dorrit. That she is convincing in the functions assigned to her, that she is presented with an economy and tact damagingly lacking in *Bleak House* and *Little Dorrit*, I agree. But her 'influence' in the home, her 'growing potency'—these are very familiar Dickensian themes, and the scenes in which they are rendered did not, apparently, offer much stimulus to Dickens's inventive powers—they are for me routine performances. All this is admittedly nothing against the characterization. Sissy's quiet potency makes a significant—and of course effective— contrast with the aggressiveness and bluster of Gradgrind

[1] P. 235.

and Bounderby, the tension of Louisa, the sullenness of the whelp. Nor do Sissy's actions—consisting as they do mostly of nursing, receiving confidences, understanding, and being patient—strike us as inept or trivial or sentimental mani-festations of what is lacking in the Utilitarian home. Without being really powerfully rendered, they suffice. But surely, were we to seek words to define the general effect of Sissy in 'terms of sensation', the words 'rich' and 'lustrous' would hardly come to mind. I cannot see how, in the structure of Dr. Leavis's argument, this fails to be an important consideration.

We are faced again with Dickens's attitude towards women, though there is some admixture of his attitude towards ser-vants too. Again we accept Dickens's limitations, so under-standable and even commendable in view of their important connexions with the very sources and methods of his genius. We are the more easily led to accept these limitations by the tact and flexibility of the organization of *Hard Times*. But Dickens's familiar performance of his familiar routine—the growing potency of the small, quiet, maternal woman—simply cannot avail itself of the implications which Dr. Leavis finds in the earliest description of Sissy. Dickens could not invent, or approve of, a Maggie Tulliver—or even a Mary Garth. A dark-haired and dark-eyed girl child, seen and felt as capable of richness and lustre, is allowable, but the adult version of these qualities can for Dickens issue forth only in criminal action. The unsuccessful and over-cautious over-development of Bella Wilfer is an exception that proves the rule.

A different kind of exception, and a thoroughly winning and beautiful one, is the licence allowed the women in the Horse-riding, with whom Sissy Jupe is of course connected.

Meanwhile, the various members of Sleary's company gradu-ally gathered together from the upper regions, where they were quartered, and, from standing about, talking in low voices to one another and to Mr. Childers, gradually insinuated themselves and him into the room. There were two or three handsome young women among them, with their two or three husbands, and their two or three mothers, and their eight or nine little children, who did the fairy business when required. The father of one of the families was in the habit of balancing the father of another of the families on the top of a great pole; the father of a third family often made a pyramid of both these fathers, with Master Kidderminster for the apex, and himself for the base; all the fathers could dance upon rolling casks, stand upon bottles, catch knives and balls, twirl hand-basins, ride upon anything, jump over everything, and stick at nothing. All the mothers could (and did) dance, upon the slack wire and the tight rope, and perform rapid acts on bare-backed steeds; none of them were at all particular in respect of showing their legs; and one of them, alone in a Greek chariot, drove six in hand into every town they came to. They all assumed to be mighty rakish and knowing, they were not very tidy in their private dresses, they were not at all orderly in their domestic arrangements, and the combined literature of the whole company would have produced but a poor letter on any subject. Yet there was a remarkable gentleness and childishness about these people, a special inaptitude for any kind of sharp practice, and an untiring readiness to help and pity one another, deserving often of as much respect, and always of as much generous construction, as the every-day virtues of any class of people in the world. (VI) (p. 35)

The dignity and wit and finesse with which the sexual freedom of these women is described needs no exegesis—we are reminded that the limited Dickens was also the rebellious Dickens. But Dr. Leavis makes no mention of this element in his admirable reading of the passage:

Their skills have no value for the Utilitarian calculus, but they express vital human impulse, and they minister to vital human needs. The Horse-riding, frowned upon as frivolous and wasteful by Gradgrind and malignantly scorned by Bounderby, brings the machine-hands of Coketown (the spirit-quenching hideousness of which is hauntingly evoked) what they are starved of. It brings to them, not merely amusement, but art, and the spectacle of triumphant activity that, seeming to contain its end within itself, is, in its easy mastery, joyously self-justified. In investing a travelling circus with this kind of symbolic value Dickens expresses a profounder reaction to industrialism than might have been expected of him. It is not only pleasure and relaxation the Coke-towners stand in need of; he feels the dreadful degradation of life that would remain even if they were to be given a forty-four hour week, comfort, security and fun.[1]

Again, an illuminating reading, yet the word 'triumphant' seems to me slightly to exaggerate the dimension of the

---

[1] Pp. 231–2.

meaning here, and in any case the 'triumphant activity' of the Horse-riding makes really no further appearance in the moral fable. Dickens has another job in mind for the Horse-riding, the job of embodying the kind of gratuitous kindness which derives from spontaneous fellow-feeling and cannot be accounted for by the Utilitarian calculus. This kind of spontaneity is by no means unrelated to the brilliant circus tricks of the performers, and indeed the relationship is made in the passage quoted. But when we see the kindness of the Horse-riding later, we see it embodied chiefly in the figure of Sleary, and we are accordingly conscious mostly of the meanings enforced by this character. The scenes in which Sleary helps Gradgrind get Tom out of the country derive their meaning from the eminently theatrical contrast between practical hard-headed Gradgrind (now menaced by his prize pupil Bitzer) and sloppy, lisping Sleary. That is, the main accent is on brandy and water; positively 'triumphant activity' comes only in the miniature comic form of the polka-dancing horse. Dickens's point is the surprising *practicality* of the incompetent-seeming Sleary, and the surprising *usefulness* of the horse that can dance the polka. This does not in any important way *feel* inconsistent with Dickens's earlier view of the Horse-riding which emphasizes, as Dr. Leavis points out, the fact that the skills of the Horse-riding contain their end within themselves (and are therefore 'wasteful' in terms of Gradgrind's algebra). In another sort of novel it might feel inconsistent; in the Dickens theatre we see exactly where the case is going, we adjust easily to a familiar effect and a familiar meaning. These final scenes are completely successful, but they are much more limited in symbolic implication than Dr. Leavis's analysis suggests.

In focusing so emphatically on Sissy's richness and lustre and the Horse-riding's triumphant activity, Dr. Leavis overestimates the degree to which Dickens keeps his symbolic intentions continuously in hand throughout the moral fable. The flashes of insight are indeed there, and there is also the wonderful capacity for realizing them in language. Dickens is indeed in these respects a poet of almost Shakespearian calibre. But an essential characteristic of Shakespeare, too, is his regular achievement of complex continuities, and it would seem right to note, in the middle even of the most enthusiastic praise of

Dickens, that Dickens does not share this characteristic. It is surprising and odd that he does not, but that is exactly the point of the present study of the Dickens problem.

What Dickens does not do is the kind of thing Shakespeare is doing in, for instance, this one short speech from *Measure for Measure*. Isabella has just found her best persuasive vein in the 'man, proud man' speech, and it is Lucio's next aside to her that I quote:

> O, to him, to him, wench; he will relent.
> He's coming, I perceive't. (II. ii. 124–5)

The ease and finesse with which this complex meaning is achieved is almost uncanny. For the single, unemphatic word 'wench' is resonant to a degree which justifies the claim that the entire play is concentrated and alive in it. The word is spoken 'in character', but there is much more to it than that. The exaggerated courtesy with which Lucio addressed Isabella in their first encounter is gone, and his word now expresses a comradely solidarity with her; the burden of her eloquence has no significance for him, but its intensity satisfies him that she is working with him in the good cause of saving his friend's life. His word also, and easily, conveys the casual, callous, and slightly contemptuous good fellowship he likes to feel towards women. But the extraordinary power of the word derives from the fact that Isabella happens to be arousing sexual desire in Angelo by her angry eloquence—she has indeed from his perverse perspective become a 'wench'.

Even Shakespeare himself did not very often achieve the incandescent economy of complex dramatic poetry which gives the word 'wench' so much resonance. But Shakespeare is full of effects similar in kind, and it is the existence of such effects which leads us to posit behind the work of art an imagination 'possessed by a comprehensive vision'. Dr. Leavis is wrong, therefore, to use these words to account for the economy in *Hard Times*. That Dickens's imagination was of a very high order everyone agrees; that he was capable of being possessed by visions of people and things has often been recognized—George Lewes's term for it was 'hallucination'; and that this possession was expressed in a verbal medium of almost Shakespearian range, flexibility, and power Dr. Leavis,

above all others, has made clear. But a distinction must be
made. The large-scale structures into which Dickens organized
these thousands of visions are not the work of such possession (*Great Expectations* is the curious exception to this rule).
Dickens's vision of Sissy Jupe's rich dark vitality fades completely; Bitzer's 'lightness' reappears mostly as a tag which
Dickens's concentration on other purposes did not allow him
the energy to bring to real life again. The economy of *Hard
Times* is not the Shakespearian resonance; it is rather a matter
of keeping singlemindedly, professionally, theatrically to the
succinct directness which Dickens's instinct told him was
right for his theme.

The economy of *Hard Times*, moreover, is a special and
brilliant effect in the Dickens theatre, and it is offered as
loudly and distinctly, and as proudly, as any of Dickens's
other effects. Who could fail to hear this in the very first
chapter, which I quote in entirety?

'Now, what I want is, Facts. Teach these boys and girls nothing
but Facts. Facts alone are wanted in life. Plant nothing else, and
root out everything else. You can only form the minds of reasoning
animals upon Facts: nothing else will ever be of any service to them.
This is the principle on which I bring up my own children, and this
is the principle on which I bring up these children. Stick to Facts,
Sir!'

The scene was a plain, bare, monotonous vault of a schoolroom,
and the speaker's square forefinger emphasized his observations by
underscoring every sentence with a line on the schoolmaster's
sleeve. The emphasis was helped by the speaker's square wall of a
forehead, which had his eyebrows for its base, while his eyes found
commodious cellerage in two dark caves, overshadowed by the
wall. The emphasis was helped by the speaker's mouth, which was
wide, thin, and hard set. The emphasis was helped by the speaker's
voice, which was inflexible, dry, and dictatorial. The emphasis was
helped by the speaker's hair, which bristled on the skirts of his bald
head, a plantation of firs to keep the wind from its shining surface, all covered with knobs, like the crust of a plum pie, as if the
head had scarcely warehouse-room for the hard facts stored inside.
The speaker's obstinate carriage, square coat, square legs, square
shoulders,—nay, his very neckcloth, trained to take him by the
throat with an unaccommodating grasp, like a stubborn fact, as it
was,—all helped the emphasis.

'In this life, we want nothing but Facts, Sir; nothing but Facts!'

The speaker, and the schoolmaster, and the third grown person present, all backed a little, and swept with their eyes the inclined plane of little vessels then and there arranged in order, ready to have imperial gallons of facts poured into them until they were full to the brim. (I) (pp. 1–2)

This covers one and one-sixth pages in the *New Oxford Illustrated Dickens*. Chapter II covers six pages, and ends thus:

He [Mr. M'Choakumchild] went to work in this preparatory lesson, not unlike Morgiana in the Forty Thieves: looking into all the vessels ranged before him, one after another, to see what they contained. Say, good M'Choakumchild. When from thy boiling store, thou shalt fill each jar brim full by-and-by, dost thou think that thou wilt always kill outright the robber Fancy lurking within—or sometimes only maim him and distort him! (II) (p. 8)

On page eight, then, the burden of Dickens's moral fable is already before us in outline, and in the third chapter we begin immediately to see the way the lives of Louisa and Tom Gradgrind have been in fact maimed and distorted. The virtue of this rapidity of demonstration, as a theatrical effect, goes without saying, and the prose in which it is rendered is as fully alive as Dr. Leavis claims it to be—the result is a very brilliant work of art. But Dr. Leavis's praise nevertheless carries the wrong implication: 'Actually, the Dickensian vitality is there, in its varied characteristic modes, which have the more force because they are free of redundance: the creative exuberance is controlled by a profound inspiration.'[1] I cannot take this in the spirit in which Dr. Leavis meant it, because the control seems to me skilfully chosen by a professional arguer rather than irresistibly compelled by a profound inspiration. Moreover, the vitality is Dickensian in another way besides the one Dr. Leavis suggests. He writes that the 'spirit-quenching hideousness of [Coketown] is hauntingly evoked' and one would agree but for one familiar proviso:

It had a black canal in it, and a river that ran purple with ill-smelling dye, and vast piles of building full of windows where there

[1] P. 228.

was a rattling and a trembling all day long, and where the piston
of the steam-engine worked monotonously up and down like the
head of an elephant in a state of melancholy madness. (ii) (p. 22)

The spirit responsible for the elephant doesn't sound in the
least 'quenched', and we are in his theatre; we are not inside
the scene, participating in it with inward imagination, but
securely and happily outside, being the audience for a master
of language.

Fact, fact, fact, everywhere in the material aspect of the town;
fact, fact, fact, everywhere in the immaterial. The M'Choakumchild
school was all fact, and the school of design was all fact, and
everything was fact between the lying-in hospital and the cemetery,
and what you couldn't state in figures, or show to be purchaseable
in the cheapest market and saleable in the dearest, was not, and
never should be, world without end, Amen. (v) (p. 23)

The *primary* impression, surely, is of the impudent vitality of
the performing voice, enjoying its indignation and confident
of its power to denounce and banish what makes it so angry.
The voice is evoking an image of a kind of death in life, but we
make only a theatrical contact with that illusion. Perhaps
when Dickens himself saw the real Coketown, his spirit actually
was quenched for a moment, as it never had been by the dense
and irregular squalor of the London slums; when he heard the
voice of the Utilitarian calculus in action, and learned about
its educational theory, perhaps he did indeed realize that so
misguided a theory of education, systematically run by well-
intentioned technicians, could do far more serious damage to
children than what Peepy Jellyby or Rob the Grinder experienced. And it might conceivably have happened that for
once, in the face of this serious menace to human freedom,
Dickens could lay aside his theatrical habits to render a
dramatic evocation that could really haunt his readers. But
the facts are otherwise. The systematic regularity of Coketown
is powerfully registered, but so is that elephant in a state of
melancholy madness. And in Gradgrind's voice, all the old
Dickensian joy in mimicry is audible. The old habits remain,
and it is not in the least to be regretted. What the description
of Gradgrind's physical appearance, quoted above, performs
before us is harsh and grim, and the eyes which 'found

commodious cellerage in two dark caves, overshadowed by
the wall', seem to promise a really cruel nature. But when the
fable requires that Gradgrind be essentially a good man, with
kind instincts and loving concern for his children hidden from
them and from himself, Dickens's method of rendering this is
his old one: as in the description of Bleak House, a new room
is added for the new purpose, and Gradgrind is rapidly fitted
out with a heart. The heart really works, Dickens makes us
believe in it, and the rhetorical point (that it is *surprising* to
discover how kind a man Gradgrind really is) is successfully
rendered by the theatrical device. The artist is in confident
control of his argument, and accordingly when Gradgrind's
heart is in full anguished operation, in those last scenes, his
grim appearance has become invisible and his strident voice
inaudible—they were verbal masks and they have been expertly laid aside.

Dr. Leavis praises the success with which Dickens 'recon-
ciles' his various characteristic modes in this novel, and one
agrees that the reconciling is done with great finesse. One
agrees, too, that it is the continuing and copious vitality of
expression that most obviously carries us through. But such
reconciling is made possible by the essential theatricality
of the whole illusion, so different from the realistic art of
George Eliot and the conventional poetic art of *Measure for
Measure*. Casaubon's deep eye-sockets are not often brought
to our attention after we have made contact with his inner life,
but what they have been discovered to mean about his nature
survives, and George Eliot's continuing vision of Casaubon
invariably comprehends the implications of this physical
identity. Likewise with Bulstrode's bloodless energy, the
mechanical regularity of his utterance, the significance of
which is always before us in a comprehensive vision, even
when we have been admitted to the choosing and suffering
self. But such realistic art requires little of the 'reconciling'
Dr. Leavis speaks of. *Measure for Measure* does, and despite
Dr. Leavis's cogent arguments there remains some question
whether that reconciling has been fully achieved, whether
the structure and texture of this conventional and formal
poetic drama has been finely enough 'worked'. In central
and crucial respects, nevertheless, *Measure for Measure* is

undoubtedly a work of comprehensive vision. The last act takes (perhaps not quite successfully) a perspective on Angelo and Isabella which makes any realistic demands for cause-and-effect continuity of characterization irrelevant, yet there is a continuity and it is dramatic and organic. There are many perspectives on Isabella—as she enters the nunnery, as her passionate moral indignation inflames Angelo's lusts, as she scarifies her brother's hesitations with such hideous confidence, as she enters into the Duke's benevolent deceit, as she begs for Angelo's life, and as she presumably accepts the Duke's offer of marriage. All these different perspectives and modes of illusion are held together in a complex, ambiguous, and comprehensive vision of a certain moral identity. And the unity of Angelo's identity in the play is more obviously successful, though perhaps somewhat less interesting. Moreover, the change of heart of these two characters, though it is not presented to us in anything resembling the continuous realistic illusion of George Eliot, nevertheless is known to us as the organic movement of an inner life. The mind behind this play is concerned about and practised in the dramatic mediation between conflicting impulses. But the impulse which produced 'Facts, facts, facts' is not brought into harmony with Gradgrind's love for his children. It is simply condemned, and we are satisfied, for we know—and willingly accept the fact—that the mind behind those brilliant last scenes, in which Bitzer's bloodless arguments menace the broken Gradgrind, is not a mind interested in or capable of such mediation.

9

LITTLE DORRIT

To read *Little Dorrit* is to realize that some surprisingly complex and ambiguous things can take place in the Dickens theatre. The old consistent clarities of approval and disapproval have in this novel disappeared: we meet characters about whom it is difficult to make up our minds, and these characters are facing situations correspondingly ambiguous. The voice of the narrator, and his devices, force these complexities and ambiguities very strongly on our attention. The world has begun to seem a much more difficult place to the great virtuoso, we discover, and this discovery is deeply moving, for it is impossible to enter the Dickens theatre without forming a warm attachment to the great theatrical artist himself. But what is in this respect moving will not necessarily yield satisfying results. In *Little Dorrit* Dickens's newly dark and complex view of his world remains an unassimilated malaise; it is not transmuted into a successful work of art.

It seems on the contrary to have inhibited the freedom of his creative energy, though it is of course difficult to distinguish cause from effect in such a manner. At any rate, although the voice in *Little Dorrit* is rendering what it sees and feels with remarkable energy still, all too often we sense a note of strain instead of the old spontaneity. Not that Dickens's indignant rhetoric is more insistent than it was in *Bleak House*—nothing could be more insistent than the attack on Chancery. But in *Little Dorrit* the rhetoric moves less rapidly and with a diminished inventiveness; the loud voice is now often a comparatively heavy and sluggish one, with the result that its burden seems compulsive, even cranky, when before it had seemed on fire with its subject. A more crucial failure in creative energy, though, is the fact that the new awareness of complexity has not bred appropriately new methods of operation in the Dickens theatre. It is not surprising that

Dickens should have been unable to invent new bottles for
his new wine, but it is nevertheless dispiriting to see new
insights 'processed' in the old way—I use the word deliberately
to suggest that in *Little Dorrit* Dickens's method of rendering
character and action is close to seeming as mechanical and
automatic as the system which he continues to attack. The
habits of the Dickens theatre itself begin to seem a kind of
prison, almost as life-destroying as the habits engendered in
the Marshalsea. Again and again Dickens notifies us of his
intention to render complex and ambiguous psychological
states; we are repeatedly advised to suspend judgement, to
go slowly in ascribing blame and praise in this dark and
disordered world. But the theatrical artist cannot take his
own advice because he doesn't know how; he cannot keep
himself from rendering complex personalities in his old
brilliant style. The result is continued discordance and often
simple inconsistency. We feel that Dickens has not imaginatively grasped his characters as whole persons. Nor has he
grasped his entire world as a whole; for the studied ambiguity
of certain elements in the world of *Little Dorrit* is interrupted, to
our embarrassment and confusion, by single-minded denunciations in the old style.

Yet because we remain, for all the new complexities of
purpose, in the Dickens theatre, we rarely experience the
quality and intensity of discomfort from the imbalances of
Little Dorrit that we experience in, say, a late James novel.
Little Dorrit remains a remarkably interesting performance
as a whole and it includes some of Dickens's most brilliant
things; and, as in all the other novels, some of these brilliant
things are performed in what amounts to perfect isolation.
Mrs. General, Mrs. Gowan, and Mrs. Merdle are memorable
performances by the great virtuoso, but despite their clear
connexion with the large structure of the novel, they really
could have appeared in any other Dickens novel, and in fact
they recur in our memory exactly as if they did appear in
any other novel. Many of the failures of the novel exhibit the
negative side of this same principle: we easily acknowledge
their *inferiority* to the best Dickens performances, pay our
respects to what is interesting and effective in them, and
wait for the next show.

Thus the opening of the third chapter presents no difficult problem to the habitué of the Dickens theatre:

It was a Sunday evening in London, gloomy, close and stale. Maddening church bells of all degrees of dissonance, sharp and flat, cracked and clear, fast and slow, made the brick-and-mortar echoes hideous. Melancholy streets in a penitential garb of soot, steeped the souls of the people who were condemned to look at them out of windows, in dire despondency. In every thoroughfare, up almost every alley, and down almost every turning, some doleful bell was throbbing, jerking, tolling, as if the Plague were in the city and the dead-carts were going round. Everything was bolted and barred that could by possibility furnish relief to an overworked people. No pictures, no unfamiliar animals, no rare plants or flowers, no natural or artificial wonders of the ancient world—all *taboo* with that enlightened strictness, that the ugly South Sea gods in the British Museum might have supposed themselves at home again. Nothing to see but streets, streets, streets. Nothing to breathe but streets, streets, streets. Nothing to change the brooding mind, or raise it up. Nothing for the spent toiler to do, but to compare the monotony of his seventh day with the monotony of his six days, think what a weary life he led, and make the best of it—or the worst, according to the probabilities.

At such a happy time, so propitious to the interests of religion and morality, Mr. Arthur Clennam, newly arrived from Marseilles by way of Dover, and by Dover coach the Blue-eyed Maid, sat in the window of a coffee-house on Ludgate Hill. Ten thousand responsible houses surrounded him, frowning as heavily on the streets they composed, as if they were every one inhabited by the ten young men of the Calender's story, who blackened their faces and bemoaned their miseries every night. Fifty thousand lairs surrounded him where people lived so unwholesomely, that fair water put into their crowded rooms on Saturday night, would be corrupt on Sunday morning; albeit my lord, their county member, was amazed that they failed to sleep in company with their butcher's meat. Miles of close wells and pits of houses, where the inhabitants gasped for air, stretched far away towards every point of the compass. Through the heart of the town a deadly sewer ebbed and flowed, in the place of a fine fresh river. What secular want could the million or so of human beings whose daily labour, six days in the week, lay among these Arcadian objects, from the sweet sameness of which they had no escape between the cradle and the grave—what secular want could they possibly have upon their seventh day? Clearly they could want nothing but a stringent policeman. (I. iii) (pp. 28–29)

As this proceeds, we note without particular emphasis that it is only a moderately good Dickensian performance. Closer inspection would reveal some disturbingly symptomatic weaknesses. A conventionally earnest tone, rather like that of a newspaper editorial in the old-fashioned style, produces a momentary deadness in certain phrases: 'relief to an overworked people' and 'the spent toiler'. And this earnestness is not well adjusted to the sarcasm which surrounds it: 'at such a happy time, so propitious to the interests of religion and morality', and later 'these Arcadian objects, from the sweet sameness of which . . .'. The mixture of tones makes the sarcasm seem merely an habitual tic, like that of a tiresome person in real life; and habitual sarcasm also seems untruthful. In this context, what would elsewhere be agreeable Dickensian playfulness ('the ugly South Sea gods' and the 'ten young men of the Calender's story') sounds a bit like professional whimsy rather than spontaneous wit. But I have exaggerated the weaknesses and over-emphasized what is symptomatically unharmonious in the passage. The theatrical identity of the passage, the job it is doing, is what most occupies our mind; and we can see that it works well enough at that job even while we are noting its inferiority to Dickens's best performances.

When Arthur Clennam's perspective on this city scene is next developed, Dickens's procedures, and their effects, are his usual ones.

Mr. Arthur Clennam sat in the window of the coffee-house on Ludgate Hill, counting one of the neighbouring bells, making sentences and burdens of songs out of it in spite of himself, and wondering how many sick people it might be the death of in the course of the year. As the hour approached, its changes of measure made it more and more exasperating. At the quarter, it went off into a condition of deadly-lively importunity, urging the populace in a voluble manner to Come to church, Come to church, Come to church! At the ten minutes, it became aware that the congregation would be scanty, and slowly hammered out in low spirits, They *won't* come, they *won't* come, they *won't* come! At the five minutes, it abandoned hope, and shook every house in the neighbourhood for three hundred seconds, with one dismal swing per second, as a groan of despair.

'Thank Heaven!' said Clennam, when the hour struck, and the bell stopped.

But its sound had revived a long train of miserable Sundays, and the procession would not stop with the bell, but continued to march on. 'Heaven forgive me,' said he, 'and those who trained me. How I have hated this day!'

There was the dreary Sunday of his childhood, when he sat with his hands before him, scared out of his senses by a horrible tract which commenced business with the poor child by asking him in its title, why he was going to Perdition?—a piece of curiosity that he really in a frock and drawers was not in a condition to satisfy— and which, for the further attraction of his infant mind, had a parenthesis in every other line with some such hiccuping reference as 2 Ep. Thess. c. iii. v. 6 & 7. There was the sleepy Sunday of his boyhood, when, like a military deserter, he was marched to chapel by a picquet of teachers three times a day, morally handcuffed to another boy; and when he would willingly have bartered two meals of indigestible sermon for another ounce or two of inferior mutton at his scanty dinner in the flesh. There was the interminable Sunday of his nonage; when his mother, stern of face and unrelenting of heart, would sit all day behind a bible—bound, like her own construction of it, in the hardest, barest, and straitest boards, with one dinted ornament on the cover like the drag of a chain, and a wrathful sprinkling of red upon the edges of the leaves—as if it, of all books! were a fortification against the sweetness of temper, natural affection, and gentle intercourse. There was the resentful Sunday of a little later, when he sat glowering and glooming through the tardy length of the day, with a sullen sense of injury in his heart, and no more real knowledge of the beneficent history of the New Testament, than if he had been bred among idolaters. There was a legion of Sundays, all days of unserviceable bitterness and mortification, slowly passing before him. (i. iii) (pp. 29–30)

These are familiar Dickensian ironies again, though rather heavy ones—'a piece of curiosity that he really in a frock and drawers was not in a condition to satisfy', 'which, for the further attraction of his infant mind, had a parenthesis in every other line with some such hiccupping reference as 2 Ep. Thess. c. iii. v. 6 & 7'. We do not credit these intentionally amusing things to Arthur Clennam's point of view or to his state of mind. Clennam is made gloomy and depressed by these bells, his mind can by no means manage the confident poise of irony, much less the explicit humorous intention of these particular examples of Dickensian humour. If no important sense of discrepancy arises, it is because we are in the Dickens theatre. The irony, and the general theatrical nature of the passage as a whole, the sense that a certain kind of writing is being accomplished—this does, of course, keep us from any really inward view of Clennam. But a truly inward view of character is, of course, not in the least what we expect to find in the Dickens theatre: we 'believe in' Clennam in the familiar Dickensian way.

From this point on, however, irony noiselessly disappears from Dickens's early presentation of Clennam, and in his portrait of this depressed mind and spirit Dickens keeps fairly consistently to a grave decorum. There are touches of 'fancy', to be sure, in passages which are for the most part rendered from Clennam's sombre perspective:

Down in the cellars, as up in the bed-chambers, old objects that he well remembered were changed by age and decay, but were still in their old places; even to empty beer-casks hoary with cob-webs, and empty wine-bottles with fur and fungus choking up their throats. There, too, among unused bottle-racks and pale slants of light from the yard above, was the strong room stored with old ledgers, which had as musty and corrupt a smell as if they were regularly balanced, in the dead small hours, by a nightly resurrection of old bookkeepers. (I. v.) (p. 54)

This is not Clennam's fancifulness, but no important disruption of the mode of illusion is experienced by the reader.

Nor does this really happen when Clennam goes to visit his old love, Flora Casby, now Flora Finching. Dickens's success here is the result partly of some artful manœuvring, but mostly of the very nature of our mode of belief in the Dickens theatre. When the experience is finished, Dickens has this to say about Clennam's response to it:

Left to himself again, after the solicitude and compassion of his last adventure [the meeting with Cavaletto], he was naturally in a thoughtful mood. As naturally, he could not walk on thinking for ten minutes, without recalling Flora. She necessarily recalled to him his life, with all its misdirection and little happiness.

When he got to his lodging, he sat down before the dying fire, as he had stood at the window of his old room looking out upon the blackened forest of chimneys, and turned his gaze back upon the gloomy vista by which he had come to that stage in his existence. So long, so bare, so blank. No childhood; no youth, except for one remembrance; that one remembrance proved, only that day, to be a piece of folly. (I. xiii) (p. 164)

Dickens goes on to assert that Clennam's response to this disillusionment was a 'healthy' one: his belief 'in all the gentle and good things in life' rescues him 'to judge not, and in humility to be merciful, and have hope and charity'. 'A disappointed mind he had, but a mind too firm and healthy for such unwholesome air. Leaving himself in the dark, it could rise into the light, seeing it shine on others and hailing it.' This passage leads directly into Clennam's vision of Little Dorrit herself as the 'answer' to his disillusionment (though of course he fails to understand the vision). The language with which Clennam's views are rendered is obviously in consonance with the figure of Little Dorrit; it is just as obviously in no very perfect consonance with what the audience has experienced in the interview with Flora. This again is a demonstration of the methods of the Dickens theatre.

Flora Finching is one of Dickens's greatest comic creations, which is to say that we are not in the least surprised to find that what takes place in her scenes is like what happens in any 'star' performance. When great comedians sign contracts to appear in so-called plays, they make one iron-bound stipulation (though this may be perfectly tacit): the story must always yield to the star, if there is any conflict between them. In the Dickens theatre the big star is Dickens himself, and we have seen how, in the account of Clennam's religious education, the hero of the story actually yielded to Dickens; in the present instance, Dickens just as successfully engineers the process whereby the 'hero' and the 'story' both yield to the temporary star. First we hear, quite straightforwardly, that 'Flora, who had been spoiled and artless long ago, was determined to be spoiled and artless now. That was a fatal blow.' (I. xiii) (p. 150) Dickens keeps Clennam's shock and embarrassment briefly before us, until the new show is well under way. Then, if by chance we are in the least uncertain of our correct response, there is this:

With these words, and with a hasty gesture fraught with timid caution—such a gesture had Clennam's eyes been familiar with in the old time—poor Flora left herself, at eighteen years of age, a long long way behind again; and came to a full stop at last.

Or rather, she left about half of herself at eighteen years of age behind, and grafted the rest on to the relict of the late Mr. F.; thus making a moral mermaid of herself, which her once boy-lover contemplated with feelings wherein his sense of the sorrowful and his sense of the comical were curiously blended. (I. xiii) (p. 155)

With the image of Clennam's habitual depression well out of our minds, the way is prepared for the production of Flora's comic side-kick, Mr. F.'s Aunt.

All this is accomplished with great skill, and the rich performance by Flora Finching does not prevent us giving Clennam's more serious sentiments their due. But the fact that Clennam is involved (as he is several times) in such theatrical proceedings does silently qualify the mode of our knowledge of him. Clennam is not the hero of *Little Dorrit* in the sense that we come to know the meanings of the novel and its world through a consistent imaginative engagement with his consciousness. In the scene with Flora, indeed, he is reduced to a generalized neutrality, he is pure audience. We continue to know as a fact that he was the boy-lover of this great *comédienne*, but we know it in no deeper way; any deeper consciousness of Clennam's particular response to Flora would inhibit Flora's performance in a way that Dickens is the last writer to be interested in. If Clennam takes Flora with his comic sense, it is not particularly *his*, it is the comic sense any neutral observer might have. And we acknowledge this by never stopping to think what function Clennam's comic sense has in his depressed mind and spirit.

Compare, as a useful example of non-theatrical art, Ralph Touchett's way of dealing with Henrietta Stackpole in *The Portrait of a Lady*. Henrietta is Isabel's old friend, and therefore an important and puzzling person for Ralph. But she is also an oddly performing 'character' for whom he is an audience; indeed, he encourages her to perform as brilliantly or as eccentrically as she can: he frankly gives her the centre of the stage. James later worried whether this characterization had not got out of hand; he confessed to having invented her

for mainly theatrical purposes, for 'entertainment', and from
the vantage-point of his later and more rigorous technical
preoccupations it might well seem that Henrietta had been
allowed too uninhibited a performance. But our less rigorous
standards find her perfectly well adjusted to the novel. The
way Ralph behaves as an audience towards Henrietta furthers
in a significant way our sense of the drama of his inner life.
His comic sense is not inconsistent with his kind of depression,
as Clennam's comic sense is to some extent with his. Ralph's
appreciation of Henrietta is an instance of his chosen detachment; and the bold playfulness with which he mocks her is
an instance of the fineness of his internal organization. Thus
we may sustain an illusion of dramatic imaginative participation with Ralph's inner life throughout Henrietta's performance, whereas Dickens's theatrical methods give us the cue
that Arthur Clennam's comic sense is something to be forgotten immediately, something not to be credited to him in
particular.

The cue is less easy to take when Dickens comes to rendering
Clennam's love for Pet Meagles. The episode is an important
one, charged with the function of showing the sickness of
Clennam's will: he cannot reach for what he desires, we are
meant to feel, and we are also shown the process by which
his admirably strong 'ethical will' (to borrow Lionel Trilling's
terminology) argues him out of feeling he deserves what he
actually is powerless to reach for.

Clennam went back to his room, sat down again before his fire,
and made up his mind that he was glad he had resolved not to fall
in love with Pet. She was so beautiful, so amiable, so apt to receive
any true impression given to her gentle nature and her innocent
heart, and make the man who should be so happy as to communicate it, the most fortunate and enviable of all men, that he was
very glad indeed he had come to that conclusion.

But, as this might have been a reason for coming to the opposite
conclusion, he followed out the theme again a little way in his mind.
To justify himself, perhaps.

'Suppose that a man,' so his thoughts ran, 'who had been of age
some twenty years or so; who was a diffident man, from the circumstances of his youth; who was rather a grave man, from the tenor of
his life; who knew himself to be deficient in many little engaging
qualities which he admired in others, from having been long in a

distant region, with nothing softening near him; who had no kind
sisters to present to her; who had no congenial home to make her
known in; who was a stranger in the land; who had not a fortune
to compensate, in any measure, for these defects; who had nothing
in his favour but his honest love and his general wish to do right—
suppose such a man were to come to this house, and were to yield
to the captivation of this charming girl, and were to persuade himself that he could hope to win her; what a weakness it would be!'

He softly opened his window, and looked out upon the serene
river. Year after year so much allowance for the drifting of the
ferry-boat, so many miles an hour the flowing of the stream, here
the rushes, there the lilies, nothing uncertain or unquiet.

Why should he be vexed or sore at heart? It was not his weakness
that he had imagined. It was nobody's, nobody's within his knowledge, why should it trouble him? And yet it did trouble him. And
he thought—who has not thought for a moment, sometimes?—
that it might be better to flow away monotonously, like the river,
and to compound for its insensibility to happiness with its insensibility to pain. (I. xvi) (pp. 199–200)

These are seriously painful feelings, and Clennam's spiritual
malaise is also a serious and central theme of the novel.
Granting the moderate success with which these feelings are
represented, what can be made of the arch questionings in the
last paragraph? Dickens makes a good deal out of them. The
next chapter is called 'Nobody's Rival'; it focuses on Clennam's
jealousy of Gowan and his refusal to recognize it for what it is;
and it ends with a conversation between Clennam and Daniel
Doyce in which Clennam, despite himself, reveals his pain:

'Ah! We see enough!' cried Arthur.

Mr. Doyce wished him Good Night, in the tone of a man who had
heard a mournful, not to say despairing, exclamation, and who
sought to infuse some encouragement and hope into the mind of
the person by whom it had been uttered. Such tone was probably
a part of his oddity, as one of a crotchety band; for how could he
have heard anything of that kind, without Clennam's hearing it
too?

The rain fell heavily on the roof, and pattered on the ground,
and dripped among the evergreens, and the leafless branches of the
trees. The rain fell heavily, drearily. It was a night of tears.

If Clennam had not decided against falling in love with Pet; if
he had had the weakness to do it; if he had, little by little, persuaded
himself to set all the earnestness of his nature, all the might of his

hope, and all the wealth of his matured character, on that cast; if he had done this and found that all was lost; he would have been, that night, utterly miserable. As it was—

As it was, the rain fell heavily, drearily. (i. xvii) (pp. 209–10)

These arch ironies work against the serious purpose of the passage. Though it was certainly not Dickens's intention, they seem to convey disrespect for Clennam's pain, and because we have to some extent become involved with that pain we are almost offended by what seems now the crude exhibitionism of the theatrical artist, so busy finding a way of playing the scene, so proud of the silly device he has invented. Our reaction is to say, 'Can't you be serious for once'?—to say it with some impatience at least, if not real distaste, and to feel not the least foolishly earnest for saying it. We realize, disconcertingly, not only the limitations but the vices of the Dickens method.

Dickens's failure at this point is in one respect not surprising, since his grasp on the whole Meagles family and what they represent is always uncertain and often distinctly inept. With these characters he has made an explicit attempt to render a complex moral situation and consequently his ineptitude is not easy to pass over with the casual disapproval usually possible in the Dickens theatre.

Dickens's rendering of Clennam's painful love for Pet Meagles is sadly like a performance by one of those actors whom Shaw described as being able to make only one or two 'points' effectively. Dickens makes a point about Clennam's state of mind; he also makes a point about the moral nature of Clennam's rival, Henry Gowan; but this is as much apparently as can be managed in theatrical terms. Yet more seems called for. Pet Meagles is aware of Clennam's love, and in a sentimental little scene Dickens makes a point about her tender awareness of his pain. But why is no point made about the meaning of Pet's choice of Gowan over Clennam? We become conscious of a certain emptiness. The way Mr. and Mrs. Meagles have raised their child (and their maid Tattycoram) has been given a good deal of explicit attention; the child's choice of a husband ought, therefore, to continue this theme; but the theatrical artist is too busy elsewhere to handle it. In non-theatrical art Pet's choice of Gowan might be expected to speak for itself, but such art is created by the sort of inward imagination of the whole situation which Dickens cannot achieve, even here where everything suggests that he wanted to.

The Meagles family (including Tattycoram and Miss Wade), like other character-clusters in the late novels, function as a theatrical machine for delivering a fairly complex meaning. But in this case the degree of complexity is so high that the machine comes to seem a clumsily complicated contraption at best and an unbalanced and self-destructive system of opposing stresses at worst. In *Bleak House* Dickens made Mr. Jarndyce's house suitable for all the people in it and for their differing interests by simply adding a separate room for each interest; Mr. Jarndyce's divided nature needs two separate rooms, though he is also represented by the whole house. This kind of contraption (while differing totally from what we ordinarily mean when we speak of symbolism) is successful enough in *Bleak House* because of the book's theme—that System simply twists and distorts and kills people by an external force. The two sides of Jarndyce's nature need have no organic connexion with each other. But in *Little Dorrit* Dickens needs some method of expressing organic connexion, because his theme is the way people imprison and corrupt themselves. To express this theme, Dickens's additive principle is quite inadequate.

Mr. Meagles comes to us first as a familiar Dickensian benevolent eccentric—systematized but not blamed for it. He is a business man who is proud of being 'practical'; the word is his keynote, and we take our cue immediately from Arthur Clennam in finding it odd, then amusing, and finally touching that he uses the word to describe his admirably loving and charitable habits. His first words show the crude, no-nonsense energy of the stereotype; but the trick with the word 'practical' begins almost immediately, and its effect is to enforce our approval of his good heart quite unequivocally. It is, of course, possible that such a response is that of a reader too long habituated to the Dickens theatre. Dickens may have hoped to set up a *critical* irony by means of the distance between the word and the acts it describes: are we not, then, to see Mr. Meagles as imprisoned in his own vocabulary and therefore to question whether his apparently good heart has not been tainted by his language? My view is, first, that the prose itself has set up a literary situation in which we simply lack the independence to derive such points unless assisted by the narrator; we are not so assisted. Second, the absolute black-and-white opposition between the word and the act strikes me as too violent to encourage anything but the simplest meaning: the machinery is working too loudly and too rapidly to allow complex critical speculation. Finally, when Clennam (our surrogate) pays attention to the word, he is not disposed to an adverse judgement. Clennam has just been telling his sad life-story, and Meagles is giving him the appropriate advice:

'That was a tough commencement. But come! You must now study, and profit by all that lies beyond it, like a practical man.'

'If the people who are usually called practical, were practical in your direction—'

'Why, so they are!' said Mr. Meagles.

'Are they indeed?'

'Well, I suppose so,' returned Mr. Meagles, thinking about it. 'Eh! One can but *be* practical, and Mrs. Meagles and myself are nothing else.' (I. ii) (p. 21)

The suggestion is that Meagles is limited in his energetic naïveté, compared with Clennam's darker wisdom and experience; but there is no implication of a more serious criticism of Mr. Meagles. Furthermore, the actions of these 'practical people', at this first encounter, are not subjected to any serious criticism for the same reasons: the machinery of Dickens's device carries us too rapidly through them to allow for anything but the simplest reading—what these 'practical' people do is not motivated by what are ordinarily understood as 'practical' motives, but comes spontaneously from good and loving impulses.

When Clennam encounters Mr. Meagles back in England, and in the company of Daniel Doyce, a definite criticism is voiced. Mildly stated, it makes a strong effect, though it is simply added to what went before:

Clennam could not help speculating, as he seated himself in his room by the fire, whether there might be in the breast of this honest, affectionate, and cordial Mr. Meagles, any microscopic portion of the mustard-seed that had sprung up into the great tree of the

Circumlocution Office. His curious sense of a general superiority to Daniel Doyce, which seemed to be founded, not so much on anything in Doyce's personal character, as on the mere fact of his being an originator and a man out of the beaten track of other men, suggested the idea. (I. xvi) (p. 194)

A curious thing is happening here. Mr. Meagles's annoying behaviour towards Daniel Doyce would seem to derive precisely from the myth that inventive men of original genius, like Doyce, are not 'practical'. Mr. Meagles actually feels inferior to Doyce because he himself lacks inventiveness, but he comes to feel superior by exploiting the myth that men like Doyce would get nowhere but for the practicality of business men. This point is soundly made, yet curiously the word 'practical' is never brought into play in order to make it. I confess that I do not know what to make of the odd blurring of effect caused by this omission. Did Dickens want us to 'see it for ourselves'? The pointedness of the devices in the Dickens theatre does not forbid us to see for ourselves, but it does keep us from feeling satisfied and secure in doing so. If on one page we are enjoying the certainties of our habitual relationship with the great virtuoso, we cannot lose those certainties without feeling insecure. And we take our revenge, as it were, by ascribing our insecurity to uncertainty on the part of the narrator.

This uncertainty reaches very serious proportions in Dickens's rendering of the Meagles's relationship with Tattycoram. In his introduction to *Little Dorrit* in the *New Oxford Illustrated Dickens*, Lionel Trilling speaks of the 'remarkable number of false and inadequate parents' in the novel, and includes the Meagles among them: 'No reader of *Little Dorrit* can possibly conclude that the rage of envy which Tattycoram feels is not justified in some degree, or that Miss Wade is wholly wrong in pointing out to her the insupportable ambiguity of her position as the daughter-servant of Pet Meagles.' (xi) Mr. Trilling is surely right in his reading, even though what he implies damages his claim that in *Little Dorrit* there is a successful management and working out of psychological insights to which he admiringly calls attention. Our sense that Tattycoram's envy is justified 'in some degree', and that Miss Wade's message is not 'wholly' wrong, is, as

Mr. Trilling's qualifying phrases perhaps unconsciously suggest, not a secure sense.

The Meagles lack imagination, the capacity to enter into or even to worry about the inner life of others. They trust their own certitude about their warm feelings and good intentions, but the way they treat their servant shows that this complacent certitude gets in the way of moral self-scrutiny. Dickens wants to say, it seems to me, both that warm feelings and good intentions are the best we have and that they are not enough; and one wants to go along with this. It is not only that he lacks the vocabulary and habit of mind needed to render this ambiguous judgement with the quiet, rueful detachment appropriate to it; it is also that his theatrical habits work actively against a proper rendering of it. His methods did not permit a creative 'study' of human behaviour. He had to act it out immediately, to find a device for performing it with brilliant effect in his theatre. Accordingly he invented the highly effective device of the word 'practical' to act Mr. Meagles out in language. But it is too effective. It creates an amused and affectionate approval of Mr. Meagles which amounts to a vivid summing-up, a brilliant finality of understanding, to which further qualifications cannot be made without a sense of blurring or even of contradiction. When those qualifications are energetically forced upon us we simply feel insecure.

With Miss Wade Dickens is rather more successful. If he cannot manage to embody the right attitude towards the Meagles, he can achieve a fairly convincing embodiment of a wrong attitude. Miss Wade is puzzling to think about and impossible to argue with. Give her an inch and she will take a mile: if you recognize the justice of her view of the world you are faced with the problem of deciding where to stop, for you also recognize that her view of the world is too systematic; but if you refuse to admit the justice of her position you are reprehensibly defending another version of System. This is what the characters in *Little Dorrit* feel about Miss Wade and what, in an innocent process of imitative form, the readers are brought to feel; and it is a just response to a convincing image of human behaviour. Furthermore, Dickens has a convincing answer to Miss Wade's view of the world. Tattycoram goes to live with Miss Wade, seduced by her message, and it is only her daily experience with Miss Wade that can effect her release from this new prison:

'I am bad enough, but not so bad as I was, indeed. I have had Miss Wade before me all this time, as if it was my own self grown ripe—turning everything the wrong way, and twisting all good into evil. I have had her before me all this time, finding no pleasure in anything but keeping me miserable, suspicious, and tormenting as herself. Not that she had much to do, to do that,' cried Tattycoram, in a closing great burst of distress, 'for I was as bad as bad could be. I only mean to say, that, after what I have gone through, I hope I shall never be quite so bad again, and that I shall get better by very slow degrees. I'll try very hard. I won't stop at five-and-twenty, sir. I'll count five-and-twenty hundred, five-and-twenty thousand!' (II. xxxiii) (pp. 811–12)

No analytic process can resolve the problem presented by Miss Wade. It is only as Tattycoram sees Miss Wade's identity as a whole that she can understand it; and understanding comes, as it must and as it legitimately can with Tattycoram, in the form of simple rejection.

Yet Dickens's idea about Miss Wade is more interesting to talk about than to experience in the Dickens theatre, which, when it comes to implementing such ideas, turns out to be in the hands of a rather limited and conventional theatrical stock-company. However original, subtle, and exploratory the script may be, the performance of it will be in the hands of the regular troupe of players, and the role of Miss Wade goes inevitably to the actress we have seen as Lady Dedlock and Edith Dombey. The sad truth is that Dickens's rendering of his original idea is rather too much a matter of conventionally 'bitter' tones of voice, 'haughty' glances, and 'strange attentive' smiles. Occasionally this seems an interesting effect, a fresh insight into a familiar type. But it works the other way more often; we feel a gap between conception and performance, and sometimes we virtually ignore the performance, we almost wish it away, in our frank concentration on Dickens's idea. Much recent Dickens criticism adopts this attitude regularly. The Meagles group fails in an even more important respect. Dickens himself actively works against the originality and truth of his idea about Miss Wade. We are satisfied that Tattycoram has really seen Miss Wade, and that such a total and instinctive vision of her whole behaviour is the only way of dealing with such principled and systematic distortion. But Mr. Meagles is not satisfied by this answer, nor, apparently, is Dickens: neither of them can resist pointing the moral of the tale in the face of our understanding that no moral is possible. I quote the whole distressing passage:

Mr. Meagles, looking through the bars of the window, saw her pass out of the Lodge below him into the prison-yard. He said gently, 'Tattycoram, come to me a moment, my good girl.'

She went up to the window.

'You see that young lady who was here just now—that little, quiet, fragile figure passing along there, Tatty? Look. The people stand out of the way to let her go by. The men—see the poor, shabby fellows—pull off their hats to her quite politely, and now she glides in at that doorway. See her, Tattycoram?'

'Yes, sir.'

'I have heard tell, Tatty, that she was once regularly called the child of this place. She was born here, and lived here many years. I can't breathe here. A doleful place, to be born and bred in, Tattycoram?'

'Yes indeed, sir!'

'If she had constantly thought of herself, and settled with herself that everybody visited this place upon her, turned it against her, and cast it at her, she would have led an irritable and probably an useless existence. Yet I have heard tell, Tattycoram, that her young life has been one of active resignation, goodness, and noble service. Shall I tell you what I consider those eyes of hers that were here just now, to have always looked at, to get that expression?'

'Yes, if you please, sir.'

'Duty, Tattycoram. Begin it early, and do it well; and there is no antecedent to it, in any origin or station, that will tell against us with the Almighty, or with ourselves.' (II. xxxiii) (pp. 812–13)

This is worse than inept. We have no alternative but to take the sermon as the official moral of Tattycoram's story, sponsored by the management. When Dickens says that Mr. Meagles makes his point 'gently', the word is an unequivocal theatrical badge to show that he is in the right. Yet the sermon is inappropriate in several ways. Since Tattycoram has already fully and convincingly described her conversion, Mr. Meagles's sermon about duty seems a work of pharisaical supererogation worthy of Mrs. Pardiggle herself—it is hard to see how the generous Dickens could have been guilty of such tactlessness. Moreover, the question of where Tattycoram's duty, or rather, since she is a servant, her 'duties' lie has been precisely the question at issue. Finally, Mr. Meagles totally lacks the authority to deliver such sermons. Tattycoram's promise to 'count five-and-twenty thousand' expresses well enough her pleasure in returning from Miss Wade's imprisoning system to the world, and to the vocabulary, of Mr. Meagles; but it is also an unwelcome reminder of earlier doubts about Mr. Meagles's practicality. As a good audience we may have reluctantly obeyed the theatrical artist's clear instructions to forget these doubts and to co-operate in this happy reconciliation scene, but with Mr. Meagles's sermon on duty Dickens has gone too far. We don't want the sermon anyway, but if the management insists on it another actor might have been hired for the job. One is reminded of the little economies practised by the management when Mr. Wopsle played Hamlet:

The noble boy in the ancestral boots was inconsistent, represent-ing himself, as it were in one breath, as an able seaman, a stroll-ing actor, a grave-digger, a clergyman, and a person of the utmost importance at a Court fencing-match, on the authority of whose practised eye and nice discrimination the finest strokes were judged. This gradually led to a want of toleration for him, and even—on his being detected in holy orders, and declining to perform the funeral service—to the general indignation taking the form of nuts. (*Great Expectations*, XXXI, pp. 239–40)

Our sense that Dickens himself is sponsoring Mr. Meagles's sermon is confirmed also by the fact that Mr. Meagles points to the heroine of the novel as an example of right behaviour. But the process works in the other direction too, and Dickens's uncertainty at this point extends to his treatment of his hero-ine, with whom we must now concern ourselves.

Mr. Trilling's defence of Dickens's characterization of Little Dorrit is a bold one:

We must accept—and we easily do accept, if we do not permit critical cliché to interfere—the aesthetic of such an imagination, which will inevitably tend to a certain formality of pattern and to the generalization and the abstraction we have remarked. In a novel

in which a house falls physically to ruins from the moral collapse of
its inhabitants, in which the heavens open over London to show a
crown of thorns, in which there are characters named nothing else
than Bar, Bishop, Physician, we are quite content to accept the
existence of a devil. And we do not reject, for all our inevitable
first impulse to do so, the character of Little Dorrit herself. Her
untinctured goodness does not appal us or make us misdoubt her,
as we expect it to do. This novel at its best is only incidentally
realistic, its finest power of imagination appears in the great
general images whose abstractness is their actuality, like Mr.
Merdle's dinner parties, or the Circumlocution Office itself, and
in such a context we understand Little Dorrit to be the Beatrice
of the Comedy, the Paraclete in female form. Even the physical
littleness of this grown woman, an attribute which is insisted on
and which seems so likely to repel us, does not do so, for we perceive
it to be the sign that she not only is the Child of the Marshalsea, as
she is called, but also the Child of the Parable, the negation of the
social will.[1]

Mr. Trilling is arguing that those who object to the characterization of Little Dorrit are judging in terms of crude
principles of verisimilitude, which are irrelevant in this case
because they are irrelevant to everything else in a book that
proceeds by symbolic rather than by realistic methods. It is
an elegantly economical proof of Dickens's success, but not a
sound one. The truth is far too puzzlingly tangled to allow
much elegance or economy.

The novel is usually a realistic form because, as Mr. Trilling himself has argued, its ordinary concern is with 'manners
and morals', with the actualization of intellectual, moral, and
spiritual values in everyday life. But all novels, of course, need
not share this concern, and Mr. Trilling suggests that Dickens
can legitimately ignore the identity and behaviour of Amy
Dorrit as it would be seen in the perspective of everyday social
life. She may be thought of as existing in a meta-social, meta-
physical, meta-moral realm of being, though Mr. Trilling would
not, of course, claim that these words are really appropriate
to Dickens's imagination. When Mr. Trilling suggests that
Little Dorrit is like the Holy Spirit, the Paraclete, he means
that she embodies a 'grace' which flows into Clennam's soul

---

[1] Introduction to *Little Dorrit*, *The New Oxford Illustrated Dickens* (London,
1953), xv–xvi.

and renews it in a mysterious process not accountable for
in social terms. Or she is like Beatrice in that she is to be
known in symbolic contemplation rather than in a realistic
social or sexual interrelationship. It is true that in rendering
many of Little Dorrit's actions Dickens has sought to introduce a special radiance: he has consistently 'glorified' her
presence and her actions. She is a socially insignificant presence at all times, and yet she is repeatedly given a special
attention which her social identity could not command. She
is timid and weak, yet she passes through dangerous situations
with a security which cannot be accounted for in social terms.
She is protected both by the mysterious power of her innocence
and by odd guarding presences. She is valued by people who
value nobody and nothing else. She has, in a word, extraordinary spiritual power, and it is implied that this is true
precisely because she has no social power at all.

Even so, Mr. Trilling's response is rather to Dickens's evident
intention than to his achievement. In the first place there is a
certain lurid glow in what passes for radiance in the Dickens
theatre. Ruskin regretted that Dickens always chose 'to speak
in a circle of stage fire', and the sad fact is that we are often
only too conscious that Amy Dorrit's halo is the work of the
lighting technician. A more important weakness is that Dickens
cannot seem to invent anything in Little Dorrit to glorify
except approved moral—and social—behaviour. Little Dorrit
is an unquestioningly loving daughter, a loyal sister, a persevering worker; she is unfailingly kind to her comic suitor,
respectful towards patronizing Mrs. General, infinite in love
and patience with Maggy. She is the complete embodiment of
the Victorian domestic and social virtues, and one's objection
is not that the Victorian virtues are less than in the highest
degree admirable but that they belong to just that social
world to which according to Mr. Trilling Little Dorrit does not
belong. We are dealing with the same impulse that produced
conventional Victorian language about 'the sanctity of the
home', and Tennyson's praise of Hallam:

> For can I doubt, who knew thee keen
>   In intellect, with force and skill
>   To strive, to fashion, to fulfil—
> I doubt not what thou wouldst have been:

A life in civic action warm,
    A soul on highest mission sent,
    A potent voice of Parliament,
    A pillar steadfast in the storm.[1]

Tennyson's unction is no better perhaps than Dickens's stage
lighting, but it is no worse, and it is hard to see why a critic
whom one would imagine to be less than pleased with Tennyson's language should be so pleased with Dickens's. Dickens
has not imagined an identity for Amy Dorrit which would
seem genuinely to inhabit a realm of being different from the
social and personal realm: he has taken conventional images of
conventional moral and social excellence and imparted to them
a radiance which is strictly the work of his own will and his
own theatrical method.

But a far more serious objection to Mr. Trilling's argument is that Dickens himself raised the question of the social
identity of Little Dorrit. We crudely realistic readers are not
to be blamed. We might leniently accept most of the characterization as the best that the Dickens theatre can offer in the
way of the 'Paraclete in female form'. But at the end of the
novel Dickens explicitly denies that Little Dorrit inhabits a
realm of being different from the social realm. The facts of the
case are these: Clennam is from the beginning highly responsive to the beauty and the value of Little Dorrit's identity,
but this does not 'save' him. She is rather too much a Beatrice,
a Paraclete in female form: this is the meaning conveyed by
her physical littleness, her identity as 'the child of the Marshalsea'. Clennam's salvation in prison comes with the discovery
that he loves Little Dorrit and that she loves him. Despite the
reticence of the novel, we have no alternative but to identify
this love with sexual and social and personal love. Clennam's
earlier love for Little Dorrit could not save him: he could
not, by communing with the good in contemplation, gain the
wholeness and health and innocence of will that would enable
him to live productively in the corrupted social world (and,
of course, there is no other world but the social world for him
to choose in this novel). He has known for a long time that he
loves Little Dorrit and that she loves him, as a father loves

---

[1] *In Memoriam*, CXIII. 5–12.

and is loved by his child. But only an adult, personal, wilful, sexual, sharing and mutually knowing love will save him, and to offer Little Dorrit this kind of love has seemed to him simply unthinkable, because it would be a violation of innocence and purity. The end of the novel simply says that Arthur Clennam learns that Little Dorrit is not a child but a woman, and my view is that the reader doesn't believe it.

The sleight of hand by which Dickens distracts our attention in this crucial passage is surely one of his most meretricious effects. When Little Dorrit appears to Clennam in his room in the Marshalsea (xxix) she seems to materialize as 'a living presence' out of his dream of her: this could be a sound beginning for the intended metamorphosis from symbolic image into social reality. He hesitates in addressing her, not being sure what name to call her: this figures both as a preparation for his new view of her as a woman and as the beginning of a new difficulty about her supposed wealth and social position. An explicit statement soon follows:

She looked something more womanly than when she had gone away, and the ripening touch of the Italian sun was visible upon her face. But, otherwise she was quite unchanged. The same deep, timid earnestness that he had always seen in her, and never without emotion, he saw still. If it had a new meaning that smote him to the heart, the change was in his perception, not in her. (II. xxix) (p. 757)

We are told explicitly that Clennam's view of her has changed, and we are soon explicitly told what the change is. But here Dickens abandons the 'child-woman' antithesis for a 'rich-poor' antithesis, and I am bound to say that I get the point of the new language without finding Dickens's choice of it anything but deplorable. Whereas Clennam had earlier found it unthinkable that he might ever possess the 'child', he now conceives of the possibility but rejects it out of shame. Dickens's device for getting this across is to have Little Dorrit offer Clennam her money, which means nothing to her except in so far as it expresses her love (that is, she offers her sexual and personal innocence which means nothing to her except in so far as it expresses her love), and to have Clennam reject the offer on the grounds that, despite her love, he 'must not' as a gentleman 'descend so low as that, and carry you—so dear, so generous, so good—down with me' (that is, he must not corrupt her innocence with his guilty experience). Now it is true that Clennam's financial ruin is identified in a confused and confusing way as something close to moral disgrace: that he, with his experience of the world and in particular of the Circumlocution Office, should succumb to the temptation of investing in the Merdle enterprises does carry with it the suggestion of suicide, of a sin against self and life. The point is by no means successfully made; it seems an intuition that Dickens could not work into an organic relationship with other more conscious and deliberate points he wanted to make about Merdle and Clennam. But whatever we feel about Clennam's financial ruin, he has expiated it in prison; he does not yield to despair but continues to think vaguely of Little Dorrit. Moreover, his scruples against taking her money are, by theatrical devices, very firmly defined as both a noble delusion and as merely temporary. And when Little Dorrit reveals that she has lost her fortune, he readily accepts her hand in marriage. In terms of the Dickens theatre, this conclusion means that Clennam has realized that he will not be violating Little Dorrit's innocence by possessing her because they are both 'poor', whatever that may imply. But here the theatrical mode fails us. The womanliness of Little Dorrit has not been embodied in significant images and we are left in exasperated disbelief. We are very far this time from sharing the great virtuoso's pride in his legerdemain.

In speaking of the failure of these pages I do not mean to suggest that it is not a remarkably interesting and indeed a moving failure. Mr. Jarndyce's offer of marriage to Esther Summerson, her acceptance of the offer, the devices by which she is released from this ridiculous and repellent 'problem'—these pages in *Bleak House* are beneath serious discussion and do not command serious attention as we read; we need not offer to become involved because the virtuoso is so clearly uninvolved himself. But now and then one becomes engaged with Clennam's inner life in *Little Dorrit,* and one always senses that Dickens has registered in this characterization his deepest and most personal moral questioning. This impression persists even at those moments when the public performer seems, with his clever devices, to be doing his level best to destroy it. Much of the characterization amounts to a highly original and moving expression of the human condition. Arthur Clennam, the man with no will, is a subject that George Eliot, one suspects, could not even have seen, much less handled: her very commitment to the traditional disciplines of the sympathetic imagination locked her into a vocabulary of moral conflict which could find no place for the language necessary to describe Clennam. And one could say the same of James. Dickens's innocence of the conventional spiritual exercises released him from the vocabulary of moral conflict and in so doing brought to his attention moral *condition* as a subject. But if Dickens's rendering of Clennam's condition is in many ways (in rendering of posture, gesture, tone of voice) successful and beautiful, nevertheless he wanted more; he wanted to believe in the possibility of change of condition. And if it is not surprising that the only kind of drama he could enact in his theatre was the artificial algebra of wealth and poverty which I have described, it is certainly, and in the most urgent way, regrettable.

It must be the moving and impressive originality of Dickens's conception of Clennam towards which the recent apologists for *Little Dorrit* are drawn. The problem remains why it is so hard to admit the essential failure of the novel as a whole, and in particular the failure of Dickens's rendering of Clennam's salvation. I see the over-emphatic and misleading excitement about Dickens's symbolic structures not as a way of defending the success of the late novels but rather as a means of evading the issue: in Mr. J. Hillis Miller's book evasion of judgement is almost total, and Mr. Trilling raises the issue only to condescend to it. But why evade judgement, unless you believe that judgement of success and failure is necessarily mean-spirited, ungenerous, even sterile? Unless you fear that the very act of literary judgement commits you to mandarin æsthetic testing that will violate the spirit of Dickens? It is this fear which seems sterile: the necessity of judging the end of *Little Dorrit*, on the contrary, comes naturally and with a considerable force. It is just because we assent to Dickens's image of the sick will as a deep and imaginative insight that we hasten, in the most unlettered eagerness, to assess his version of salvation. If we care at all about Arthur Clennam, if we in the least degree see his condition as relevant to our own life and to the life of the times, then we simply want to know the answer to it. If an answer is given, and it doesn't work, we can say as much; and we must say it, for not to do so would be to say that art doesn't matter.

PART III

DICKENS'S CIVILIZATION AND ITS DISCONTENTS

10

GREAT EXPECTATIONS

Great Expectations, Dickens's masterpiece, is like all of his
novels a performance in the Dickens theatre. As usual, a
primary object of our attention as we read is the great
theatrical artist himself, who clearly wants his presence to be
felt, who overtly and audibly performs before us some brilliant
routines and contrivances in order to command attention and
applause. But in this particular novel the whole performance
comes to us as the full-scale impersonation of a single man
and a single voice. The great virtuoso appears on stage in the
theatrical disguise of a man called Philip Pirrip who purports
to be telling us his story, reporting his observations of men and
manners, and moralizing on his own career. This illusion—that
we are hearing a man called Pip speaking to us—is most skilfully contrived to give the impression of consistency, but it
gives that impression only to the reader who is at ease in the
theatricality of the occasion, as indeed all of Dickens's novels
work only for readers accustomed to the Dickens theatre.
Dickens's impersonation of the voice and point of view of Pip
is a theatrical mask which he manipulates with the utmost
dexterity when it is needed. But it is not always needed, and
when it is quietly laid aside the skilful reader experiences no
inconsistency. No reader accustomed to Dickens's theatrical
art has ever been offended or even mildly puzzled to find that
much of *Great Expectations* is spoken by the typically Dickensian voice—that of an acknowledged and self-confident master
of language and narrative technique who quite audibly and
quite unremittingly seeks to amuse, excite, and move his
readers. Who has ever 'believed' that the famous comic set-
pieces—Trabb's boy or Mr. Wopsle's *Hamlet*—were the work
of a man named Philip Pirrip, called Pip?

The theatrical nature of the whole novel is evident on the
very first pages, as it would have to be.

My father's family name being Pirrip, and my christian name Philip, my infant tongue could make of both names nothing longer or more explicit than Pip. So, I called myself Pip, and came to be called Pip.

I give Pirrip as my father's family name, on the authority of his tombstone and my sister—Mrs. Joe Gargery, who married the blacksmith. As I never saw my father or my mother, and never saw any likeness of either of them (for their days were long before the days of photographs), my first fancies regarding what they were like, were unreasonably derived from their tombstones. The shape of the letters on my father's gave me an odd idea that he was a square, stout, dark man, with curly black hair. From the character and turn of the inscription, '*Also Georgiana Wife of the Above*,' I drew a childish conclusion that my mother was freckled and sickly. To five little stone lozenges, each about a foot and a half long, which were arranged in a neat row beside their grave, and were sacred to the memory of five little brothers of mine—who gave up trying to get a living exceedingly early in that universal struggle—I am indebted for a belief I religiously entertained that they had all been born on their backs with their hands in their trousers-pockets, and had never taken them out in this state of existence. (i) (p. 1)

Reading this first paragraph, we believe that we are hearing the voice of a man named Philip Pirrip, who is telling us how he came to be called Pip because that is how it really happened. We never, from this point on, consciously doubt the narrator's fidelity to the facts of his life. Yet already in the second sentence of the second paragraph the author's fidelity to the facts has been joined by another motive: the voice of Pip tells us how he derived his first fancies about his family not only because that is how it really happened, but because it happened in a charming, amusing, and touching way. The voice, then, is no longer simply telling the truth; it is, without in the least seeking to disguise this motive, attempting to make a certain effect on us, and of course we do not fail to yield our immediate co-operation. We know ourselves to be in the presence of a writer with designs on us, an accomplished, self-conscious stylist, and we are glad to be. As when a good story-teller of our acquaintance tells us an incident from his childhood, we do not actually disbelieve what he is saying. If we stopped to think we might say, 'Yes, this could be the actual truth', or

'No, he's dressing it up—I wonder what the actual truth is.'
But the point is that we do not stop to think, which is to say
that we are doing something else which is different from the
kind of thinking which could be also termed believing. We
are accepting, we are seeing the point, we are enjoying, we are
applauding. We are in a theatre.

By the next page we are ready to accept this sort of thing:

A fearful man, all in coarse grey, with a great iron on his leg. A
man with no hat, and with broken shoes, and with an old rag tied
round his head. A man who had been soaked in water, and smothered
in mud, and lamed by stones, and cut by flints, and stung by
nettles, and torn by briars; who limped, and shivered, and glared
and growled; and whose teeth chattered in his head as he seized
me by the chin. (1) (p. 2)

Far from its being offensive, we recognize the mannered self-
consciousness of this prose as a brilliant style successfully
deployed. In the Dickens theatre style is neither conventional
nor functional, but an object of attention and pleasure in
itself. Meanwhile there is the man being so brilliantly described,
whose existence we credit, whose vivid figure we seem actually
to see. And at the end of the paragraph there is again Pip, and
the story proceeds. The highly stylized ordering of visual im-
pressions in this description of the convict is not implausible
as a child's view, if we stop to think. Nor is it particularly
plausible. But we do not stop to think: Pip has necessarily
disappeared from our consciousness in order to allow the style
full play. If we willingly return to being conscious of Pip when
the theatrical artist tells us to, our obedience is in ratio to
the theatrical artist's security and confidence. But it is we who
have initially given him licence to call the tune; just as, in our
living room with our amusing friend, it is we who give him the
licence to entertain us.

Later in the story where more is at stake and the theatrical
artist is called on for swifter and more ingenious manipulations,
there is a proportionately greater danger that the lines of communication between the artist and his audience will tangle. But
the description of Mrs. Gargery's funeral, for instance, is beautifully secure.

It was the first time that a grave had opened in my road of
life, and the gap it made in the smooth ground was wonderful. The

figure of my sister in her chair by the kitchen fire, haunted me night and day. That the place could possibly be without her, was something my mind seemed unable to compass; and whereas she had seldom or never been in my thoughts of late, I had now the strangest idea that she was coming towards me in the street, or that she would presently knock at the door. In my rooms too, with which she had never been at all associated, there was at once the blankness of death and a perpetual suggestion of the sound of her voice or the turn of her face or figure, as if she were still alive and had been often there.

Whatever my fortunes might have been, I could scarcely have recalled my sister with much tenderness. But I suppose there is a shock of regret which may exist without much tenderness. Under its influence (and perhaps to make up for the want of the softer feeling) I was seized with a violent indignation against the assailant from whom she had suffered so much; and I felt that on sufficient proof I could have revengefully pursued Orlick, or any one else, to the last extremity.

Having written to Joe, to offer him consolation, and to assure him that I would come to the funeral, I passed the intermediate days in the curious state of mind I have glanced at. I went down early in the morning, and alighted at the Blue Boar, in good time to walk over to the forge.

It was fine summer weather again, and, as I walked along, the times when I was a little helpless creature, and my sister did not spare me, vividly returned. But they returned with a gentle tone upon them, that softened even the edge of Tickler. For now, the very breath of the beans and clover whispered to my heart that the day must come when it would be well for my memory that others walking in the sunshine should be softened as they thought of me.

At last I came within sight of the house, and saw that Trabb and Co. had put in a funereal execution and taken possession. Two dismally absurd persons, each ostentatiously exhibiting a crutch done up in a black bandage—as if that instrument could possibly communicate any comfort to anybody—were posted at the front door; and in one of them I recognized a postboy discharged from the Boar for turning a young couple into a sawpit on their bridal morning, in consequence of intoxication rendering it necessary for him to ride his horse clasped round the neck with both arms. All the children of the village, and most of the women, were admiring these sable warders and the closed windows of the house and forge; and as I came up, one of the two warders (the postboy) knocked at the door—implying that I was far too much exhausted by grief, to have strength remaining to knock for myself.

Another sable warder (a carpenter, who had once eaten two geese for a wager) opened the door, and showed me into the best parlour. Here, Mr. Trabb had taken unto himself the best table, and had got all the leaves up, and was holding a kind of black Bazaar, with the aid of a quantity of black pins. At the moment of my arrival, he had just finished putting somebody's hat into black long-clothes, like an African baby; so he held out his hand for mine. But I, misled by the action, and confused by the occasion, shook hands with him with every testimony of warm affection. (xxxv) (pp. 264–5)

The relevant critical question here is how it happens that when Dickens swings into his brilliantly professional comic rendering of the funeral itself, we do not experience a disturbing mixture of modes. Except for its masterly economy, this comic funeral might have appeared in *The Pickwick Papers*: it is a virtuoso's performance in the style for which the generally received name is 'Dickensian'. The name of the virtuoso is—needless to say—not Philip Pirrip. These 'two dismally absurd persons', these 'sable warders', the 'black Bazaar' which Mr. Trabb is holding 'with the aid of a quantity of black pins'—Dickens would be far from flattered if we failed to recognize from whose shop these wonderful specimens have come. How, then, can this material seem to follow suitably after four paragraphs which render Pip's inner responses to his sister's death?

The answer, of course, is that these responses have been rendered in a mode which discourages sympathetic dramatic participation in Pip's inner life. We believe in these inner events and they have their effect, but they do not constitute an inner drama, nor does this fact impress us as a failure in Dickens's art. Indeed, the voice of the narrator does not seem really to want us to engage dramatically with Pip's inner life: it wants us to look at the whole business from quite a different perspective.

The narrative voice of Pip which we hear in *Great Expectations* is consistently that of an older, wiser man looking back on youthful follies. But it is not the voice of a man who, in any specific way, shows the markings of having been through the particular experiences of Pip which form the body of the novel; it is not the voice of a man who has been shaped into a special and individual kind of maturity by special experiences. The voice of Pip is, in a word, the voice of a stock-character. It is a decidedly traditional impersonation of middle-age looking back on youth that Dickens is performing here; and, despite the far greater range of event and of feeling in Dickens's book, the identity of Pip as an older man looking back is not unlike that of Justice Shallow:

> The same Sir John, the very same. I see him break Skogan's head at the court gate when 'a was a crack not thus high; and the very same day did I fight with one Samson Stockfish, a fruiterer, behind Gray's Inn. Jesu, Jesu, the mad days that I have spent! And to see how many of my old acquaintance are dead! (*Henry IV, Part II*, III. ii. 32–38)

The tradition of the Seven Ages of Man is not far away. And what in Dickens's work looks like an exception to this actually proves the rule. The remarkable sensitivity to the feelings of children, for which Dickens has rightly received so much attention and praise, is quite unlike Joyce's rendering of Stephen as a child in *A Portrait of the Artist as a Young Man*. It is in relationship to the traditional attitude towards such things that Dickens is calling *special attention* to the actuality of a child's sufferings or the oddity of a child's motives:

> If a dread of not being understood be hidden in the breasts of other young people to anything like the extent to which it used to be hidden in mine—which I consider probable, as I have no particular reason to suspect myself of having been a monstrosity— it is the key to many reservations. I felt convinced that if I described Miss Havisham's as my eyes had seen it, I should not be understood. Not only that, but I felt convinced that Miss Havisham too would not be understood; and although she was perfectly incomprehensible to me, I entertained the impression that there would be something coarse and treacherous in my dragging her as she really was (to say nothing of Miss Estella) before the contemplation of Mrs. Joe. Consequently, I said as little as I could, and had my face shoved against the kitchen wall. (IX) (p. 61)

In the ironically undercutting phrase 'entertained the impression' Dickens is affirming the traditional view that children are not to be taken seriously, while at the same time speaking out against it. Pip's feelings are described in the context of the traditional view of youth and age, which is almost antithetical to the familiar romantic and modern conception of the drama of the individual consciousness. We believe that Pip is telling about things that actually happened to him, but we believe more consciously that he is doing so because of the many odd and amusing and frightening and *generally significant* things that happened, not at all because his is a unique individual consciousness with a unique inner drama. Along with the happenings themselves, the narrator is careful to report his own reactions and responses to them; but nothing could be further from the 'egotistical sublime' that the mature Pip's traditional attitude towards the history of his inner life. Dickens's impersonation of Pip's narrative voice is an entirely theatrical performance in a traditional mode, and it is for this reason that Pip's account of his early feelings can seem perfectly at home with the other performances taking place in the Dickens theatre.

In Pip's responses to his sister's death, the local manifestations of this general perspective are abundantly visible. The seriousness of Pip's feelings are, for instance, delicately undercut by a *pianissimo* note of burlesque, which is entirely gratuitous and unmotivated in dramatic terms: 'and I felt that on sufficient proof I could have revengefully pursued Orlick, or any one else, to the last extremity'. The anger against Orlick, as I shall show later, is an extremely important element in the thematic structure of the novel, but Dickens's style at this juncture does not, to say the least, invite us to take it seriously. Moreover, the phases of psychological event in these four paragraphs come to us as an oddly linear structure. They simply succeed each other on the stage of Pip's consciousness, and Dickens emphasizes this structure by the use of short paragraphs. Now this is by no means an unconvincing or implausible registration of the structure of psychological states, and may even be more plausible than the more complexly dramatized non-linear structure to which we are accustomed in dramatic art. But in fact we *are* accustomed to a non-linear structure, and the result is that Dickens's structure does not invite us to dramatic participation: we note the interest, the oddity, the humour, the validity of these stages in Pip's consciousness with the same amused and interested detachment with which they are offered to us.

Thus the professional brilliance of the funeral scene does not interrupt a sustained dramatic illusion, because there is no such illusion to interrupt. As the successive stages of Pip's responses to his sister's death merely follow each other, each one completely displacing what has gone before, likewise the comic funeral displaces what has preceded it. Observe that the mildly satiric point which informs the whole description is as exempt from dramatic significance as the comedy itself. It is with the greatest affection and pleasure that Dickens is mocking—if he is mocking—the mechanical pomposity with which these provincials celebrate their sorrow; yet even this delicate modulation of tone would not answer if we chose to stop and think about the exact significance of Mrs. Gargery's death to all concerned. But neither the satire nor the comedy rises from within a dramatic situation; nor do they cut across the scene in dramatic irony. The whole procedure is, so to speak, sponsored directly by the management.

It is noteworthy that during the funeral itself 'Pip the snob' makes no appearance, and yet no very serious dramatic significance of this fact comes to our attention. Pip's responses to Mr. Trabb and company show the decent embarrassment and constraint which anyone might feel:

When I had spoken to Biddy, as I thought it not a time for talking, I went and sat down near Joe, and there began to wonder in what part of the house it—she—my sister—was. (XXXV) (p. 265)

In this progress I was much annoyed by the abject Pumblechook, who, being behind me, persisted all the way, as a delicate attention, in arranging my streaming hatband, and smoothing my cloak. (XXXV) (p. 266)

These are plausible and exact details; but if we were reading non-theatrical art we might well ask exactly what relationship Pip's decent and modest demeanour at his sister's funeral has with the airs and graces he has picked up since his great expectations arrived. A plausible answer to the question might be that Pip has been 'softened' by the thought of his own death. But it is not to be expected that our minds, so fully occupied by the candid comic intentions of this performance in the Dickens theatre, would ask such questions.

It is only when the stage has been cleared of Mr. Trabb and the rest that there is room again for Pip's airs and graces, which reappear as fluently as they had before been suppressed: 'He was very much pleased by my asking if I might sleep in my own little room, and I was pleased too; for, I felt that I had done rather a great thing in making the request.' (XXXV) (p. 267) And there follows an encore of the comic duet between Pip's snobbish pomposity and Biddy's deflating diffidence.

'Biddy,' said I, 'I made a remark respecting my coming down here often, to see Joe, which you received with a marked silence. Have the goodness, Biddy, to tell me why.'

'Are you quite sure, then, that you WILL come to see him often?' asked Biddy, stopping in the narrow garden walk, and looking at me under the stars with a clear and honest eye.

'Oh, dear me!' said I, as I found myself compelled to give up Biddy in despair. 'This really is a very bad side of human nature! Don't say any more, if you please, Biddy. This shocks me very much.' (XXXV) (p. 270)

A less experienced theatrical artist might have complicated his description of Mrs. Gargery's funeral by the counterpoint of Pip's pretentiousness and a richer effect might have been gained, in the sense that Mozart's orchestral writing in *Idomeneo* is richer than his orchestral writing in *The Magic Flute*. But as we hear the orchestral detail with an incomparably greater clarity and more powerful effect in *The Magic Flute*, so we hear the separate points of Dickens's maturest theatrical art more clearly because of his skilful economy.

Pip, as a character who behaves in a particular way and sees and feels things in a particular way, appears on the stage of the Dickens theatre only intermittently. Often his place is taken by someone only conventionally called Pip, who functions as a decent, neutral audience for the performances of other characters. Often Dickens, the theatrical artist himself, appears on stage in person to give a full-fledged Dickensian rendition of some event, some character, which is connected with Pip only in the sense that it is Pip's physical point of view from which we are looking at what happens. Dickens shuttles freely between these three modes and takes us with him easily, every time. Sometimes his choice of mode for a particular scene might seem puzzling, if we thought about it, because it lessens the intensity of the scene, or fails to capitalize on a comic opportunity. But the skilful strategies of the theatrical virtuoso are usually trustworthy.

'Pip the Snob' appears mostly when Pip is dealing with people associated with his past and with the forge; this is the whole point about his snobbishness, of course. And we are never surprised to find him being merely an audience for Mr. Jaggers or Mr. Wemmick in the city. But when Mr. Wopsle comes to town, and calls himself in his new role as actor to the attention of Pip in his new role as young gentleman, we might expect a comic duet between these two pretenders. Instead, Dickens chooses to let Mr. Wopsle give a solo performance, to cast Pip in the role of discreet, decent, and kind observer, and to render the performance of *Hamlet* in his own loud and brilliant professional manner. These seem sound and intelligent professional choices, but another similar instance is perhaps less successful. When Joe comes to town and is, as Pip's voice tells us, made uncomfortable and awkward by Pip's city manners, these manners are not themselves rendered concretely but only asserted. We actually see and hear very little to criticize in Pip's behaviour, since our attention is fully occupied by Joe and his hat. That this should be so, that we should not be allowed really to experience Pip's 'betrayal' of Joe at this moment, is understandable in view of the nature of theatrical art and is not felt to be a weakness in the scene. But it is at such moments that one realizes that, judged by the standards of non-theatrical art, Dickens's achievement is of a very special kind. Consider how intensely painful the scene would be if Pip's snobbishness were concretely rendered, how deep the shame that could have been communicated to us by setting out the scene dramatically; and then how mild, in comparison, the emotions are in the scene as it is, how easy, how familiar, how undisturbing the shame actually expressed.

The truth is that there is no very great dramatic pressure in the entire rendering of Pip's betrayal of Joe through snobbery, his realization of that snobbery and his penitence. Yet this is the explicitly stated moral burden of the whole novel. *Great Expectations* is a novel in which the official meaning is not rendered from the inside and is not present before us continuously in a dramatic illusion of reality: it is merely one of the many routines out of which the novel is

constructed and is really on a par in that respect with the
description of Mrs. Gargery's funeral and Mr. Wopsle's *Hamlet*.
It is a performance, an impersonation, a mimicking of moral
self-discovery to which the natural theatrical response is one
of pleasure in the tact and delicacy of tone with which the
whole enterprise is carried out. I do not mean to suggest that
one observes and assesses the performance callously, without
being moved by the sentiments which are given so refined a
theatrical embodiment. As Dr. Johnson said of Gray's 'Elegy',
that it voiced sentiments to which every bosom returned an
echo, so we can acknowledge and share the explicit emotional
and moral 'meaning' of *Great Expectations*, while at the same
time recognizing that our mode of response to these humane
and familiar sentiments is a theatrical one.

Consider the frame of mind with which we contemplate
Pip's feelings towards the end of his moral progress:

What remained for me now, but to follow him to the dear old
forge, and there to have out my disclosure to him, and my penitent
remonstrance with him, and there to relieve my mind and heart
of that reserved Secondly, which had begun as a vague something
lingering in my thoughts, and had formed into a settled purpose?

The purpose was, that I would go to Biddy, that I would show
her how humbled and repentant I came back, that I would tell her
how I had lost all I once hoped for, that I would remind her of our
old confidences in my first unhappy time. Then, I would say to her,
'Biddy, I think you once liked me very well, when my errant heart,
even while it strayed away from you, was quieter and better with
you than it ever has been since. If you can like me only half as well
once more, if you can take me with all my faults and disappoint-
ments on my head, if you can receive me like a forgiven child (and
indeed I am as sorry, Biddy, and have as much need of a hushing
voice and a soothing hand), I hope I am a little worthier of you
than I was—not much, but a little. And, Biddy, it shall rest with
you to say whether I shall work at the forge with Joe, or whether
I shall try for any different occupation down in this country, or
whether we shall go away to a distant place where an opportunity
awaits me which I set aside when it was offered, until I knew your
answer. And now, dear Biddy, if you can tell me that you will go
through the world with me, you will surely make it a better world
for me, and me a better man for it, and I will try hard to make it a
better world for you.'

Such was my purpose. After three days more of recovery, I went down to the old place, to put it in execution. And how I sped in it, is all I have left to tell. (LVII) (pp. 447–8)

Here again, stopping to think would undermine serious belief in Pip's change of heart, in his relationship to Biddy, and in the actuality and significance of this whole mode of representing Pip's inner life. What keeps us from stopping to think is the explicit theatrical intention and the thoroughly traditional perspective of the narrator: every detail in the prose is contrived to notify us that Pip is in a familiar theatrical condition —he is riding for a fall. The soft, cozy tone in 'the dear old forge' and 'my penitent remonstrance'; the plangent rhythms of the speech—the aria—which Pip is rehearsing, with its fluent pieties about an 'errant heart' and the hope of 'a better world' and a 'better man'—all this mimics 'repentance come too late' so loudly and distinctly, but also so easily and with such familiar public sentiment, that any serious inspection of the repentance and the hope would be an act of disobedience, a denial of the theatrical artist's voice.

Dickens's loudest cue of all towards our proper response is his first: the 'rhetorical' question with which the passage begins. With this device, Dickens asks for and receives our collaboration with his theatrical purpose, which is to make us know what is going to happen so that we can take the right attitude towards it: sad and affectionate recognition of a familiar pattern. The tone of the passage is quiet, but our response to 'What remained for me now'? is the distinct realization that something quite different from his expectations is in store for Pip. The effect of the rhetoric is to keep us, with the narrator, at a considerable distance from any kind of dramatic engagement in these, Pip's last great expectations. The expectations are, to be sure, *particularized*—Pip hopes to marry Biddy. But I need hardly at this juncture emphasize that the reader does not and cannot take Pip seriously as he reads about these hopes, because he completely lacks the dramatic wherewithal to do so. Judged by the standards of non-theatrical art, this passage would be one of the most disastrous failures of actualization in the history of the novel; for it is literally inconceivable to us that Pip should think of

marrying Biddy, with whom he has not the slightest hint of
the appropriate relationship, and seriously to believe that he
is hoping for and expecting this inconceivability would be to
think of him as virtually insane. No reader has ever made this
mistake. One can perhaps imagine a reader who might at this
point have 'had enough' and who would then reject the passage
as overdone; but if he had had enough, he would also know
exactly what he had been having and what was now being
offered. Pip's purpose to marry Biddy stands for a certain kind
of hope: he has given up for ever the hope of getting what he
really wanted, and now is trying to get back what he could
have had before. We know in advance that this too will be
unavailable and we know it so well that it would never occur
to us to attempt to go through the experience *with* him.

It is because what is true about Pip's thoughts and feelings
in this passage is true about them throughout the novel, that
I have called Dickens's entire rendering of Pip's career and of
its moralization a theatrical one. If it moves us deeply, if its
traditional pattern, perspective, and moral realizations escape
the charge of sentimentality, that happens because they are
being performed in the Dickens theatre, where a certain
easiness of pathos and a traditional and commonplace wisdom
about life are appropriate. The lack of dramatic depth is
acceptable because the centre of our attention is once again,
as in all Dickens's performances, first the great virtuoso
himself, and then the tact, the delicacy of touch, the clarity
and sweetness of tone with which he is performing his set-
piece of traditional moral self-discovery. A comparison with
Gray's 'Elegy' or Pope's *Pastorals* is again in order. To those
who would complain at the familiarity of the images, the lack
of inward imagination in these poems, the impossibility of
dramatic engagement with their moral meanings, the answer
would be to call attention to the perfection of the poet's tone,
which creates in itself the theatrical circumstances in which
these poets perform, with superb resources and with the most
highly refined taste and tact—which are after all moral
characteristics of high value—their familiar material. That
something of the equivalent taste and tact is visible in *Great
Expectations* I am taking for granted.

.   .   .   .   .   .

But the theatrical story and the theatrical meaning which make up the surface of *Great Expectations* is not the whole story nor the whole meaning of this curiously resonant novel. The surface is performed with a fine consistency and it has been found not only satisfactory but beautiful by most readers. Here, for instance, is an account of what is important about *Great Expectations* in the words of a highly competent reader:

> Yet at the heart of *Great Expectations* are all those obvious sorts of greatness which embarrass the modern critic—convincing and often profound characterization, a moving and exciting story, and a world observed with both literal and moral fidelity. More particularly, a boy is corrupted by great expectations into becoming an ungrateful snob, but is eventually saved by his love for the convict who had been his unknown patron. There needs no explicator to tell us what is primarily great about Miss Havisham and her decaying house, or about so explicit a scene as Pip's coldly unknowing reception of the returned Magwitch, cold until 'I saw with amazement that his eyes were full of tears'. Tears such as Magwitch weeps leave us moved and shamed.[1]

This is the way Mr. Christopher Ricks begins an essay in which he examines Dickens's successes and failures in getting Pip to take the right tone towards his bad behaviour and towards his salvation. To Mr. Ricks this question is important because one of the book's triumphs of art is that 'we feel so little malice toward Pip, who has behaved so badly', and I presume that most readers will accept Mr. Ricks's reading of the novel and the terms in which he praises it. Yet I would argue, on the one hand, that this language takes the novel too seriously, since it fails to recognize the easiness of the pathos; and on the other hand, that it doesn't take it quite seriously enough, since it really fails to get to the heart of the novel's meaning. In the passage I have just been examining, Mr. Ricks's reading would fail to account for two important facts. Granted that we are moved by Pip's disappointment at the collapse of his last great expectation; but if we compare it for a moment with our response to, say, Mr. Bulstrode's weeping at the collapse of his great expectations we may well find ourselves preferring to reserve the words 'moved and shamed' for writing of that kind.

[1] Christopher Ricks, *'Great Expectations'*, *Dickens and the Twentieth Century*, ed. John Gross and Gabriel Pearson (London, 1962), p. 199.

George Eliot's non-theatrical art achieves intensities of
dramatic engagement which, if we compare them with our
responses to Pip's career, will be in great danger of making the
latter seem, to use the ugly word frankly, sentimental. With
Mr. Bulstrode we experience pity and fear to an intense degree: we are repelled from him in painful distaste, we are
drawn towards him in painful understanding and pity: we are
moved and shamed indeed. That Mr. Ricks does not, in his
essay, risk such a comparison is but another instance of the
Dickens problem.

Mr. Ricks's reading of the novel would also fail to take care
of another fact about Pip's last disappointment. And this, I
think, is a much more understandable failure, since the novel
itself, and Dickens himself, have not really taken care of it
either. This is not the Dickens problem, therefore, but the
problem of this particular novel. I am referring to the fact
that Pip hardly responds at all to the discovery that Biddy
has already married Joe: nor does the author, nor do we the
readers. There might have been a particularly cruel irony here,
there might have been some particularly intense and painfully *shameful* resentment in Pip's response to it—there might
have been at least *something* in the way of response. But there
is really nothing.

Nor, of course, do we miss anything. In raising the possibility
of these responses I am, in the terms of theatrical art, illegitimately stopping to think when the prose itself has not asked
me to. But if we do not stop to think it is not only because
the theatrical situation is clear to us, as I have argued, but
also because Pip's response to this disappointment is entirely
consonant with everything else he does in the novel—we do
not expect him to feel resentment, nor do we expect Dickens
to point up the irony of the discovery. If we did, then, seriously
stop to think, the easy answer to our questioning would be,
'What's so surprising? Pip is like that and has always been.'
Yet this fact about Pip—that he is 'like that'—is substantially
a *secret* in the novel. We know it because we feel it, yet it almost
never comes to our consciousness, nor is it likely that it came
to Dickens's consciousness either. Yet it is the most important
fact about *Great Expectations*.

Great Expectations, I suggest, means more than Dickens's

explicit intentions achieved and therefore more than he knew. Its deepest and most interesting meanings are unconscious ones. But these unconscious meanings are successful meanings: they are genuinely created and achieved and brought to unity and harmony in a living work of art. Dickens could only 'express' these meanings whereas we can 'know' them: or rather he could express them whereas we can only know them. *Great Expectations* is the one novel by Dickens that is a deeply and organically imagined criticism of life. It is the theatrical rendering of a story which contains, deep within itself, a symbolic structure of deep imagination, in comparison with which the plots of all Dickens's other novels stand revealed as conscious structural contraptions to support consciously contrived theatrical scenes and rhetorical arguments. The plot of *Great Expectations* resembles that of Dickens's other novels by virtue of his continuing predilection for lurid conventional theatricalities: disguises, thrilling discoveries, long-lost secrets, midnight encounters, and the like. But these familiar theatrical elements are in *Great Expectations* motivated and organized from within, rather than constructed and assembled for overt theatrical or argumentative purposes. They grow into a living thing, a genuine fable, which comes to be a vision and a criticism of life, not a series of rhetorical 'points' but a harmonious and organically alive work of the imagination. Indeed, the lack of rhetorical argument in *Great Expectations* is the first evidence of its essentially organic nature.

Every reader will have observed that, though this novel touches on the law, on prison, on mechanical behaviour of all kinds—familiar Dickensian themes—it is oddly uninterested in making a rhetorical attack upon these social evils. The theatrical mode of seeing and performing this material closely resembles Dickens's methods in *Bleak House*, with the single difference that these evils are not the objects of explicit critical attack in *Great Expectations*. Wemmick will be a sufficient example. He is one of the most brilliantly rendered of Dickens's mechanical men: his 'post-office' face, his collection of 'portable property', his organized inhumanity to Jaggers's clients, and, of course, his double life—these are virtual distillations of Dickens's earlier efforts in this direction. Yet nothing is clearer than that we are never asked by the prose to want all this to be changed. I do not mean to suggest merely that we like Wemmick the way he is, because he so vividly performs his own nature—as in *Bleak House* no one would (in the theatrical context) want Mr. Vholes to be changed, because he performs his Vholes-like nature so well and with such fresh inventiveness at every moment. With Mr. Vholes we can combine this attitude quite comfortably with another attitude: that of wanting the world to be different, of wanting nobody to have to be like Mr. Vholes, of wanting Richard Carstone to be saved from the clutches of 'respectable men' like Mr. Vholes—and we take this latter attitude in easy obedience to the audibly insistent rhetoric of criticism in the theatrical artist's voice. But with Mr. Wemmick there is no such rhetoric. Nor with Mr. Jaggers, Mr. Pumblechook, Mr. Trabb, Mrs. Pocket.

The meaning of *Great Expectations* is correspondingly different from the meaning of the other mature novels. *Bleak House, Hard Times, Little Dorrit, Our Mutual Friend*—all these portray a world in which human freedom and happiness is threatened by wrong systems, wrong institutions, bad habits, bad values, bad people. And the portrait of this world becomes Dickens's rhetorical instrument for attacking these wrongs. But *Great Expectations* offers a new portrait. Dickens's new insight discovers a world in which human freedom and happiness are frustrated not by social wrongs, not by bad habits, but by the opposite, by the best and most demanding ideals of society. Pip is frustrated by people and by habits and by values which he, Dickens, and the reader all take to be good rather than bad. Moreover, the final statement of the significance of Pip's experiences articulates a moral attitude which we agree is good. Yet we feel that it is also a frustrating attitude, and the tone of the whole work confirms us in this opinion. Dickens's new insight into his world, in short, is an embodiment of Freud's theme in one of his most important works, *Civilization and its Discontents*.

I have argued that if we should stop to think about the curious emptiness of Pip's response to Biddy's marriage, it would immediately occur to us that the response is not in the least surprising, since we have known all along that Pip is like that, that something is missing in him. We have also known the identity of that something, though we may never have named it consciously. One name for it would be 'force of will', but a more accurate and illuminating word is 'libido'. We have known from the beginning of the novel that what is missing from Pip's life is any free expression of libido, and that it is missing because it is held in contempt and horror by the ideals of the civilization within which Pip tries to make a life for himself. It must have been for this reason that Dickens was drawn to the characterization, as he was earlier drawn to Arthur Clennam and was later to Eugene Wrayburn. But *Great Expectations* differs from the novels which surround it. Although Pip is, beneath the surface of the novel, known to us as 'the man without will, the man who cannot act', yet on the surface of the novel he is defined as 'the man who wanted and acted wrongly'. *Great Expectations* is the deepest of Dickens's visions of the discontents of civilization because of this unemphasized contradiction: the traditional moralization of its surface allowed Dickens unconsciously to render in the structure of his story itself that final pessimism about the possibility of human happiness which, in combination with his regretfully humorous acceptance of this condition, is his deepest criticism of life.

Who, then, is Pip? What is he like? Pip speaks of himself as being 'morally timid and very sensitive' and gives a reason for it: 'My sister's bringing up had made me sensitive'. (VIII) (p. 57) But 'within myself, I had sustained, from my babyhood, a perpetual conflict with injustice'. We hear of these things at an early point in the narrative when Estella has just humiliated Pip. His response is classic:

> I got rid of my injured feelings for the time, by kicking them into the brewery wall, and twisting them out of my hair, and then I smoothed my face with my sleeve, and came from behind the gate. The bread and meat were acceptable, and the beer was warming and tingling, and I was soon in spirits to look about me. (VIII) (p. 58)

The young animal returns to the hope of free expression of impulse by means of the bread and meat which operate directly on the animal spirits through the animal body. But it is the animal body which had been insulted before—'And what

coarse hands he has! And what thick boots!' And the meat
and bread had been given 'as insolently as if [he] were a dog in
disgrace'. (VIII) (p. 57)

Here is the hero, and now a few elementary facts about his
circumstances. His home had been 'sanctified' by a 'giant' of
a man who is emasculated by fear of his own capacity for
violence. In the first long discussion between Pip and Joe
Gargery, Joe puts this fear into significant language:

> 'And last of all, Pip—and this I want to say very serous to you,
> old chap—I see so much in my poor mother, of a woman drudging
> and slaving and breaking her honest hart and never getting no
> peace in her mortal days, that I'm dead afeerd of going wrong in
> the way of not doing what's right by a woman, and I'd fur rather
> of the two go wrong the t'other way, and be a little ill-conwenienced
> myself. I wish it was only me that got put out, Pip; I wish there
> warn't no Tickler for you, old chap; I wish I could take it all on
> myself; but this is the up-and-down-and-straight on it, Pip, and
> I hope you'll overlook shortcomings.' (VII) (p. 45)

That this is the clearest possible instance of civilization producing discontent is a point that Dickens enforces by what
follows:

> Young as I was, I believe that I dated a new admiration of Joe
> from that night. We were equals afterwards, as we had been before;
> but afterwards, at quiet times when I sat looking at Joe and
> thinking about him, I had a new sensation of feeling conscious that
> I was looking up to Joe in my heart. (VII) (ibid)

The net result of this 'new admiration' is to perpetuate the
injustice of the Tickler and at the same time to frustrate any
animal conflict with that injustice. The image of gentle Joe
sanctifies the home at the same time as it inhibits free expression of impulse; and when we read later that Pip has lost
the early vision of the forge as 'the glowing road to manhood
and independence' (XIV) (p. 100) we are in no moral perplexity
about this 'miserable' change.

Into Pip's discontent at the forge breaks the promise of
great expectations—freedom, release, money. Pip can become
a gentleman and he can win Estella. The dream here is
perfectly ambiguous: the new money will make it possible to
conquer the animal completely, the coarse hands and thick

boots, the coarse and common flesh of the blacksmith; but it is also a gift of energy and potentiality. It leads to self-subduing work (the study with Mr. Pocket which Pip undergoes so dutifully and so successfully). But Pip hopes it will also magically confer at the end a new influx of free animal energy, the possibility of free expression of libido: Pip's money will win Estella. The unapproachable Estella, however, proves to be a deeply frustrating riddle: she herself is a product of 'the old wild violent nature' of her criminal mother and father, and she can be possessed only by 'heavy' brutish Bentley Drummle, whom she hates and who beats her. Pip remains a gentlemanly friend, with whom she holds familial, affectionate, and genteel converse.

All this is doubly confirmed by the fact that the great expectations are discovered to derive from the wild and violent Magwitch who eats like a dog (III) (p. 16), makes a mechanical animal sound when moved by gentle sentiments (ibid.), is like a 'terrible beast' (XXXIX) (p. 304), and lays on Pip's shoulder a hand which 'might be stained with blood'. (XXXIX) (p. 306) Once the source of the money is discovered, Pip is instantly sure that he 'can take no further benefits from' Magwitch and this seems perfectly correct from the point of view of 'civilization'. Legally speaking, Magwitch's money is immoral money when it is in England; and it is implied that Herbert (who also finds convicts a 'degraded and vile sight') shares Pip's conviction that the money must not be used. Pip's heart softens towards Magwitch, to be sure, but not until Magwitch's appearance and manner, too, have softened; indeed, the gentle old man whom Pip loves at the end is simply not a violent wild beast but another version of gentle Joe. Pip had pleased the convict at first by his gentleness and his childish sense of honour, his decency, that is by virtue of his 'civilization'; but we know of the fear that played so important a part in this childish honour. When Magwitch returns, he is delighted that he has 'made a gentleman', and he watches Pip's style as if it were an exhibition. Pip has learned this lesson well, too, and actually has the good manners and decent refined instincts which Magwitch likes to see, and which amount to civilization. But even before Magwitch has softened, Pip's loyalty to Magwitch amounts to the

moral obligation of not betraying a man who loves him and
depends on him and who will virtually commit suicide if Pip
lets him down. Again civilization wins out, but there is blood-
fear too. The violence of the convict, the blood on his hands,
figure both as a horror and a lure. Blood and violence produce
power and satisfaction and are in fact in this story the only
means towards fruition. But violence is a deceptive lure in two
senses: the power offered is useless because it comes through
blood, and the violence itself disappears into the final gentleness of Magwitch's demeanour and behaviour before Pip, so to
speak, has a chance to face it and accept it.

Through the whole story, Pip is always called on for the
special kind of hard work that goes to make up this civilization. When Miss Havisham orders Pip to 'play' in her presence,
the irony would seem sufficiently obvious, and the ambiguity
of Pip's 'service' for Miss Havisham is in fact very richly
worked out. What he is asked to do requires difficult self-
control and deliberate application (the fascination of the house
adds to the tension, to the pressure on Pip, who must retain
his obedient good manners in this weird atmosphere), yet he is
made to feel embarrassed and clumsy in accepting the wages
for this really difficult work. With Miss Havisham, indeed,
he is always 'working'. When he discovers the facts of his
great expectations, civilization demands that he forgive Miss
Havisham rather than hate her. He manages to produce only
a mild reproach before his 'better nature' comes into evidence:
'It was a weak complaint to have made, and I had not meant
to make it.' (XLIV) (p. 341) And in the next breath he is
pleading with Miss Havisham to do the decent thing by Mr.
Matthew Pocket, and to continue his own secret financial
support of Herbert. A few chapters later, when Miss Havisham
asks him to forgive her, he is ready with the touchingly
honourable reply: 'There have been sore mistakes; and my
life has been a blind and thankless one; and I want forgiveness and direction far too much, to be bitter with you.' (XLIX)
(p. 377) Soon afterwards Pip has the 'work' of rescuing Miss
Havisham from the flames.

Here, then, is the basic fable of *Great Expectations* and the
vision of life and criticism of life which it embodies. It is the
story of a hopeful young man with a strong animal body and

powerful desires who is called on at every turn to display, in
the commonest actions of his everyday life, the ideals of the
civilization into which he was born: continual self-restraint,
self-control, forgiveness of enemies, fortitude in withstand-
ing—not heroic combat, which would be invigorating—but
boredom and frustration and insult. He is this perfect model
of moral deportment because he is 'morally timid and very
sensitive'—because he is so utterly persuaded of the validity of
these ideals that he never finds any adequate opportunity for
expressing, or even recognizing, his own interests and his own
self. Although he has within himself 'sustained . . . a perpetual
conflict with injustice', this conflict, because his civilization
never offered him a vocabulary for articulating it, was always
turned against himself. In his youth it took the form of
'kicking [his] injured feelings into the brewery-wall, and twisting them out of [his] hair'; when he grows up he inevitably
turns his frustrations against himself in the form of continual
remorse and guilt. Looking everywhere around him and in
particular at the people responsible for his continued frustrations, he can find no one to blame: but this is true only because
he is imbued with the moral obligation of understanding and
forgiving. Moreover, there is no conceivable alternative to his
sense of horror and repulsion about the one source of power
apparently available in this civilization: blood, wildness, and
violence. It never occurs to him that these horrors are really
'human', that they are in any way worthy of respect. Pip is an
obedient child of civilization; the fact that he is also a human
animal, with many and complex impulses which breed animal
needs and glamorous hopes and great expectations—this fact
leads to the melancholy, mildly humorous acceptance of the
world's insufficiency which is the novel's guiding tone and
final meaning.

We come now to investigating how the great virtuoso of
the Dickens theatre proceeded once he had accepted from his
imagination this strange and beautiful material. Although he
may not have consciously understood the implications of his
fable, nevertheless as a theatrical artist he knew and understood its structure and implemented it with every resource at
his command. He knew what elements in the fable were related
to what other elements; and he used all his old devices, but

with a new subtlety and refinement, to make these relationships clear and effective.

Let us look first at an element in the novel which is incomprehensible and unparaphraseable except in terms of the large unconscious meaning I have sketched out. Indeed, it was in trying to puzzle out the meaning of this element that I was initially led to understand what the whole novel was about. I refer to the character of Orlick, about whom a few facts will be in order.

Orlick shares with Joe Gargery, Abel Magwitch, and Bentley Drummle (and with Jaggers too) a most important characteristic: he is physically powerful, definitely larger and stronger than Pip. He is also, like Joe and Pip, a blacksmith; he lodges out on the marshes; he pursues Biddy; he insults Mrs. Gargery, fights with Joe and is beaten by him, then attacks Mrs. Gargery with a convict's leg-iron and brings her to powerless inarticulateness but also into an odd subservience to him. He goes to work for Miss Havisham and eventually ties up with Compeyson; he is seen lighting Drummle's cigar at the Blue Boar; he attacks Pip himself, on the marshes, just before the final catastrophe with Magwitch (revealing at this point that it was he who had hidden on Pip's staircase). Lastly and most important, he is the only person in the novel towards whom Pip feels hatred ('violent indignation') and the only person whom Pip deliberately decides to fight. In sum, he is connected to the forces of violence in the novel at every point. Yet nothing Orlick does could, strictly speaking, be called necessary to the action; and his final appearance, when he lures Pip down to the marshes and attacks him, must have seemed to many readers simply far-fetched.

Orlick is the single exponent of violence in the novel who is viewed without ambivalence. He is absolutely evil, absolutely brutish, and by the same token absolutely dangerous: towards him alone, therefore, can Pip behave without civilization in an instinctive act of animal violence which is simple self-preservation. But though Pip's feelings towards him are unambivalent, his function in the novel is not so simple. For though one might think that he drains off Pip's violence, the fact that he is not really involved in the action but only attached to it at many points means that nothing is effectively drained off. Pip is saved from Orlick's animal violence, by Trabb's boy and Herbert and Startop, before Pip can put his own violent indignation into action.

Indeed this whole episode is curiously self-defeating. It is the only occasion on which Pip is helped by any one in a way which he can accept (Magwitch's blood-money must be rejected), yet that he should be helped by Trabb's boy, ineffectual Herbert and Startop with his 'woman's delicacy of feature'—this has a way of suggesting a cryptic allegory and denying it at the same time; in any case the effect is a halfhearted and debilitating irony. Yet a kind of purgation is effected: after a period of delirium, Pip sleeps soundly, awakens 'strong and well', and carries out the plan with Magwitch with strength and certainty—though, significantly, he does none of the physical work, since he has burned his arm working for Miss Havisham and civilization. Of Orlick we are told only that Pip and Herbert 'relinquished all thoughts of pursuing Orlick at that time'. We hear nothing of Pip's feelings about Orlick from this point, nor of his feelings about the way in which he was saved from both Orlick's violence and the expression of his own: Pip passes immediately into a state of anxiety concerning his duty to Magwitch. Yet there might be a larger meaning in the fact that Pip awakens 'strong and well'. He has not been in any continuous company with Magwitch for several chapters, but he has been collecting information about Magwitch's past. Now, after the Orlick episode, his relationship with Magwitch is continuously gentle and sympathetic: one might feel that the battle with Orlick had indeed purged Pip's fear and horror of Magwitch. But actually Magwitch had appeared to him 'softened' before the episode with Orlick. And after Magwitch's capture and death, Pip must again sink into delirium before he is free and penitent.

The truth is that Pip has no continuing and developing relationship with Orlick, and that Orlick has only the sketchiest independent identity in the novel. Orlick is really only a name given to some actions; he is a theatrical handyman assigned certain tasks in the novel. This is acceptable in the Dickens theatre because these actions take care of feelings generated by the fable but never really engage Pip's attention. Something of the same could be said about Biddy, but even

Biddy is given a slightly more solid and independent identity. She is connected with Pip's early world, though to be sure somewhat loosely, since she is only 'Mr. Wopsle's great-aunt's granddaughter'. Her physical appearance as a child shows, it is true, no very active creative effort on Dickens's part: 'she was most noticeable, I thought, in respect to her extremities; for her hair always wanted brushing, her hands always wanted washing, and her shoes always wanted mending and pulling up at heel'. But Biddy is at least planted in the story at an early point, whereas Orlick is not brought on stage until the last minute before his services are required: he is hurriedly though acceptably fitted out with a special 'slouch' and pushed immediately into action.

The action for which Orlick is needed consists of insulting Mrs. Gargery, being beaten by Joe for doing so, and then felling Mrs. Gargery with a 'tremendous blow' from a convict's leg-iron. When these important things happen, Pip is no longer a child: he has been apprenticed to Joe and thus officially designated a man. The point is that he is grown-up enough to be independent of his sister's tyranny, and since one does not imagine her temper to have improved the simplest way of expressing this is to say that he is big and old enough to insult and even strike Mrs. Gargery himself. The odd fact is that once Pip has ceased to be a child the narrator never records any of his feelings about his sister until Orlick insults her: all Pip's dealings are with Joe. But once Orlick has acted, there is the following very interesting material:

> With my head full of George Barnwell, I was at first disposed to believe that *I* must have had some hand in the attack upon my sister, or at all events that as her near relation, popularly known to be under obligations to her, I was a more legitimate object of suspicion than any one else. But when, in the clearer light of next morning, I began to reconsider the matter and to hear it discussed around me on all sides, I took another view of the case, which was more reasonable. (XVI) (p. 112)

Then, after it is discovered that the assailant has used the convict's leg-iron:

> It was horrible to think that I had provided the weapon, however undesignedly, but I could hardly think otherwise. I suffered

unspeakable trouble while I considered and reconsidered whether
I should at last dissolve that spell of my childhood and tell Joe
all the story. . . . In addition to the dread that, having led up to
so much mischief, it would be now more likely than ever to alienate
Joe from me if he believed it, I had a further restraining dread that
he would not believe it, but would assert it with the fabulous dogs
and veal-cutlets as a monstrous invention. (xvi) (p. 114)

Later, when Mrs. Gargery's temper is found to have improved and when she repeatedly asks Orlick to appear before
her and repeatedly tries to conciliate him, with the bearing of
a 'child towards a hard master', these results are recorded
merely as surprising oddities, with no further comment about
their significance. Mrs. Gargery again disappears from our
view until her death, which is treated in the interesting way I
have discussed above.

It is hard to describe the way one understands what is going
on here without at the same time suggesting one of two wrong
possibilities: either that the understanding reader is a 'knowing'
reader, a tedious parlour-analyst, unable to keep Freud out of
his mind for a moment, or that the text is somehow inadequate
and unsuccessful. Let me suggest, in dealing with the first wrong
alternative, a way in which we definitely do *not* understand
what is happening. We do not say that it is 'really' Pip who is
feeling the rage against his sister and that Orlick is acting
it out in a kind of allegorical psychomachia. The theatrical
nature of Dickens's impersonation of Pip effectively disallows
any such analysis of his inner life, which simply does not exist
in this kind of theatrical art. Indeed, it is the frank theatricality of the whole passage which keeps us on the right track,
forbids us to attempt any irrelevant deep analysis, and yet
allows us to know the significance and the rightness of the
sequence of events and feelings here recorded. As Orlick begins
to insult Pip's sister, we feel that this is something that someone might do, something that even ought to be done: the
impulse towards this particular act of violence is something
that has been generated by the fable and is perfectly ready
to hand. Dickens tacitly supports this feeling by his description, cooly amused and utterly unsympathetic, of the process
by which 'instead of lapsing into passion, [Mrs. Gargery] consciously and deliberately took extraordinary pains to force

herself into it, and became blindly furious by regular stages'. Next, we easily get the point of Joe's dutiful defending of his wife's honour and good name, and therefore we can go along with Dickens's non-committal comic rendering of the fight and the peaceable aftermath, in which Joe and Orlick share a pot of beer from the Jolly Bargeman. After Orlick has struck Mrs. Gargery down, we are not surprised to find Pip feeling guilty, because guilt again is a feeling generated by the event itself, and also because Pip's guilt is clearly identified as 'wrong' in two ways suitable to theatrical rendering: his imagination has been inflamed by Mr. Wopsle's reading of *George Barnwell* and his sister has been struck down with the convict's leg-iron with which he thinks he has a guilty connexion. Observe that both of these theatrical 'pretexts' for Pip's false sense of guilt have an underground connexion with the general fable: Pip has been tyrannized over, not only by his sister, but by Mr. Wopsle and the convict, in relation-ship with both of whom he has had to be exactly as much an obedient little boy as with his sister. Thus we come out of this particular piece of violence with firm understanding of and sympathy with this mild-mannered young apprentice, who is constantly tyrannized over by other people's worked-up passions and persecuted by his own false guilts, against which his whole civilization forbids him to take violent action.

When we read that Mrs. Gargery's temper has been improved by the attack and that she stands in a subservient relationship to her attacker, we feel the pressure of the irony although we do not consciously define the source of it to ourselves. The prose sets out these developments in a tone of blandly curious interest in their oddity and this is beautiful and right because the significance of these developments *is* curious and odd in the sense that it is completely useless to Pip. The change in Mrs. Gargery partly shows that Joe was wrong when he apologized to Pip for not having come to Pip's aid during Mrs. Gargery's rampages. His argument was that she would only have visited her wrath more violently on Pip himself, but we see now that if he had hit her hard enough her temper would have improved. But the fact that she might also have been knocked into permanent idiocy is an adequate theatrical image of the moral impossibility of this mode of treatment;

and again we leave the scene with all our feelings taken care
of and our sense of Pip's dilemma, the dilemma of the discontents of civilization, strong and clear.

It is impossible to say how much Dickens knew of what he
was accomplishing, though this uncertainty does not disturb
us as we read. I believe that Dickens certainly shared with his
theatrical creation, Pip, the taboo against striking a woman,
particularly the woman who figures in some respects as the
mother in the fable, and he was probably quite incapable of
allowing even the thought of striking a mother to come to the
surface of his mind. One feels no condescension towards him
because of this kind of piety: it is partly historical accident
and partly a condition of his free communication with his
public in the Dickens theatre. Such pieties are still virtually
obligatory in theatrical art: remember, as the exception that
proves the rule, how W. C. Fields prided himself on being the
first actor ever to strike a child in the movies. But condescension is out of the question in view of the success with which
Dickens's theatrical resources in this passage embody a very
rich range of insight and understanding of these difficult matters
without straying from the theatrical mode or straining it.

We can now define Orlick as the embodiment of pure and
uninhibited libido. His curious lack of organic relationship to
the plot of *Great Expectations*, the arbitrariness of his actions
if judged by the standards of non-theatrical art, are in no way
disquieting because the fable demands that the free expression
of libido should be impossible and virtually inconceivable in
the civilization he is describing. Indeed, the rudimentary details
of Orlick's character and physical appearance show this too,
for Orlick's self-expression is hardly 'free': he is always forced
into a sadistic mode. Even his sexual pursuit of Biddy is a
matter of sinister shadowings and slouchings and lurkings.

Having little organic relationship to the plot, the characterization of Orlick is released for other duties; and the interconnexions between Orlick and the other characters function
as so many sign-posts to the structure. Orlick's fight with Joe
brings Joe's great strength to our consciousness just when it
is necessary that we be reminded how little possibility for
free action and expression the 'dear old forge' actually represents. Without this vivid reminder, we might miss the irony in

Dickens's continual references to the 'womanly tenderness' of Joe. Joe's association with Orlick is only one of the many devices which keep Dickens's very complicated handling of the gentle blacksmith from going wrong. For Joe is called on to be, by turns, a rather bewildering variety of things: he is very strong, he is proud, he is strong in 'self-restraint', he is weak in failing to help Pip, he is Pip's father (as we feel) yet Pip's equal and a child, he is a ridiculous fool, he is emasculated, he is capable of being a strong husband to Biddy and of fathering a child whose name happens to be Pip—he is, in short, an ideal image of pastoral civilized manliness and an utterly useless and frustrating model for any spirited young human animal. Dickens means all of these things, and he expresses them successfully in a unified image in the theatrical mode, and the number of these meanings is a concrete piece of evidence of the richness of his insight. Joe's relationship to Orlick helps.

Orlick's association with Magwitch also helps to fix and clarify the ambiguity of another important figure in Pip's landscape. The theatrical charm of Magwitch, even when we first see him, is as dangerous to Dickens's total meaning as it is important to it. Consequently, the connexion between Magwitch and Orlick is useful in fortifying our sense that Magwitch is wild, violent, bloody, murderous, coarse, and common. Orlick lives on the marshes and attacks Pip there: Magwitch is always associated with the marshes and the Hulks. Orlick frightens Pip when he is a child: 'he gave me to understand that the Devil lived in a black corner of the forge, and that he knew the fiend very well: also that it was necessary to make up the fire, once in seven years, with a live boy, and that I might consider myself fuel'. (xv) (p. 105) Magwitch had threatened Pip at the very beginning of the novel with a similar picture: 'There's a young man hid with me, in comparison with which young man I am a Angel. That young man hears the words I speak. That young man has a secret way pecooliar to himself, of getting at a boy, and at his heart, and at his liver.' (i) (pp. 3–4) And the fact that Orlick enters Compeyson's service, as Magwitch had before, diminishes very slightly the fullness of our sympathy for Magwitch as someone helplessly seduced by an evil man.

I offer the character of Orlick and the uses to which he is put as confirmation of my reading of the fable of *Great Expectations*; conversely, only by reading the fable in this way, and by understanding Dickens's theatrical procedures, can one accept Orlick at all as a successful contrivance. Judged by the standards of non-theatrical art, Orlick cannot be taken seriously as a fully-realized character in a self-developing dramatic action. But in the Dickens theatre we are accustomed to theatrical standards, to a different mode of illusion. We believe in the existence of *all* the characters and *all* the events only because they are being impersonated for us there and then by the visible and audible skill of the theatrical artist. He is appearing before us in person to tell us a story and to make us believe it. Granted that Orlick appears very late in the action and seems to have been dressed for his role rather hastily, nevertheless theatrical art allows for such things with no very important disturbance of its mode of illusion, as long as the effect is then vividly brought into theatrical being. As for what Orlick means, our recognition and acceptance of that is like the photographic positive of the negative that we can suppose took place in Dickens's mind as he wrote. He found that he needed—in order to make the story 'feel right'—certain actions and somebody to do them. We can articulate this need as Dickens, perhaps, could not have. He needed an act of violence against Pip's sister, he needed another wild and violent man against whom Pip could always feel a violent indignation: he needed to show the impossibility of any legitimate expression of libido in this civilization. He needed Orlick and the improvisation came off. At the end of the first episode with Orlick, we know and feel some important things: that the world would be a freer place if Mrs. Gargery could be knocked into submission; that it takes a thoroughly murderous and hateful man to do such a thing; that Pip could certainly never do it; that the frustrations in Pip's life are permanent and irreducible. All this comes through to us in feeling, however little of it we may consciously articulate. Our attitudes have been successfully shaped by Dickens's deeply imagined fable, however theatrically that fable has been performed.

An 'unintegrated' character like Orlick is acceptable in

Great Expectations only because of the sureness of Dickens's
touch as a theatrical artist and by no means because the whole
novel is carelessly made. On the contrary, *Great Expectations*
is for the most part very sensitively organized, though its
mode remains a theatrical one. Everyone who knows the work
is familiar with the multiplicity of interconnexions between
the various elements in the novel, particularly those between
the violent characters. The revelation of Estella's parentage,
for instance, needs no discussion, nor do any of the other
larger interconnexions. That these are often of a lurid melodramatic cast will surprise no one accustomed to the Dickens
theatre. In the other mature novels, lurid revelations are
made acceptable by the clarity of the theatrical artist's
argumentative intentions, his campaign to show the universality of the evil influence of the law, or respectability, or
false charity. But in *Great Expectations* these lurid interconnexions, by virtue of the deep movements of the basic
fable, come to the reader's attention with something like
the sudden mysterious but natural rightness of revelations
in a dream. Esther Summerson, in *Bleak House*, is connected
with Lady Dedlock and with Jarndyce and Jarndyce by
heavy-duty theatrical cabling in comparison with which
some of the interconnexions in *Great Expectations* seem like
the sinuous tendrils of a growing vine.

There is, to be sure, plenty of sturdy melodrama mixed in:
'What *was* it that was borne in upon my mind when she stood
still and looked attentively at me? . . . What *was* it?' (xxix)
(p. 224) Or 'What *was* the nameless shadow which again in
that one instant had passed?' (xxxii) (p. 250) But what of the
following?

> 'Do you know what I touch here?' [Miss Havisham] said, laying
> her hands, one upon the other, on her left side.
> 'Yes, ma'am.' (It made me think of the young man.)
> 'What do I touch?'
> 'Your heart.'
> 'Broken!' (viii) (p. 53)

Dickens has his plot well in hand: Magwitch did in fact have
with him on the marshes a young man, Compeyson, who was
Miss Havisham's young man who broke her heart, and Pip

has seen this young man and felt his heart 'shoot'. Dickens
could produce this little stroke later as evidence that he
played fair in his theatrical mystifications. But the truthfulness of the detail is much more sensitive and natural than
this plot meaning, and derives from the emotional undercurrents
of the fable itself, of which though the story may have been
all that Dickens knew it was certainly not all that he expressed.

An exceptionally delicate move in Dickens's theatrical
strategy is made in the description of Joe's fight with Orlick:
'But, if any man in that neighbourhood could stand up long
against Joe, I never saw the man. Orlick, as if he had been
of no more account than the pale young gentleman, was very
soon among the coal-dust, and in no hurry to come out of it.'
(xv) (p. 108). One fight reminds Pip of another he has chronicled before—the connexion says no more than this. But in
leading our thoughts momentarily to the pale young gentleman,
Herbert Pocket, Dickens reminds us of the difference between
Pip's attitude towards violence and Herbert's. Pip fights with
Herbert during his second visit to Miss Havisham. Estella,
who remarked scornfully about Pip's coarse hands and thick
boots during his first visit, now will not even condescend to
speak to him, but takes him down into the yard and feeds
him 'in the former dog-like manner'. As he wanders about he
meets the 'pale young gentleman'. Their fight is described
with overtly amusing intention and both Dickens and Pip
are perfectly non-committal about its meaning: the episode
remains in the reader's mind as charming and funny, but it
has done its thematic work efficiently all the same.

Herbert is a 'gentleman' and he fights like a gentleman.
He is 'at once light-hearted, business-like and bloodthirsty';
he sponges himself with a 'great show of dexterity' and
inspires Pip 'with great respect' as he plays the game 'with
the greatest satisfaction in seconding himself according to
form'. Pip, morally timid and very sensitive, is both frightened
by this violence and 'respectful' of the gentlemanly style—this
is the quintessential expression of his dilemma; but the most
important feeling, not surprisingly, is shame over his own
victory: 'He seemed so brave and innocent, that although I
had not proposed the contest, I felt but a gloomy satisfaction
in my victory. Indeed, I go so far as to hope that I regarded

myself, while dressing, as a species of savage young wolf or other wild beast.' (xi) (pp. 85–86) When Estella lets him out at the gate, 'there was a bright flush upon her face, as though something had happened to delight her', and she lets Pip kiss her. We know she has been watching the fight, but Pip does not; yet even if he did know, we feel, his response would be the same: 'I kissed her cheek as she turned it to me. I think I would have gone through a great deal to kiss her cheek. But, I felt that the kiss was given to the coarse common boy as a piece of money might have been, and that it was worth nothing.' (xi) (p. 86) The only feeling that remains for Pip from the whole episode is shame and guilt and fear: 'I felt that the pale young gentleman's blood was on my head, and that the Law would avenge it.' (xii) (p. 87)

The general tone of the scene is cheerful and amused, with plenty of comic hyperbole. Yet Pip's melancholy dilemma is at the same time clear. There is power in the coarse hands and thick boots, and that power is recognized and rewarded by the beautiful Estella; but it is she who has scorned the source of the power and Pip is already so committed to self-restraint that any expression of that power, except in pure self-defence, is taboo.

Herbert Pocket's later career continues the implications of this first appearance. The logic of events proposes him as an image of the good life and Pip feels respect for him at the end of the novel. But in various ways Herbert cannot serve adequately in this role and we feel Pip to be underselling himself and his own expectations when he honours as his better the pale young gentleman whom he so easily defeated. When we first see Herbert as a grown man he is described in a way which relates back to his style in the fight:

There was something wonderfully hopeful about his general air, and something that at the same time whispered to me he would never be very successful or rich. . . . He was still a pale young gentleman, and had a certain conquered languor about him in the midst of his spirits and briskness, that did not seem indicative of natural strength. (xxii) (p. 167)

This delicate and kind image of Herbert's lack of vital impulse remains in force with the reader even when it is apparently being denied, at the very end of the novel:

Many a year went round, before I was a partner in the House; but I lived happily with Herbert and his wife, and lived frugally, and paid my debts, and maintained a constant correspondence with Biddy and Joe. It was not until I became third in the Firm, that Clarriker betrayed me to Herbert; but, he then declared that the secret of Herbert's partnership had been long enough upon his conscience, and he must tell it. So, he told it, and Herbert was as much moved as amazed, and the dear fellow and I were not the worse friends for the long concealment. I must not leave it to be supposed that we were ever a great House, or that we made mints of money. We were not in a grand way of business, but we had a good name, and worked for our profits, and did very well. We owed so much to Herbert's ever cheerful industry and readiness, that I often wondered how I had conceived that old idea of his inaptitude, until I was one day enlightened by the reflection, that perhaps the inaptitude had never been in him at all, but had been in me. (LVIII) (pp. 455–6)

Herbert's physical and spiritual identity, the quality of his happiness, the regularity of his industry and its appropriate reward, the self-deprecating decency with which Pip admires him and takes a willing second place to him—all this serves to define the world of the novel, the civilization of which Pip has experienced so poignantly the discontents and to which he is now making a modest and melancholy adjustment. Herbert does not cut very deeply into life's possibilities. He is surely Dickens's most sympathetic mechanical man, but he remains a mechanical man for all that; and his honest and hopeful industry and courtesy are firmly—though unargumentatively—associated with his pallor and his conquered languor. Herbert's lack of vital impulse is, indeed, reminiscent of Bitzer's in *Hard Times*, but it is not produced as evidence for any case against System: we know it only by the dimension, the scale of our interest in and respect for Herbert's world. Herbert's life is a good life, but it takes place in a small pale world; his 'ever cheerful industry and readiness' justifies respect without commanding any very positive admiration; it is understandable, and right, for Pip to adjust to this world, but it would be wrong for him to do so with any more enthusiasm than he in fact shows.

It is the tone of Pip's acceptance of Herbert's world as the right one that enables the reader to pay an equal attention to Pip's explicit moralizing of his experience and to the novel's deeper theme. 'I must not leave it to be supposed that we were ever a great House, or that we made mints of money': the mild, rueful, rather tired voice joins with us in the comfortable sort of *contemptus mundi* suitable to the popular theatre. In this paragraph Dickens goes out of his way to avoid the irony for which he has nevertheless provided the materials. Whether or not Herbert would still be 'looking about', had it not been for Pip's secret generosity, whether his industry would have anything to work with—these questions seem simply not to interest Pip. There is nothing sly in the rhetoric; we are not even invited to make the ironic point for ourselves. But the materials are there and the fact that they are not exploited figures as an unemphatic expression of Pip's weariness. Likewise, Pip's dutiful repudiation of his earlier (and, we feel, considerably more accurate) reading of Herbert's nature comes to us with a qualification, in the word 'perhaps', which certainly does not direct us to entertain any ironic suspicion of what Pip is doing. The word reflects Pip's modest and mature mildness, which no longer needs or wants confident certainties. But the word also points up Pip's, and Dickens's, avoidance of any strenuous Victorian imperatives about work and duty. We are not bullied out of our slightly different view of the matter. Pip calls attention to abilities and habits and values which we believe Herbert to have and which we believe to be good. Nothing is forced: Dickens does not claim for Herbert anything like power, or beauty, or high spirits. But we know that Pip has at least thought himself to be in hopeful contact with power and beauty, and we know him to have—somewhere inside him, in his physical body alone perhaps—a deeper, stronger, animal nature, a richer capacity for intense experience, than Herbert. So, as we listen to Pip tell us what he has learned through suffering— that the old way of life was the best and that he was wrong to have given it up for the hope of great expectations—we assent to all this as plausible and see that it makes his life possible; but we know—we hear in the tone of all the last pages—that something is missing, something is unrealized, some force in Pip has remained untapped.

11

OUR MUTUAL FRIEND

The disappearance of overt social criticism in *Great Expectations*, which allowed Dickens access to his deepest vision of the discontents of Victorian civilization, proved to be temporary. In *Our Mutual Friend*, the last finished novel, Dickens returned to the purposes and to the structural methods of *Little Dorrit*.

Both works are built on the same large scale, both interweave several lines of action into what explicitly offers itself as indictment of an over-systematized and corrupted society, both are dominated by large guiding symbols, and both are insistently serious works in the sense that they are continuously informed by Dickens's consciousness of the difficulty of moral choice in a corrupted world. And in neither work does this serious and difficult material prove completely congenial to Dickens's habitual artistic methods. There is, however, one important distinction to be made. Since in *Little Dorrit* the inappropriateness of Dickens's theatrical methods produced jarring discords, it might seem an admirable development that *Our Mutual Friend* is not marred by such outright miscalculations. But the studied consistency of texture, the restraint of verbal devices, the patient concern for continuity of plausible action which characterize some sections of *Our Mutual Friend* prove to be achievements of taste which have been gained at the expense of inventiveness and creative vitality. Or that may mean simply that Dickens's enormous energy was at last beginning to fail.

The opening chapter of *Our Mutual Friend* sets up a familiar theatrical situation: the virtuoso is beginning one of his large-scale works in a familiar way, by evoking a suspenseful mysteriousness in an exotic setting. But the performance seems, in the inevitable comparison with earlier performances, remarkably quiet. We hear nothing as insistently brilliant as the copious verbal configurations of the opening of *Little Dorrit* or the touching and grotesque details of the opening of *Great Expectations*. Yet we do encounter familar rhetorical structures:

In these times of ours, though concerning the exact year there is no need to be precise, a boat of dirty and disreputable appearance, with two figures in it, floated on the Thames, between Southwark Bridge which is of iron, and London Bridge which is of stone, as an autumn evening was closing in.

The figures in this boat were those of a strong man with ragged grizzled hair and a sun-browned face, and a dark girl of nineteen or twenty, sufficiently like him to be recognisable as his daughter. The girl rowed, pulling a pair of sculls very easily; the man, with the rudder-lines slack in his hands, and his hands loose in his waistband, kept an eager look-out. He had no net, hook, or line, and he could not be a fisherman; his boat had no cushion for a sitter, no paint, no inscription, no appliance beyond a rusty boat-hook and a coil of rope, and he could not be a waterman; his boat was too crazy and too small to take in a cargo for delivery, and he could not be a lighterman or river-carrier; there was no clue to what he looked for, but he looked for something, with a most intent and searching gaze. The tide, which had turned an hour before, was running down, and his eyes watched every little race and eddy in its broad sweep, as the boat made slight headway against it, or drove stern foremost before it, according as he directed his daughter by a movement of his head. She watched his face as earnestly as she watched the river. But, in the intensity of her look there was a touch of dread and horror. (I. i) (pp. 1–2)

This list of speculations about the boat and its purpose is a piece of theatrical strategy which could have been written by no one but Charles Dickens, yet Gissing could not have objected in this instance that Dickens, the delighted spectator, has interposed his pleasure, his invention, his wit between us and the scene. Similarly, as we note in the last sentence of the paragraph the economy of the narrative exposition, and the quietness of the cadence, we are aware that this is not quite the 'loud and distinct' effectiveness of the familiar Dickensian style: there is a restraint here, new to the Dickens theatre.

The question is whether restraint is an advantage to a style which has remained theatrical, and for me the answer is that it is not. It is almost as if Dickens had become respectable, for what tastefulness in the theatrical style yields is sadly like the genteel finish of academic landscape and genre painting, sadly changed from the free and natural idiom of *Great Expectations*, which can be equally quiet and equally economical: 'The marshes were just a long black horizontal line, then, as I stopped to look after him; and the river was just another horizontal line, not nearly so broad nor yet so black; and the sky was just a row of long angry red lines and dense black lines intermixed.' (I) (p. 4) Nothing in *Our Mutual Friend* shows the vitality or power of this boldly simplified expressionistic landscape. Instead we find, later in the first chapter, this sort of thing:

But, it happened now, that a slant of light from the setting sun glanced into the bottom of the boat, and, touching a rotten stain there which bore some resemblance to the outline of a muffled human form, coloured it as though with diluted blood. This caught the girl's eye, and she shivered. (I) (p. 2)

The intention is to make our flesh creep and also to write with quiet good manners: it is not a happy combination, since it produces little evocative energy, and more than a little vagueness. The whole chapter sets its mysterious scene before us with nothing more interesting than such tasteful competence.

Tasteful competence is also the most that can be claimed for the important and much admired line of action which is initiated in this first chapter: the salvation of Eugene Wrayburn through the love of Lizzie Hexam. Here is faint praise indeed, and I will readily agree that certain elements in this line of action are worthy of more. Wrayburn's bored carelessness is rendered with real, and for Dickens with surprising, finesse. In his engagingly spirited and good-tempered mockery of himself, of his background, of his profession and its prospects, one hears the very accents of an intelligence and energy which has nowhere to go, no worthy object to fix on. The repeated interchanges between Wrayburn and Lightwood are recognizable as set pieces without losing their plausibility as conversations between sophisticated young men. Though Wrayburn and Lightwood use the same idiom, a fine distinction between them is drawn: Wrayburn clearly has a greater capacity for passion and moral seriousness. We believe that he is capable of being saved, and that salvation must and can come through the river and through Lizzie Hexam—this is one of Dickens's most imaginative symbolic inventions. But Dickens's rendering of the river and of Lizzie Hexam herself fails to capitalize on the potentialities of these symbols, and the salvation of Eugene Wrayburn turns out to be a tastefully managed diagram of symbolic intention rather than the fully realized and powerful symbolic action it could have been and probably set out to be. Sympathetic critics, however, have credited it with being entirely successful.

The circumstances that bring Eugene Wrayburn to the river, his first impression of the river life, his attraction to Lizzie Hexam and the growing depth and seriousness of his interest in her, the complications caused by Bradley Headstone—this structure of action and attitude makes up the scenario of symbolic action. The meanings suggested by the scenario are extremely interesting ones. Eugene Wrayburn is capable of a life of deep feeling and purpose, and we see too that through his profession, the law, he retains a significant connexion with the fundamentals of life and death, mercy and justice. But the connexion is all but vestigial. As the novel opens, the most that Wrayburn seems to have to hope for is a sterile stewardship, arranging in a seemly ritual the money relationships of the upper classes. He cannot take this prospect seriously, nor can he feel anything but scorn for the 'social contract' of marriage towards which his 'respected father' is pushing him. Accordingly, his energy goes into a witty satire of his class and its idols. Then, in a casual accident which yet has a significant relationship to his professional skills, he is brought to the river and to the life of the people who work on it and with it; he finds his salvation, and his life, in encountering the dangers of the river, in almost losing his life in the river, and in being rescued by Lizzie Hexam, one of the river-people.

The river, therefore, stands for what the upper classes of London have lost significant contact with: emotional and physical vitality, natural rhythms, physical labour and its attendant skills and strengths, seriousness of ambition and purpose, meaningful knowledge of death and therefore of life.

But the river represents these values in a highly ambiguous way; hence its value as a symbol. The river-people have been both brutalized and corrupted by the upper classes, who have systematically exploited the river and its people and then turned their backs on the results. The river is befouled by the wastes of commerce on which the civilization of the upper classes depends, yet the upper classes assume no responsibility for the moral corruption of people condemned to work in these sewers. Eugene Wrayburn's capacity for life, his hunger for deep feeling and purpose, makes him accessible to what is valuable in the river and its people, makes him fall in love with Lizzie Hexam; but to win her he must not only fully share his life with her, that is, marry her, but he must encounter and pass through the violence and brutality and corruption of the river-life. The vision expressed by this symbolic scenario amounts to social prophecy: the condition of England can be saved only by a new and deep amalgamation of the classes. This will be no easy matter, Dickens's symbolic structure suggests, for what the upper classes must 'marry' is no pastoral version of the unspoiled simplicity and closeness to nature of the lower classes, but the foul and brutalized result of their own exploitation.

Now it seems to me unquestionable that this is what the river in *Our Mutual Friend* was meant to stand for. If one can thus know what the symbol means, then that meaning has been at least in some measure expressed. And so it has, of course. Yet at many significant junctures in this novel, we are conscious rather of what the expression could and should have been than of what it triumphantly is. Take Bradley Headstone, for instance. That Eugene Wrayburn, pursuing with aristocratic carelessness the beautiful Lizzie Hexam, should find himself rivalled by this solemnly self-educated, morose, and furious schoolmaster; that he should, in his love of the girl who seems to him unequivocally beautiful, healthy, and good, find himself involved with this man to the point of being in actual danger of physical violence from his twisted nature; that he should have to face this without allowing it to damage his image of Lizzie Hexam—here surely is a remarkably stern and perceptive symbolic account of what the regeneration of the upper classes may cost. But these meanings are only hinted at, if the sad truth is not that they must be quite independently—and therefore illegitimately— manufactured by the reader himself. For the relationship between Wrayburn and Headstone rarely comes to real expression. In Chapter VI of Book IV, for instance, it is in the midst of Wrayburn's rather formal inner debate with himself about his future course of action with Lizzie Hexam that Headstone strikes. We know, from several obvious hints, that Headstone is near; but nothing in Wrayburn's inner debate makes a significant connexion with Headstone. His sinister presence then produces only a melodramatic tension. When the violence does come, this is how it is described:

He had sauntered far enough. Before turning to retrace his steps, he stopped upon the margin, to look down at the reflected night. In an instant, with a dreadful crash, the reflected night turned crooked, flames shot jaggedly across the air, and the moon and the stars came bursting from the sky.

Was he struck by lightning? With some incoherent half-formed thought to that effect, he turned under the blows that were blinding him and mashing his life, and closed with a murderer, whom he caught by a red neckerchief—unless the raining down of his own blood gave it that hue.

Eugene was light, active, and expert; but his arms were broken, or he was paralysed, and could do no more than hang on to the man, with his head swung back, so that he could see nothing but the heaving sky. After dragging at the assailant, he fell on the bank with him, and then there was another great crash, and then a splash, and all was done. (IV. vi) (p. 698)

This is all, and not only is it not enough—it is really nothing. Again one hears an inept combination of the old impulse to make a thrilling effect and the new impulse to write with economy and restraint: the impulses naturally cancel each other out. No detail of Wrayburn's actions or feelings has the least symbolic or thematic significance. His act of looking at the reflected night in the water, his 'half-formed thought' that he has been struck by lightning, these create a merely local effect and surely not an impressive one. Yet the event is a crucial one in Wrayburn's salvation by Lizzie Hexam, and the truth is that whatever meaning we can derive from it is strictly our own work.

The same thing is true of the whole chapter. The setting is a pure and peaceful rural stretch of the river, near a little country village: this ought to mean something about what Lizzie represents to Eugene, and probably was intended to, but that meaning is not rendered. Actually the scene takes place in this setting because Lizzie has been forced here to avoid Wrayburn's advances—a plausible motive which only confuses the main lines of the symbolic action. Moreover, so feeble is Dickens's grasp on his symbolic action at this point that after an adequate opening paragraph establishing the peace and plenty of the scene by the river he takes time out for a humorous account of village amusements: dogs, fiddlers, and a little Fair. This is a mild version of a familiar Dickensian routine which is given a familar point by some satire against some of Dickens's oldest enemies, those puritans who close the museums on Sunday:

All this was a vicious spectacle, as any poor idea of amusement on the part of the rougher hewers of wood and drawers of water in this land of England ever is and shall be. They *must not* vary the rheumatism with amusement. They may vary it with fever and ague, or with as many rheumatic variations as they have joints; but positively not with entertainment after their own manner. (IV. vi) (p. 690)

The satire has no clear relationship to the symbolic action which is the main concern of the chapter.

Even the dialogue between Lizzie Hexam and Wrayburn in this scene does not activate the symbolic implications of the river. Dickens's rendering of Lizzie Hexam, in fact, is weak throughout the novel. It is true that we learn what the river means most tellingly from some of the things that Lizzie Hexam does, but these meanings are reduced to the most conventional terms by what Dickens has decided she should *be*. It is in her actions primarily that we see that the story of Eugene Wrayburn's salvation is not a piece of social realism, a study of the problem of the aristocrat who falls in love with a girl from the lower classes. The story of Eugene Wrayburn is social vision, not social realism; its purpose is not a study of Eugene's difficulties but a vision of his needs. The heart of this symbolic action is the fact that

Lizzie Hexam rescues Wrayburn from death by virtue of the
skills she has learned on the river, which she could not have
learned amid the sterile refinements of upper classes' life. She
represents what the upper classes need: vitality, fullness of
physical life, the vital skills of work, the capacity for full
experiencing of life and death in fundamental terms—from
these implications, in turn, we learn what the river means.
Correspondingly, when we see that it is in pursuing her that
Eugene Wrayburn finds his first purpose in life we understand
that this vital sense of purpose has communicated itself to
him. In terms of social realism we would observe only that
Wrayburn has fallen in love with an attractive girl who
happens to be from a different class.

Now, granted that this scenario of a symbolic action is a
work of prophetic vision, the trouble is that the theatre in
which it was staged was the Dickens theatre. Dickens's
theatrical habits led him to his familiar method of expressing
his meanings *serially*, as strong and effective single points.
When he came to Lizzie Hexam, Dickens had already seen
her manipulating the boat: this was the basis of the vision,
no doubt. Accordingly the descriptions of her 'lithe' movements with the oars, while surely less powerful than such
things would have been earlier in Dickens's career, nevertheless serve successfully to embody the positive physical and
emotional resources with which Eugene Wrayburn has
lost real contact. Beyond this one point, however, there
is a great falling off. Lizzie's familial piety, her loyalty to
Jenny Wren, her earnestness in arguing against Wrayburn's
seductive pursuit—these are right feelings and attitudes, but
their rendering is seriously cramped by Dickens's commitment
to a negative point about Lizzie Hexam which he initiates
in the first chapter by describing the 'dread or horror' in the
'intensity of her look'. Dickens has chosen to isolate this
child of the river from any taint of the brutality, the violence,
the corruption to which nature has been perverted by class
exploitation. Gaffer Hexam's trade of robbing dead bodies
in the Thames is a luridly effective image of the moral degradation of the lower classes which serves well enough for its
local purpose, but it has all the customary inflexibility of
Dickens's theatrical effects. One understands why he felt it

necessary to separate unequivocally this image and that of Lizzie Hexam, and to characterize her by speech, manner, and feelings which show that she has not been corrupted by her father's trade. Apart from the lithe action of rowing the boat, Lizzie Hexam's identity in the first chapter and throughout the novel is an image of conventional womanly modesty and gentleness, refined in speech, unwavering in her practice of the familiar Victorian virtues. One's objection is not to these admirable virtues, but to the way they work against the rendering of Lizzie's vitality and passion. As in *Little Dorrit*, we are asked to believe that salvation can come through conventionally approved moral behaviour and we cannot believe it.

Dickens's vision of Lizzie Hexam's vitality was probably inhibited by his old need to keep the good woman free from any taint of egotistic wilfulness, from any hint of aggressive sexual passion. His mimicry, as usual, proceeds for the most part in negative terms. There are some hesitant moves towards a positive identification of Lizzie's vitality: when Eugene Wrayburn spies on her through the window in Book I, Chapter XIII, he looks 'long and steadily' at 'a deep rich piece of colour, with the brown flush of her cheek and the shining lustre of her hair, though sad and solitary, weeping by the rising and the falling of the fire'. This is reminiscent of the first image of Sissy Jupe in *Hard Times* and the same failure to capitalize on the 'lustre' occurs in both books. Dickens's reticence in such matters makes him render Wrayburn's interest in Lizzie from this point on in completely abstract terms—her 'beauty' is mentioned rather than expressed, Wrayburn is touched by her spiritual qualities only and by her evident love for him; and in the climactic scene by the river she repeatedly gives Wrayburn 'earnest, supplicating looks', and speaks with the noble pleading rhetoric of the lady-like stage heroine.

'Think of me, as belonging to another station, and quite cut off from you in honour. Remember that I have no protector near me, unless I have one in your noble heart. Respect my good name. If you feel towards me, in one particular, as you might if I was a lady, give me the full claims of a lady upon your generous behaviour. I am removed from you and your family by being a working girl.

How true a gentleman to be as considerate of me as if I was removed by being a Queen!' (iv. vi) (p. 693)

This is dreary stuff by any standard and for Lizzie Hexam
it is dreary in a particularly wrong way. These genteel accents
contradict the image of Lizzie's litheness at the oars. There
can be no significant salvation for Wrayburn through the love
of a girl who talks like this.

The passion that Lizzie Hexam might well have expressed—
but pointedly does not express—in the scene by the river is
anger rather than 'earnest supplication'. For she belongs to a
group of characters who are like the Rouncewell family in
Bleak House in that both groups are instances of the special
device for rendering complex attitudes that Dickens substi-
tuted for the dramatization of the inner life. In the Rouncewell
family Dickens embodied with fair success a complex attitude
towards the aristocracy; the group of characters consisting
of Lizzie Hexam, Bella Wilfer, Jenny Wren, Charley Hexam,
and Bradley Headstone expresses an even more complex and
ambiguous attitude towards anger, and in particular the anger
occasioned by social injustice. The theme is a familiar one
in Dickens and this character-cluster in *Our Mutual Friend*
thus represents Dickens's last word on a theme about which,
probably more than any other, he maintained a continuing inner
debate. If it is by no means a fully successful and persuasive
last word, it is a very interesting and affecting one.

The splendour of Micawber's outburst against Uriah Heep
is justly famous. Mr. Micawber's great pun brings to a particularly exhilarating climax one of the most frequently repeated routines in the Dickens theatre: the routine in which
a villain is allowed an extraordinarily long rope for acting
himself and his villainy out, thereby working up the audience's
anticipation of his predictable downfall into an equally
extraordinary state of frustration, so that the long delayed
event comes with an almost orgasmic force. (Pecksniff's self-
recovery is merely a new twist of the same routine.) This
quasi-sexual pattern is common enough in almost all comic
art, but there is a special reason why Dickens was so good at
it and so inexhaustible in finding new ways of varying it. Anger
was surely his ruling passion, and one recognizes instinctively

that the overthrow of comic villains in his novels amounts to a uniquely spontaneous and regenerating sublimation of anger. This same spontaneity makes the angry rhetoric of *Bleak House* and *Hard Times* an act of life itself rather than an aggressive sermon, and I have argued that it is the impetuosity and fire of this rhetoric which validates the unusual simplicity of the moral and social criticism in these middle-period novels.

Complications arose in regard to organized class anger and to anger in women. Doubtless it was a quite ordinary horror of mob riots, and the whole nineteenth century's memory of the French Revolution, that was responsible for Dickens's rather unimaginative and conventional approval of the good, patient, independent workman. But the angry brickmaker in *Bleak House* is given the floor against Mrs. Pardiggle in a superb tirade which clearly has Dickens's support, although the patience of the brickmaker's wife is given a more explicitly labelled moral admiration. Dickens's fear and distrust of mob anger, moreover, derives a certain generosity and validity from his contempt for Parliamentary government and his exemption from any respectable reverence for symbols of state: the only organization he really trusted was the Dickens theatre. His official recommendation for people suffering social injustice at the hands of public institutions was always an untheoretical quietism of the domestic life, a recommendation which takes its permanent authority from his remarkable certainty about the absolute value of food and warmth. And this recommendation holds for the heroes and heroines of the novels too: Allan Woodcourt and Esther Summerson, Arthur Clennam and Little Dorrit 'go down' into an uneventful domestic life which, as Dickens imagines it, is totally insulated from social and political pressures and concerns. Even Arthur Clennam's quiet 'I want to know' is really rejected. But then these heroes and heroines are people we don't take quite seriously. Nor need we, for opposed to this official recommendation is the splendid energy of the virtuoso's rhetoric in *Bleak House* and *Hard Times* and occasionally in *Little Dorrit*, a rhetoric which 'punishes' injustice very thoroughly in exactly the energetic style which is not allowed to the heroes and heroines. And in all three books there are exhilarating comic downfalls arranged for some of the social tyrants:

Bucket's brisk manhandling of the Smallweeds and others, the overthrow of Bounderby, the shearing of Casby by the tugboat.

The anger of women presented a more deeply puzzling problem to Dickens, and the sexual significance of the problem has probably been felt by every reader. The quasi-sexual rhythmic structure in Dickens's familiar routine of the over-throw of the comic villain, and our easy understanding of its force and its meanings, shows that in comic literature in general, and in Dickens in particular, there is a very close relationship between sexual impulse and the passion of anger. That the good women in the early Dickens novels never feel or express anger, and are highly admired for this, is the exact equivalent in social terms for the fact that they are not allowed to show, in any word or gesture, any hint of sexual impulse. This is understandable and conventional enough in the work of a high Victorian novelist, nor is it surprising, granted the influence of *Pamela* and *Clarissa*, that Dickens among other nineteenth-century English novelists should have contrived long and copiously detailed accounts of the suffering under injustice of patient and loving women. The story of Florence Dombey is a vaguely social allegory rendered in terms of personal injustice and personal suffering, and the relationship between Little Dorrit and her father is of the same pattern exactly. In both instances we are as sure that the cruel father will eventually recognize the worth of his daughter as in *David Copperfield* we are sure that Uriah Heep will be exposed, or in another variant, that Emily will come to a pathetic end.

Most readers today find the tearful version of this pattern distasteful, yet the word 'sentimental' does not answer ex-actly. We need that word to distinguish between, for instance, the sufferings of Jo the Tough Subject in *Bleak House* and the sufferings of King Lear, yet most of us think that Jo is mostly all right, while Florence Dombey is mostly all wrong. In both instances, if we judge them by the standards of non-theatrical art, the 'cause' of the suffering is unquestionably felt to be the writer himself. Compare, for instance, the sufferings of Fanny Price in *Mansfield Park*. This is not an entirely success-ful work, when all is said and done, but it is not a theatrical work, nor is it disfigured by Richardson's sado-masochism.

Jane Austen admires Fanny's patience, her loyalty to her 'principles', but Fanny's meekness, the success of Mrs. Norris's tyranny, the blindness of Sir Thomas, these happenings are inevitable not because they occur in the recognizable rhythm of a sentimental theatrical set-piece, but because they are in part realistically accounted for by Fanny's sickly lack of spirit (quite coolly and frankly presented) and by her social position as a poor cousin. Moreover, when Fanny explains to Sir Thomas her reasons for refusing Henry Crawford, it takes real strength and courage to withstand his implicit accusation that she is not behaving in a dutiful, grateful, and womanly way. Subdued and long-suffering as she is, Fanny is 'free', she seems to sponsor and to generate her own behaviour as we would expect in non-theatrical art, whereas Jo in *Bleak House* is visibly manipulated into suffering for effect.

Yet despite his obvious role as predestined victim, there is a certain fine resistance and independence even in Jo: he really is 'tough', he has integrity, he prefers some things to others and says so, and all this because, as we quite distinctly feel, Dickens *wants* him to and wants to admire him for it. There is, then, an important kind of balance in this characterization. But Dickens does not at all want Florence Dombey or Little Dorrit to have this kind of toughness; he pointedly deprives them of it and thereby seems to cause their suffering much more arbitrarily than Jo's. Moreover, there is something wrong with the 'moral calculus' in these long structures of frustration. These virtuous heroines are recognized in the end (as Fanny Price, too, is recognized at the end) by their bad parents, but it seems necessary to Dickens that these parents be ruined in health and spirit to make recognition emotionally satisfying, whereas Sir Thomas Bertram becomes a good parent without losing his strength of mind or body. The Dickensian heroines have already been quite sufficiently rewarded by Dickens's insistent and absolute praise for their lack of angry resentment, their loving self-effacement, whereas our feeling for Fanny Price during her suffering is, for the most part, the complex discriminating sympathy normal to non-theatrical art. The suffering of Florence Dombey and of Little Dorrit is simply not rendered with the generosity, the justice, the moral intelligence which we are accustomed to find in serious art. It does not compare, for instance, with the suffering of Catherine Sloper in *Washington Square* or of Princess Mary in *War and Peace*.

Matters are made worse by the fact that these passages in Dickens are so uninterestingly written, and what is really disturbing about them is our knowledge that so many readers read them with an energetic and wilful co-operation that is simply unwarranted by what Dickens achieved. These pathetic stories are *efficiently* managed in theatrical terms, and Dickens certainly tried to make them effective. But his conception of womanly self-effacement was a completely negative one that operated as a block to his inventiveness. And in one respect one doesn't regret the emptiness of these pages, for they show hardly a trace of that perverse ingenuity in the invention of tortures which we feel to be a sickness in the work of Richardson, Charlotte Brontë, and Tennessee Williams, among many others. The readers who thought and who continue to think that Dickens's rendering of the suffering of innocent women, in particular of innocent little girls, is deeply affecting and morally instructive are, it seems to me, so anxious to have a certain kind of experience that they will contrive to get it even in the absence of real help from the novel itself.

The simplest account of what is wrong with the suffering of Florence Dombey, Little Dorrit, and the rest is that one recognizes immediately and throughout that these heroines are doing proper 'woman's work', as that was understood by a very inexperienced and undistinguished thinker on such matters. The biographers have demonstrated that it was only late in life that Dickens had occasion to do any serious thinking and feeling about women, and it is generally accepted that the later heroines are 'more interesting' than the earlier ones. Some of the women who are taken seriously in *Little Dorrit*, *Great Expectations*, and *Our Mutual Friend* express what in the earlier works was allowed only to criminals, to lower-class prostitutes like Nancy in *Oliver Twist* or to upper class tragedy-queens like Edith Dombey and Lady Dedlock. They have become capable of passion, and it is not surprising that their chief expression of passion takes the form of anger. Mrs. Clennam, Fanny Dorrit, Miss Wade, and Tattycoram in

Little Dorrit begin the development, Miss Havisham's perpetual re-enactment of her betrayal and her training of Estella as an instrument for revenge bring this development to full flower, and in *Our Mutual Friend* the heroine herself, Bella Wilfer, was chosen for the role entirely because of her capacity for anger.

Taking angry women seriously amounts to a new and surprising development in Dickens's attitude towards the otherness of other people. To compare the results with the ordinary practices of serious art is to see clearly and sadly enough the inadequacies of Dickens's methods but also to freshen one's admiration for the unique insights afforded by those methods, and the remarkable sincerity and spontaneity with which Dickens approached this unfamiliar territory of human experience. In the earlier novels the approved kind of woman had always been the Esther Summerson kind, unfailingly and uninterestingly self-effacing and long-suffering, and although there had also been plenty of instances of the opposite kind, these had never caused any serious problems for the artist or for the audience. Haughty and cold operatic heroines, like Edith Dombey, Lady Dedlock, and to some extent Rosa Dartle are actually admired for their passionate wilfulness, but from a safe theatrical distance. They are superb performers of their roles, and since an important element of their roles is the thrilling catastrophe to which they are always known to be destined, Dickens's admiration for their strength of will costs him little. The hysterical jilts and especially the shrews are brought much closer to us. They inhabit the domestic circle rather than Lady Dedlock's glamorous realm, and the shrewish wives, far from being destined for an operatic death, are virtually immortal. But Dickens is so far from finding these women seriously difficult to deal with that his mimicry of their terrible tantrums is always unusually inventive and joyous. He very cheerfully acknowledges their capacity to make trouble because he never for a moment respects their right to do so. The Pecksniff girls are allowed an exceptional touch of pity because they got more than they bargained for. But Mrs. Snagsby in *Bleak House* is an immortal and omnipotent tyrant who needs no pity and gets none. 'Mrs. Snagsby replies by delivering herself a prey to spasms; not an unresisting prey, but a crying and a tearing one, so that Cook's Court re-echoes with her shrieks. Finally, becoming cataleptic, she has to be carried up the narrow staircase like a grand piano.' (xxv) (p. 361) Only Mr. Snagsby is at the mercy of this wonderful and terrible performer; Dickens knows how to handle her.

In *Little Dorrit*, just as the old certainties about System have been qualified by a conscious and troubled hesitancy and ambiguity, so difficult women can no longer be approached with the fearless and joyous self-confidence of the earlier novels. The behaviour of dark-haired 'passionate' Tattycoram is no comic tantrum but a disturbing involuntary rage which elicits real respect and concern along with the expected moral disapproval. Miss Wade's bitterness is genuinely puzzling, whereas the elaborate mystifications early in *Bleak House* had assured us that Lady Dedlock's frozen style would eventually be explained by a thrilling secret. The Murdstones inspire in David Copperfield an intense, pure fear, but Mrs. Clennam's coldness is a subject of painfully ambivalent meditation and questioning for her son, both as child and as man. Fanny Dorrit is perhaps the most interesting instance of the change because her more obvious similarity to the earlier comic jilts and flirts emphasizes how much closer and more respectful Dickens's observation of a familiar type has become. We side with her when she takes her revenge on Mrs. Merdle, and any simple distaste or amusement at her wilfulness is inhibited by those interesting torrents of passionate tears in the arms of her beloved Amy.

What distinguishes these characterizations from Dickens's earlier practice is the sustained questioning attentiveness with which this difficult behaviour is studied. But this is not to say that Dickens's methods have changed into those normal to serious dramatic art. In *Middlemarch* we study Mr. Bulstrode attentively and therefore return to him again and again because he is involved in a continuous action: he has experiences and makes decisions and comes to realizations and we come to know him by witnessing these acts and by participating in the inner life from which they arise. The difficult women in *Little Dorrit* are not engaged in such an action, nor do they reappear in encores of their previous performances as they would have done in Dickens's earlier novels. They reappear because their behaviour continues to be disturbing and hard to understand. Lady Dedlock's thrilling secret and Mr. Tulkinghorn's sinister plan are teasingly mystifying—we know the theatrical artist has his intrigue-plot well in hand. The behaviour of Mrs. Clennam and Miss Wade and the rest is truly mysterious and the search for an answer to it is both ingenuous and disturbed. When we take note of the fact that these mysterious and difficult people are women, we realize that the wilful, exuberant, aggressive master of the Dickens theatre is facing the otherness of other human beings in its most intensely painful and primitive form: he is facing the coldness, the bitterness, the scorn of the loved one, and wondering why these things should be.

In *Middlemarch* it is precisely when Dorothea discovers Casaubon's coldness that George Eliot articulates her supreme statement of the sympathetic imagination. Because Dorothea is deeply hurt but also deeply puzzled, she is ready to begin what in George Eliot's conception—and it is the conception of most serious dramatic art—is the normal process of emerging from moral stupidity into a morally intelligent understanding and love for other people. She is ready to try to 'conceive with that distinctness which is no longer reflection but feeling' what life feels like in Casaubon's centre of self. And George Eliot accordingly proceeds at this point to take us behind Casaubon's behaviour into the drama of his inner life.

Dickens's theatrical habits made this normal procedure unavailable to him but opened the way to another kind of insight. He did, however, achieve what looks like the first step towards the sympathetic imagination—he came to realize that cold and cruel women (and parents) had impulses and needs similar to his own and in particular that they, like himself, wanted to give and receive love. It may come as a surprise to observe that an artist so famous for his warm heart should have realized this so late in his career, but such are the facts. The explanation is simply that Dickens never lost his theatrical habits, which is to say that he never lost his belief that identity was the same thing as behaviour, nor his sense that behaviour reflected and reported in the simplest sense what people wanted to do. Holding such views, even the warmest-hearted man will inevitably see a world full of cold-hearted people: it was indeed an extraordinary leap of the sympathetic imagination that brought Dickens to realize that someone like Mrs. Clennam really did want love. But since he never lost confidence in his belief that identity was behaviour, this realization served only to increase the mystery. Unable to close his eyes to Mrs. Clennam's unremitting coldness, Dickens had no alternative but to keep staring at it until he understood it. It was, I suggest, precisely these circumstances that made it possible for him to arrive at those anticipations of the Freudian conception of neurosis to which Mr. Trilling has given admiring attention.

It is right and important to admire these insights but even more important to see that they in fact derive from the apparent limitations of theatrical art. The same thing is true of almost all Dickens's special prophetic insights. The inspired view of the inhumanity of System owes something to Dickens's incapacity for serious interest in rational social procedures and institutions; his insight into the dehumanizing power of man's tools owes something to his incapacity to imagine work from the inside; and his guess-work about Mrs. Clennam owes something to his incapacity to imagine the drama of choice in the inner life. Dickens is a puzzling artist because all these incapacities are also forms of freedom and elements of genius, for they are merely negative ways of describing the extraordinary energy of Dickens's sensuous responsiveness to his world. He never was tempted by what Santayana describes as the merely conventional and respectable objections to the comic mask:

Objections to the comic mask—to the irresponsible, complete, extreme expression of each moment—cut at the roots of all expression. Pursue this path, and at once you do away with gesture: we must not point, we must not pout, we must not cry, we must not laugh aloud; we must not only avoid attracting attention, but our attention must not be obviously attracted; it is silly to gaze, says the nursery-governess, and rude to stare.[1]

Dickens's genius lay in a radical incapacity not only to be influenced by the rules of nursery-governesses but also to

---

[1] *Soliloquies in England* (New York), 1922, p. 137.

enter the noble world of the sympathetic imagination which
may be the ideal goal of those rules. He never stopped staring
at people and it seems that neurosis is only discoverable and
definable by staring. Unable to imagine the drama of the inner
life, which is after all almost always rendered as a noble drama
of free choice, Dickens kept staring at the puzzle of Mrs.
Clennam's behaviour: she must want love and must also
intend to behave as she in fact does, yet her behaviour takes
the mysterious form of rejecting love. And Mr. Trilling has
shown that Dickens arrived at the only possible answer to
the puzzle: the insight that Mrs. Clennam's behaviour must
be motivated by a need of which she is unaware, the need to
punish herself. And he finds something of the same pattern
and the same answer to it in Miss Wade.

These remarkably perceptive insights into neurotic states
remained, unfortunately, the merest hints and guesses in
Little Dorrit, and Dickens's theatrical and moralistic habits
in fact worked actively against them. The vision of Mrs.
Clennam and the rest as neurotically self-imprisoned—together with the moral and emotional attitudes appropriate
to this vision—this kind of insight is consistently blurred and
often betrayed by inappropriate procedures in carrying it
through. Tattycoram, after what one might call her successful
psychiatric interview with Miss Wade, is forced not only by
Mr. Meagles but by Dickens himself to listen to a sermon about
duty which lacks all respect for what she has already achieved
in self-understanding. The discovery of Miss Wade's liaison
with Gowan is a particularly flagrant example of a habit to
which Mrs. Barbara Hardy has drawn attention, the habit of
tucking his 'loose ends' so carefully 'into the wrong place that
their looseness, and their mechanical structure, is revealed'.[1]
The revelation of the guilty secret for which Mrs. Clennam is
punishing herself is delivered in a style much too reminiscent
of the mystifications of *Bleak House* to harmonize with the
serious image of her neurotic self-imprisonment, and the lurid
theatricality of the Clennam house and its fall all but contra-
dicts Arthur's painful complexity of feeling about his mother.
Above all there is the stylistic and moral dissonance between

---

[1] '*Martin Chuzzlewit*' in *Dickens and the Twentieth Century*, ed. John Gross
and Gabriel Pearson (London, 1962), p. 117.

Dickens's ambiguous and half-respectful view of all these difficult, troubled, and angry women and his insistent glorifica-
tion of Little Dorrit's approved behaviour. That her perfect
love is the right response to injustice we might perhaps accept
in itself, but it does not come to us so simply. It is admired
and glorified in the midst of effective theatrical scenes which
at the same time arouse our very strong anger against the
persecutions of Mr. Dorrit and Mrs. General. It is an anger
that Dickens takes particular pains to create and is quite
successful in creating. Mr. Dorrit's soft egotism is in fact one
of the most powerfully repulsive things in his work. The result is that if we are perhaps willing to admire Little Dorrit's
loving patience as beautiful and right for her, we at the same
time recognize it as a totally impossible alternative for ourselves and for Dickens. He has played both sides against the
middle, a characteristic procedure of his which in this novel
proves seriously damaging, for it is precisely this excluded
middle that the fine ambiguity of his attitude towards the
difficult and angry women inhabits. The novel defeats itself.

In *Great Expectations* Dickens found a way of rendering his
sense of mystery about the difficult otherness of human beings
and his insight into neurotic states that was really harmonious
with his continuing theatrical habits. In a cursory inspection
the later novel might well seem to represent a falling-off in
serious psychological insight. Mrs. Clennam's psychosomatic
paralysis seems a far more serious and plausible kind of self-
imprisonment than what takes place in the fantastic atmosphere of Satis House, and Miss Wade's use of Tattycoram
(with its Lesbian overtones) is far more disturbingly mysterious
than Miss Havisham's fantastic bewitchment of Estella. But
in *Little Dorrit* psychological realism was undermined by
assertive moralizing: Dickens was a brilliant diagnostician
but an aggressively clumsy therapist, and therapy was
insistently attempted. In *Great Expectations* the diagnosis
remains in force, but Dickens has decided to abandon the
attempt at therapy, and it is this decision (an unconscious
one on Dickens's part, as I have argued) that is *symbolically*
represented by the weird, almost charming, fairy-tale atmosphere of Satis House and the fantastic relationship—as of

the witch and the sleeping-beauty—between Miss Havisham and Estella. For these images are symbolic as we ordinarily understand the word: they express Pip's vision of these women, his attitudes towards them. The lack of psychological realism has a positive value and meaning in that it expresses Pip's helplessness, his inability to conduct an active and wilful search for understanding and for cure, his melancholy and humorous acceptance of the traditional mystery of human nature, of woman and of love. The atmosphere of Satis House is also harmonious with the rendering of Mrs. Gargery and Biddy, the two other difficult women of the novel. These characters inhabit a world very different from Satis House, but they are organically connected with Miss Havisham and Estella by the similar attitude Pip takes towards them. Mrs. Gargery is as bad a parent as Mrs. Clennam but she has no guilty secret and there is no explanation for her cruelty, nor in fact is that cruelty deeply felt—it is amusingly and ruefully chronicled. Biddy is as selfless, dutiful, and patient as Little Dorrit but in her own unemphatic way she is as cold and rejecting as any other woman in the novel. Her virtues are dutifully admired rather than glorified and she remains a rather unattractive figure. The assertive approvals and disapprovals of *Little Dorrit* have disappeared as has the intensity of pain and bewilderment occasioned by cold, deceiving, and rejecting women. Pip can neither blame them nor gather much energy to try to explain them: they are simply there, a mysterious part of nature, and the fantasy imagery of the novel registers a way of living humorously and sadly with that fact.

In *Our Mutual Friend* Dickens took another important step towards the sympathetic imagination. Wrayburn's need for Lizzie Hexam's lithe strength at the oars symbolically represents a new and quite positive assessment of the passionate vitality that in the earlier novels would have seemed either unwomanly or difficult and dangerous. Even more surprising is the fact that the heroine, Bella Wilfer, is positively admired for her capacity for passionate anger. The evidence for this is indirect but persuasive:

'Pa,' said Bella, sipping the fragrant mixture and warming her favourite ankle; 'when old Mr. Harmon made such a fool of me (not to mention himself as he is dead), what do you suppose he did it for?'

'Impossible to say, my dear. As I have told you times out of number since his will was brought to light, I doubt if I ever exchanged a hundred words with the old gentleman. If it was his whim to surprise us, his whim succeeded. For he certainly did it.'

'And I was stamping my foot and screaming, when he first took notice of me; was I?' said Bella, contemplating the ankle before mentioned.

'You were stamping your little foot, my dear, and screaming with your little voice, and laying into me with your little bonnet, which you had snatched off for the purpose,' returned her father, as if the remembrance gave a relish to the rum; 'you were doing this one Sunday morning when I took you out, because I didn't go the exact way you wanted, when the old gentleman, sitting on a seat near, said, "That's a nice girl; that's a *very* nice girl; promising girl!" And so you were, my dear.' (I. iv) (p. 42)

Mr. Harmon's meaning was a bitter one, but Dickens, Mr. Wilfer, and Bella unquestionably enjoy this image of childish passion, and the rest of the characterization leaves us in no doubt that Bella is an attractive and interesting young woman precisely because of her spirit. But Dickens's moralistic habits again blur the vision: spirit is one thing but anger is another, as it turns out, and Bella's anger is often quite mechanically identified as 'bad', to use Tattycoram's servant-class phrase about herself. John Rokesmith is apparently in the same sort of painful position with Bella Wilfer that Pip was in with Estella, but the elaborate mystifications about 'our mutual friend' assure the audience that Rokesmith is really (to some extent like the Duke in *Measure for Measure*) a testing and observing rather than an experiencing character. His watchful study of Bella, although it is combined (insecurely) with his growing love for her, makes the audience realize that Bella's anger will disappear in due course, together with her love of money. Moreover, although Bella is another one of Dickens's lustrous, passionate, dark-haired heroines, much of her anger takes the form of a snappy petulance unattractive in its lack of fire and generosity of spirit.

But Bella's first expression of feelings about her ridiculous situation has some real force, eloquence, and inventiveness:

'It's a shame! There never was such a hard case! I shouldn't care so much if it wasn't so ridiculous. It was ridiculous enough to have a stranger coming over to marry me, whether he liked it or not. It was ridiculous enough to know what an embarrassing meeting it would be, and how we never could pretend to have an inclination of our own, either of us. It was ridiculous enough to know I shouldn't like him—how *could* I like him, left to him in a will, like a dozen of spoons, with everything cut and dried beforehand, like orange chips. Talk of orange flowers indeed! I declare again it's a shame! Those ridiculous points would have been smoothed away by the money, for I love money, and want money—want it dreadfully. I hate to be poor, and we are degradingly poor, offensively poor, miserably poor, beastly poor. But here I am, left with all the ridiculous parts of the situation remaining, and added to them all, this ridiculous dress! And if the truth was known, when the Harmon murder was all over the town, and people were speculating on its being suicide, I dare say those impudent wretches at the clubs and places made jokes about the miserable creature's having preferred a watery grave to me. It's likely enough they took such liberties; I shouldn't wonder! I declare it's a very hard case indeed, and I am a most unfortunate girl. The idea of being a kind of widow, and never having been married! And the idea of being as poor as ever after all, and going into black, besides, for a man I never saw, and should have hated—as far as *he* was concerned—if I had seen!' (i. iv) (pp. 37–38)

There is the engaging freedom of her speech with her father:

'Pa,' said Bella, 'we have got a Murderer for a tenant.'

'Pa,' said Lavinia, 'we have got a Robber.'

'To see him unable for his life to look anybody in the face,' said Bella. 'There never was such an exhibition.'

'My dears,' said their father, 'he is a diffident gentleman, and I should say particularly so in the society of girls of your age.'

'Nonsense, our age!' cried Bella, impatiently. 'What's that got to do with him?'

'Besides, we are not of the same age:—which age?' demanded Lavinia.

'Never *you* mind, Lavvy,' retorted Bella; 'you wait till you are of an age to ask such questions. Pa, mark my words! Between Mr. Rokesmith and me, there is a natural antipathy and a deep distrust; and something will come of it!'

'My dear, and girls,' said the cherub-patriarch, 'between Mr. Rokesmith and me, there is a matter of eight sovereigns, and something for supper shall come of it, if you'll agree upon the article.' (i. iv) (p. 40)

On the other hand, there is the emphasized 'coquettishness' and the continual business with the black curls: 'pouting again, with the curls in her mouth', and later: 'then whimpering again, and at intervals biting the curls, and stooping to look how much was bitten off'. But the violence of her affection for her little father remains engaging: 'This abrupt change was occasioned by her father's face. She stopped to pull him down from his chair in an attitude highly favourable to strangulation, and to give him a kiss and a pat or two on the cheek.' (I. iv) (p. 36) It is an interesting characterization and by no means a really unsuccessful one, but it is also quite clearly an assemblage of points rather than an image of human behaviour created out of the highest imaginative vision. The bad qualities are for the most part kept quite separate from the good ones and both are labelled unmistakably; the bad ones are readily detachable, nor is the reader in any doubt that they will eventually be detached. And when the bad qualities go, most of Bella's wilfulness and spiritedness goes along with them.

Dickens's retreat from his positive estimate of Bella's passionate anger is confirmed by the figure of Lizzie Hexam, whose total lack of anger against the injustice of her situation has the effect of admonishing Bella's bad temper by means of an ideal example of model behaviour. I have already shown that this point about Lizzie Hexam also weakens the symbolic action with Eugene Wrayburn in which she is involved. But over against Lizzie are placed her father's angry hostility to self-improvement, her brother's mean-spirited pride and shame, and Headstone's murderous rage against the gentleman with whom Lizzie has fallen in love. The result is an unusual and persuasive emphasis on class anger in the world of Podsnappery, while at the same time very heavy guns of moral sermonizing are brought to bear on this inevitable outcome of social injustice. The fantasy realm in which Miss Havisham and Estella lived was not easily accessible to moralistic assessments or recommendations, and in fact no such assessments were made: the finality of Miss Havisham's obsession is such that we do not think of her as having made a choice towards which we can direct moral 'blame', and Pip, after a momentary show of resentment, turns all his sense of frustration against himself. But in *Our Mutual Friend* human beings are quite straightforwardly defined as inhabiting the everyday world of the moral will. Anger is accepted as an inevitable product of social injustice and Dickens hints that it may be a positive sign of vitality, but it is a 'bad' emotion to encourage and human beings are presumed to be able to conquer the temptation to encourage it.

The dolls' dressmaker's anger is much less efficiently held in check by Dickens's moralistic habits than the anger of the other characters, and she is indeed one of the novel's liveliest successes. The characterization is perhaps too deliberately 'Dickensian', the sort of thing Dickens knew he was good at and knew he was expected to do. But it is also charged with a good measure of the creative energy which is painfully lacking in the rendering of Silas Wegg or Mr. Venus. Jenny Wren's speech has a vitality, a particularity of detail, a sharpness of idiom, a fullness of spirit that makes her anger seem an act of life. It has an absolute authority as a response to human suffering that is really inaccessible to moralistic thinking about character and the will to change. Furthermore, the typically Dickensian device of making her a child who speaks like a woman and who thinks of herself as a woman and of her father as a child—this device, it seems to me, entirely escapes from the limited pathetic intention it was designed, one imagines, to fulfil. Lizzie Hexam, Eugene Wrayburn, and the rest are meant to show an admirable compassion when they allow this sharp-tongued little person to lead the conversation, to dominate the scenes she takes part in; but the truth of the matter is that Jenny Wren speaks with a depth of passion that seems fully adult, and that the adults who serve her seem in truth less wise than she, less experienced, and much less forceful. Moreover Jenny Wren's paradisal dream has as much force as her anger:

'Talking of ideas, my Lizzie,' they were sitting side by side as they had sat at first, 'I wonder how it happens that when I am work, work, working here, all alone in the summertime, I smell flowers.'

'As a common-place individual, I should say,' Eugene suggested languidly—for he was growing weary of the person of the house—'that you smell flowers because you *do* smell flowers.'

'No, I don't,' said the little creature, resting one arm upon the
elbow of her chair, resting her chin upon that hand, and looking
vacantly before her; 'this is not a flowery neighbourhood. It's
anything but that. And yet, as I sit at work, I smell miles of
flowers. I smell roses till I think I see the rose-leaves lying in heaps,
bushels, on the floor. I smell fallen leaves till I put down my hand—
so—and expect to make them rustle. I smell the white and the pink
May in the hedges, and all sorts of flowers that I never was among.
For I have seen very few flowers indeed, in my life.'

'Pleasant fancies to have, Jennie dear!' said her friend: with a
glance towards Eugene as if she would have asked him whether
they were given the child in compensation for her losses.

'So I think, Lizzie, when they come to me. And the birds I hear!
Oh!' cried the little creature, holding out her hand and looking up-
ward, 'how they sing!'

There was something in the face and action for the moment quite
inspired and beautiful. Then the chin dropped musingly upon the
hand again.

'I dare say my birds can sing better than other birds, and my
flowers smell better than other flowers. For when I was a little
child,' in a tone as though it were ages ago, 'the children that I
used to see early in the morning were very different from any
others that I ever saw. They were not like me: they were not chilled,
anxious, ragged, or beaten; they were never in pain. They were not
like the children of the neighbours; they never made me tremble
all over, by setting up shrill noises, and they never mocked me. Such
numbers of them, too! All in white dresses, and with something
shining on the borders, and on their heads, that I have never been
able to imitate with my work, though I know it so well. They used
to come down in long bright slanting rows, and say all together,
"Who is this in pain? Who is this in pain?" When I told them who
it was, they answered, "Come and play with us!" When I said, "I
never play! I can't play!" they swept about me and took me up, and
made me light. Then it was all delicious ease and rest till they laid
me down, and said all together, "Have patience, and we will come
again." Whenever they came back, I used to know they were coming
before I saw the long bright rows, by hearing them ask, all together a long way off, "Who is this in pain? Who is this in pain?"
And I used to cry out, "Oh, my blessed children, it's poor me!
Have pity on me! Take me up and make me light!"' (ii. ii)
(pp. 239–40)

This dream by no means merely *longs for* happiness and peace
and quiet, but actively celebrates the richness of natural

impulse: it is a dream motivated by energy and passion and not by their opposites.

But Lizzie Hexam's (and Dickens's) attitude towards this dream is symptomatic of the whole novel's methods:

> As they went on with their supper, Lizzie tried to bring her round to that prettier and better state. But the charm was broken. The person of the house was the person of a house full of sordid shames and cares, with an upper room in which that abased figure was infecting even innocent sleep with sensual brutality and degradation. The dolls' dressmaker had become a little quaint shrew; of the world, worldly; of the earth, earthy.
>
> Poor dolls' dressmaker! How often so dragged down by hands that should have raised her up; how often so misdirected when losing her way on the eternal road, and asking guidance! Poor, poor, little dolls' dressmaker! (II. ii) (p. 243)

The word 'prettier' deserves the scorn which it is our first impulse to direct towards it: it is wrong in exactly the way one first suspects, because it substitutes a conventional, respectable, and 'aesthetic' judgement for one morally intelligent and humane. One instinctively trusts in this case the tale rather than the teller; one is on Jenny Wren's side in resisting Lizzie's blandishments. Though the teller assures us that it would be better for Jenny Wren to be won over to the prettier view of things, we are not convinced, preferring to believe and trust that better part of him that made Jenny Wren an impressive human being able to choose her own moods and her own expressions. For Jenny Wren is not a 'shrew', quaint, little, or otherwise; there is no significant perspective in the novel from which her feelings can be accused of being 'worldly' or 'earthly'; and the writer whose pleasure it is to talk about 'innocent sleep' being 'infected' by the 'sensuality and degradation' of a pitiful old drunk seems hardly the same writer who created Jenny Wren.

The passage is symptomatic of the whole novel in that it almost knowingly disgraces its possibilities. Here, then, is a novel which with respect to its scenario has at times a certain visionary richness, yet which in its working out confidently destroys this vision with arbitrary moralistic assessments and recommendations. On the one hand there is the river, with all it could stand for, Lizzie Hexam's saving vitality and an extraordinary number of images of social rage, so that we can surely describe the scenario of this novel in the terms Dr. Leavis uses (wrongly, for me) of *Hard Times*: it shows that Dickens was indeed 'possessed by a comprehensive vision'. On the other hand, however, we have the working out of the scenario: in which a combination of theatrical habits, wilful sermonizing, and failing powers defeats the possibilities of the scenario at almost every turn. It is not the moral judgements in themselves to which one objects but their flatness, the fact that they oversimplify and actually contradict the potential richness of the material. Dickens's decision to employ Lizzie Hexam as an ideal image of the proper attitude towards social injustice is acceptable in itself, but it all but defeats his other decision to make her a creature of strong vitality and physical strength and skill. That Wrayburn should fall in love with the genteel and refined earnestness of this lower-class girl is by no means implausible, but it makes his salvation a far less significant matter than the scenario seems to intend. Again, Bella Wilfer's metamorphosis into Rokesmith's sweetly affectionate wife is not implausible, but it relinquishes what is most interesting in the basic conception of her character. Indeed, it is Dickens's evident interest in plausibility of action which may have been responsible for the weakness of the novel as a whole. The restraint of the verbal devices, the care and refinement with which the successive phases of character development are engineered—these admirable concerns may have functioned inadvertently as distractions through which Dickens's vision, and his creative energy, leaked away.

To speak of Bella Wilfer's change of heart as plausible may seem odd nonsense in view of the fact that this change is brought about by the extraordinarily 'artificial' device of Boffin's impersonation of money-corruption. This action is indeed one of the oddest things in the novel, since it combines an obviously theatrical invention with a careful attempt at plausibility and continuity. It is not a very happy combination, but it is surely an extremely interesting one. For it brings us once again to Dickens's fundamental identity as a theatrical artist.

When Dickens became a thorough-going moralist, he did not cease to be a theatrical artist. That is, he did not ever learn to practise the mode of moral drama which is the norm for serious art, that mode which consists of the dramatization of moral choice in the inner life of the individual human consciousness. He did, in some degree, learn to practise the kind of moral drama which we call symbolic action, as in the scenario for Eugene Wrayburn's salvation. But his interest in this form of art was far less serious and steady than the recent critics have suggested, and his capacity to carry out his diagrams of symbolic action into large-scale structures was almost non-existent. Dickens's moral insight remained for the most part that of the theatrical artist; that is, it took the form of having overt and explicit messages to deliver to his public. His method of delivering these messages, accordingly, took the inevitable form of a straightforward public rhetoric of persuasion, and in particular the form of impersonation of, mimicry of, wrong and right behaviour. When Mr. Jarndyce sends Esther Summerson, Ada, and Richard to Mrs. Jellyby's house 'for a purpose', when Mr. Meagles, standing at the window with the repentant Tattycoram, asks her to look at Little Dorrit as a model of right behaviour, these characters are doing something entirely consistent with the moral method of the novels in which they appear. And the interesting thing about Mr. Boffin's impersonation of avarice is that he is doing *exactly* what Dickens does as a moralist: he is mimicking wrong behaviour in order to show how ugly and foolish it is.

Mr. Boffin takes a thoroughly Dickensian delight in his own performance too. But what happens on the stage of the Boffin theatre does not quite justify delight. Here is the big scene:

'You pretend to have a mighty admiration for this young lady?' said Mr. Boffin, laying his hand protectingly on Bella's head without looking down at her.

'I do not pretend.'

'Oh! Well. You *have* a mighty admiration for this young lady— since you are so particular?'

'Yes.'

'How do you reconcile that, with this young lady's being a weak-spirited, improvident idiot, not knowing what was due to herself, flinging up her money to the church-weathercocks, and racing off at a splitting pace for the workhouse?'

'I don't understand you.'

'Don't you? Or won't you? What else could you have made this young lady out to be, if she had listened to such addresses as yours?'

'What else, if I had been so happy as to win her affections and possess her heart?'

'Win her affections,' retorted Mr. Boffin, with ineffable contempt, 'and possess her heart! Mew says the cat, Quack-quack says the duck, Bow-wow-wow says the dog! Win her affections and possess her heart! Mew, Quack-quack, Bow-wow!'

John Rokesmith stared at him in his outburst, as if with some faint idea that he had gone mad.

'What is due to this young lady,' said Mr. Boffin, 'is Money, and this young lady right well knows it.' (III. xv) (pp. 595–6)

At the end of the novel Mr. Boffin reminisces about this scene, calling it his 'grandest demonstration':

Mrs. Boffin laughed heartily again, and her eyes glistened again, and it then appeared, not only that in that burst of sarcastic eloquence Mr. Boffin was considered by his two fellow-conspirators to have outdone himself, but that in his own opinion it was a remarkable achievement. 'Never thought of it afore the moment, my dear!' he observed to Bella. 'When John said, if he had been so happy as to win your affections and possess your heart, it come into my head to turn round upon him with "Win her affections and possess her heart! Mew says the cat, Quack-quack says the duck, and Bow-wow-wow says the dog." I couldn't tell you how it come into my head or where from, but it had so much the sound of a rasper that I own to you it astonished myself. I was awful nigh bursting out a-laughing though, when it made John stare!' (IV. xiii) (p. 777)

The Inimitable Boz must often have taken a similar pleasure in his own performances, and indeed he is doing so here, for he wrote Boffin's script. But 'Mew says the cat', alas, is not a very remarkable achievement and it would be both sad and misleading to end a study of Dickens's theatrical art with this mediocre performance before us if Boffin's specific reasons for self-congratulation did not reinstruct us in the fundamentals of that art. Boffin is not only delighted but astonished by his own invention: it suddenly occurred to him to say something he had never thought of before, something nobody had ever thought of before. Such astonishing inventiveness is one of the basic elements of Dickens's art. Another is what Dr. Leavis has described as Dickens's gift for registering 'with the responsiveness of a genius of verbal expression what he so sharply sees and feels'. To this I would add—though Dr. Leavis has really implied it of course—that it is the gift above all for registering what he so sharply *hears* that makes Dickens's method of characterization so successful. Boffin seems to lack this basic gift. His idiom never becomes really vivid, loud, and distinct, and in 'Mew says the cat' we note with regret that Dickens is straining unsuccessfully for what used to come with as great a spontaneity as art has ever produced. Boffin's performance troubles us because it is a tired and mediocre performance: the readers who are troubled by the fact that it *is* a performance are experiencing the Dickens problem. For Boffin is doing exactly what Dickens himself always does, and that is why a device which to readers accustomed to non-theatrical art seems artificial must have seemed the most natural thing in the world to the master of the Dickens theatre.

INDEX

PRINTED IN GREAT BRITAIN
AT THE UNIVERSITY PRESS, OXFORD
BY VIVIAN RIDLER
PRINTER TO THE UNIVERSITY